PRACTICE
WISDOM FROM THE DOWNWARD DOG

Featuring
Shirley Archer | Dana Damara | Nicole DeAvilla | Steph Ritz | Marcy Snodgrass
with essays from 43 Yogis | compiled by Jane Ashley

FLOWER *of* LIFE PRESS

PRAISE

"In this insightful account of one person's awakening to the full potential of a spiritual life, I found a rich description of Kandy Love's journey from a devastating diagnosis, to a full reevaluation of her life and spiritual practices, and finally to the incorporation of those practices into all aspects of her life. A true and exciting account of a metamorphosis from a successful yet unfulfilled life to one of sacred practice used as the cornerstone to find new strength and understanding in her life. This is truly an uplifting story and of value to all those who follow a spiritual pathway."

—Thomas Clark, Meditator

"Shirley Archer's story is heartfelt, vulnerable, and transformative! Her journey from trauma to passion and purpose is inspirational—we are lucky to have people in the world like Shirley who are willing to model the power of mindfulness and yoga to create a beautiful life that serves others, too."

—J. Amara, Yogi and Meditator

"Nicole DeAvilla dives into the most esoteric of topics and then brings it back down to earth in practical terms that can help us all have a new perspective on how we can live more abundantly in the modern world...she shows her vulnerable side in 'I Stopped and Time Stood Still' so that many can be inspired to embark on their personal journey to lead a life full of many riches."

—Rhonda Liebig, Energy Revitalizer, bestselling author of The FITT Solution, and founder of the Fresh Inspiration Show and Tour

"I was intrigued with Julianne Gillespie's metaphor: 'yoga is software for the soul'. By programming yoga with a focus on your breath and body work you can achieve a desired flow state of being and rise above the chaos. Julianne highlights how to be more present through yoga for greater happiness."

—Anne Garland, Influencer, Strategist, Author

"Flowing from the heart, Michele Tsihlas's writing style is uniquely, compellingly dynamic. This capsule of a challenging journey realizing affirmations' depths illustrates benefits of taking a mind-body stance with the postures. Michele generates hopeful motivation by sharing her insights to the potency of yoga for multi-faceted health."

—Carol Kretzmann, MS

"After reading Lee Kemter's chapter, it gives me a chance to see my world perceived in a new way. I love how she writes asking questions that allow me to understand how I move through life. This simple awareness gives me a more joyful and connected experience for the present and the future."

—Valerie G.

"In her essay 'Walking the Path of Dharma', Ananda Ma shares how people from very different backgrounds hear the call to study Yoga. The spiritual aspects of yoga are often overlooked, considered not pertinent for today, or simply not taught in favor of a more physical emphasis. Yoga is a system that ties together all human endeavors to include the most important, union with the One. Each person to some degree is on that path—some are more serious about that path and spend a life in devotion to it. Thanks to all who choose to walk that path."

—Devananda, On the path

"It's not every day that we get such deep and intimate insight into such a personal and painful journey with such courage and honesty. Andrea Trank bravely shares her journey into fear that ultimately led to illness and helps walk us through how Yoga can heal both the mind and body simultaneously. What an incredibly important lesson in today's society to understand the direct correlation between mental and emotional dis-ease and the physical manifestation of disease in the body as a result. And maybe even more important is the realization and empowering truth of how yoga can be the foundation and inspiration for self-healing."

—Monica Garcia Saenz, Author, Poet and Self-Proclaimed Advocate of Self Love

"Through personal story, scientific inquiry, and intuitive insight, Shantika has provided a clear map for how to deepen my relationship with my body and the knowledge it holds. I have been aware of my psoas peripherally through yogic movement, and this provides an opportunity to explore it in more depth with tangible reasoning, steps forward and support. I'm grateful for the thorough and concise teaching she offers, and encourage folks to see how her work might benefit them on their path."

—Megan M., Music Teacher and Artist

"I am in awe with Banton Dyer's honest and vulnerable writing in 'The Next Right Thing'. He has an uncanny ability to tell his story and simultaneously lay out a map for you in your own healing process. His story will inspire you and let you know that healing can happen no matter what your life experience has been. Amazing."

—Nicole DeAvilla, co-author *Practice*, bestselling author of *The 2 Minute Yoga Solution FAST and EASY Stress and Back Pain Relief for ANYONE at ANYTIME*, coach, essential oil educator and yoga therapist

"The heartwarming story of this yogi's journey moved me as a yoga student, yoga teacher and studio owner. Reading Paul Gemme's experience from the time he first stepped on the mat, followed by establishing a regular practice and then beginning to make the mind-body connection is a testament to the power of yoga. Every person can benefit holistically if they just continue to practice."

—Margaret Knoedler Durbas

"In 'The Garden of Love: Planting the Seeds of Intimacy', Valery Sherrin vulnerably shares her story of loss and abandonment and its impact on her self worth and identity. Through her dedication to the mat and her determination to find her inner truth, she transforms a life that was once lost and unrooted, into one in which seeds of intimacy grow through the intentional nourishment and 'mothering' of her soul. The practice of yoga becomes the fertile soil in which her soul seeds bloom to create a bountiful and beautiful harvest of hope, healing, connection, community, and love."

—Aurora Farber, Women's Leadership Coach, Writer, Speaker and modern-day Priestess, www.aurorafarber.com

"You won't read a story like Gillian Confair's in Yoga Journal, but you should! Confair describes an authentic, 'come as you are' approach to her practice and encourages others to do the same, no matter the pathway. Readers will surely relate to guilty pleasures that they've tried to suppress in the past, but this chapter may just inspire them to take a second look and see if there is something deeper there."

—Lindsey B. Jones, Community Leader and City Counselor, Cave Junction Oregon

"How inspiring of Holly Beavers! I love the reminder that the way we show up on our mat is the way we show up in life! Our mat is like a mirror and only by walking with those emotions and acknowledging them can we release them! Thank you so much for sharing your vulnerability—it makes it easier for me to be authentic with my own!"

—Kati Dirker

"Kali Carmel Cathie has the gift of taking the most profound depths of human experience and extracting it's essence. She reminds us of the primordial wisdom that is inherent in women all along, if only she trusts herself enough as she goes and grows inward. Such an exquisite tale of the feminine stirring, awakening and rising through yoga."

—Chrissy Cartwright, Mother, Superfoods Ambassador and Heart-led Entrepreneur

"Lauren's article on her 10-minute yoga practice is a great reminder that we are all in control! However busy we may get, we can all find more time to love ourselves. Lauren's message is that self-love must come first before one can be fully available to our daily lives and the people surrounding us. As Lauren explains, when we become stressed or overwhelmed, the best way to deal with it is to put it to the side and practice self-love first. In always keeping faith in ourselves, and a solid yoga routine, 10 minutes a day can be a saving grace."

—Kyle Smock

"Some writers point at the ineffable, and others can open a door, however briefly, to give readers a felt sense of Being itself. Stephanie Lopez has a unique gift to offer both as she exquisitely translates the experience of vastness into connection with our everyday selves."

—Linda Oshins, ERYT 500, Reiki Master, iRest L2 Teacher,
Author of *Pranayama: A Compendium of Practices*

"Nereyda's personal story of dealing with a debilitating disease at an early age is an inspiration to all. She opens your mind to alternative ways to manage pain and disease through Eastern philosophy and medicine. She has given us an important reminder that self-care is the most important thing you can give yourself and your loved ones. Nereyda is definitely an inspiring and resilient person."

—Sandy P. RN, BSN, PHN

"Adriana Buenaventura writes from her heart and from her own journey of moving from feeling empty and helpless to the pure joy of coming home to herself. This is about healing and taking your power back through the restorative calming yoga practice that she lives and teaches. I was completely swept up in the inspiration of possibility for all who read her moving story, and I will use Adriana's story to inspire my clients of the possibilities that lie within themselves. I feel confident that her story will also inspire you, the reader, towards something much greater for yourself or your loved ones as you discover that your past need not define you. It is what we do with it that defines us, as Adriana so expertly shows us."

—Carmen Moretti, CMS-CHt, Medical Support Clinical Hypnotherapist

"'Trusting the Process of Change' is an honest and relatable account of how yoga can be not only beneficial to one's mental health, but simply necessary for it. Anyone who has ever struggled with a life change would benefit from reading this essay. Julie Kiddoo explains how yoga is a connecting force to something bigger than oneself—and can hopefully inspire more people who have thought about practicing yoga to go for it."

—Emilia Azar

"Michelle Kahan's writing elegantly reflects the energy and wisdom that she brings to her teaching, which in my experience has uniquely helped her students explore and deepen not only their yoga practices, but also their lives."

—Steven Myhill-Jones

"Jean Edrada's story is a powerful image of her ever growing wisdom. Hers is the story of life speaking through themes, coming full circle but perpetually ending up at a deeper beginning. Jean possesses a wonderful gift in not only recognizing the wisdom spoken through her living story, but the generosity to share it with others in both words and actions."

—Charlie Werber

Are You Ready To Be A Published Author?

Books are the best business card you can have, whether you are an entrepreneur building your company, or a changemaker with a message that needs to be heard. Flower of Life Press is committed to giving voice to authors—and offering the support that is critical to birthing an authentic and powerful book.

We are ready to serve you with writing coaching, editing, and design while we provide the marketing team that will propel your journey and electrify your audience!

Check us out now at **floweroflifepress.com**—and have your book published by the team with over 3,000 books to their credit!

FLOWER OF LIFE PRESS
Voices of Transformation

Practice: Wisdom from the Downward Dog

Copyright © 2019 Flower of Life Press

All rights reserved. No part of this publication may be reproduced, distributed, or transmitted in any form or by any means, including photocopying, recording, or other electronic or mechanical methods, without the prior written permission of the publisher, except in the case of brief quotations embodied in critical reviews and certain other noncommercial uses permitted by copyright law.

The content of this book is for general instruction only. Each person's physical, emotional, and spiritual condition is unique. The instruction in this book is not intended to replace or interrupt the reader's relationship with a physician or other mental health professional. Please consult your doctor for matters pertaining to your specific health.

Book design by Jane Ashley, floweroflifepress.com
Cover and interior artwork by Whitney Freya, whitneyfreya.com

To contact the publisher, visit floweroflifepress.com

Library of Congress Control Number: 2019902950
Flower of Life Press, Old Saybrook, CT.

ISBN-13: 978-1-7337409-1-3

Printed in the United States of America

*"Do not feel lonely.
The entire universe is inside of you."*

—RUMI

CONTENTS

Note from the Publisher *by Jane Ashley* xii

The Cover Art *by Whitney Freya* xiv

FEATURED AUTHORS

Becoming Whole Again: My Journey through Trauma into Passion
and Purpose *by Shirley Archer* 1

Evolution of the Soul–Alchemy on the Mat *by Dana Damara* 9

I Stopped and Time Stood Still *by Nicole DeAvilla* 17

Listening to the Silence *by Steph Ritz* 25

Yoga Saved—and Keeps Saving—My Life *by Marcy Snodgrass* 33

CONTRIBUTING AUTHORS

Walking the Path of Dharma *by Ananda Deviika' Ma' A'charya'* 43

Emotional Range *by Holly Beavers* 51

Practice: One Bartender's Journey into Presence and Compassion
by Jessica Bell 57

Secrets of the Psoas: How This Precious and Intelligent Muscle Can Heal
Our Life as We Tend to Her With Kindness
by Shantika Bernard, PhD 63

Tantra Is Me *by Lara Brightside* 73

Coming Home into the Arms of Joy *by Adriana Buenaventura* 81

Learning to Stay: A Yogic Journey to Motherhood
by Kali Carmel Cathie 89

Finding Home Within *by Katherine Folk Clancy* 97

Yoga: The Final Frontier *by Gillian Confair* 103

Chef Yoga: The Power of a 10-Minute Daily Practice
by Lauren D'Agostino 109

Planting Seeds for New Beginnings *by Jane Del Piero* 115

The Next Right Thing *by Banton Dyer* 121

Ako ang Tulay: I Am the Bridge *by Jean Edrada* 127

Elevated Connection: A Gateway to Healing *by Jennifer Farnholz* 133

My Break-Up with Yoga and Healing a Broken Heart
by Sharon Fortier 141

A Deeper Truth: Trusting the Wisdom of the Body
by Paul Gemme 147

Yoga: A Pathway to Inner Peace *by Julianne Gillespie* 153

The Sweetness of Peace *by Heather Greaves* 159

Healing Through Stillness *by Kevin Heidt* 165

One Downward Dog at a Time *by Debbie Howard* 171

The Gifts of Practice: Inspirational Meditations and Poems
by Michelle Kahan 177

The Purifying Fire of Open-Hearted Awareness *by Lee Kemter* 185

Trusting the Process of Change *by Julie Kiddoo* 191

Daring to Trust that a Phoenix Will Rise *by Carina Lieu* 195

Mother, Loss, and Coming Home to Love: A Story About Navigating the
Unknown *by Alison Litchfield* 205

One Good Thing! *by Kirsten Livingston* 211

A Living Practice of Connection and Belonging
by Stephanie Lopez 217

Phoenix Goddess Rising: My Path to Love
by Carolina Grace Lorenzo.. 221

Enlivening the Antennae of Consciousness *by Kandy Love* 227

Cradle of Comfort *by Elizabeth McLaughlin* 233

Breath, the Divine Remedy & Poetry
by S. Pauline Michalovic...239

The Answer Is Within *by Avital Miller* 253

So I Breathe...A Journey To Inner Peace and Self-Empowerment!
by Dena Otrin...259

Goodbye Hustle: How I Discovered Life is a Forward Bend
by Danny Poole, written by Windy Cook.......................................265

Healthy Relationships: Yoga as a Portal into Your Sovereign Nature
by Rachel Romano..271

The Garden of Love: Planting the Seeds of Intimacy
by Valery Sherrin..277

The Power of a Headstand: How I Found My Self-Care Groove Again
by Debbie Sodergren 287

Before Yoga, There Was Fear: Finding My Ground on the Mat
by Andrea Trank..293

Purifying Thoughts: The Power of Positive Self-Talk and Affirmations
by Michele Tsihlas 299

Released by My Ujjayi, No Longer Prisoner of My Disease
by Nereyda Varias..305

Yoga: The Art of Release, the Art of Being
by Debra MicheLLe Vegh..311

Getting Lost: A Homecoming *by Eliza Whiteman*........................317

Grace of Pain *by Sasanna Yee*..323

Note from the Publisher

BY JANE ASHLEY

The idea for this collaborative book, *Practice: Wisdom from the Downward Dog*, came to me last year while holding a downward facing dog pose in a yoga class. It was Day 1 of a 40-Day Yoga challenge I was participating in.

Even though I'd been practicing yoga on and off for years, I'd fallen off the horse when my husband and I became full-time caregivers for his elderly mother with Alzheimer's. Three years later, I'd finally found my way back to the mat, and in that moment in downward dog, suddenly my awareness blew open and I *remembered*.

I remembered the crystalline structure of my bones. I remembered my body as a receiver and transmitter of energy. I felt energy flowing in and out of different meridians in my body. I felt a deep drop down, as if my Soul had "fallen" into every cell of my body. It was a quantum leap into presence. I was being held by the Divine.

My imperfect yoga practice had propelled me into a whole new experience of embodied Grace. I finally understood yoga as a portal into my own evolution— this went *well* beyond the physical practice.

It's well past midnight as I put the final touches on *Practice: Wisdom from the Downward Dog*, and I am struck by the joy I'm feeling.

If truth be told (and it always should!), I questioned my sanity several times during the "birthing" of this book. *"50 authors? Seriously?!? What was I thinking when I came up with this idea? 20 would have been plenty, Jane!"* echoed through my mind.

It's 1:00am when it becomes clear I'm not going to finish by 11pm as I had told my husband. He's used to it by now—and he knows what it means to me to be publishing this book and following my calling.

Yes, I could have chosen 20 stories, and had a few more hours of time for myself—but that's not me, and that's not why I do this.

My journey as a publisher is about giving voice to others—and my passion for this work grows as my community of New Evolutionaries expands with authenticity and purpose.

These stories matter—and my life is richer for having the chance to share the sacred space of creativity with each yogi whose words are captured within these pages you hold.

I am so proud to share each bit of wisdom with you, and thrilled to introduce these amazing authors to you! Each offering is unique, yet tied together by the transformative power of Yoga.

If you are experienced in Eastern philosophy, you'll resonate with the journey—and if you are new to Yoga, I hope the vibration that holds these stories together motivates you to become more aware of the beautiful current of your breath, and perhaps you'll step onto a yoga mat, too.

Here's the thing about Yoga: there is no judgment in the studio. It's a personal journey with no finish line, and everyone is welcome, so grab a mat, open your heart, and *practice dropping in...*

Before long, the magic begins to take hold, the energy flows, and life changes. Despair turns to hope, tragedy heals, and a renewed purpose raises the vibration—opening the door that awaits anyone willing to embrace the yogic practice of turning inward to cultivate the awareness of oneself as a Divine Being.

THE COVER ART
"YELLOW TARA"
BY WHITNEY FREYA

I began my yoga practice the same year I began my painting practice. Both were completely new to me and each have guided me through my life's journey with wisdom and inspiration that transcends this linear reality. The blank canvas and the open yoga mat, both have been a magic carpet on which I have traveled to higher realms, dimensions and levels of consciousness. Both have reminded me to stay present, to honor my strength, my heart, and my intentions. I believe both are portals to living at a higher level of vibration, one that releases fear and struggle and embraces the infinite possibility and pure love.

"Yellow Tara," the painting on this book cover, is the result of my intention to create spiritual, material and etheric abundance. Yellow Tara is an aspect of Lakshmi, the Hindu Goddess of abundance and prosperity. She is first, the creatress of spiritual, energetic and emotional abundance. She can guide you to aligning with the vibration of abundance so that all you see is this energy overflowing all around you. From this place, material abundance becomes as natural as the abundance of leaves on the trees, or grains of sand on the beach.

This painting existed for months as an example of a "first layer" in my teaching process. I knew I wanted to paint Yellow Tara on this canvas and had an image I had printed hanging from a magnet for a year or more. I would catch a glimpse of the canvas, as it lay propped against the kitchen wall amongst other canvases in varying stages of creation, and somehow know that it had a life of its own.

Then, one morning without any warning, I found myself picking her up off the floor, retrieving my inspiration from the magnet board, and in fewer brush strokes than I ever would have imagined possible, she just burst into being. It was like she painted herself!

She taught me that these desires we have, the ones that are seeded deep in our heARTs, WILL GROW to fruition, and that they follow a higher timeline. She has reminded me over and over that our plans and expectations are better served when we hold on loosely to timelines and TRUST.

May this "Yellow Tara" bathe you in the truth of the abundance that is swirling all around you. May she guide your thoughts and awareness towards ALL that is available to you. May she strengthen your heART, allowing your passions, desires and inspirations to illuminate your highest life's path. And so it is.

Explore a new reality with **Whitney Freya** and contact her about commissioning your own personalized Yellow Tara painting at WhitneyFreya.com.

Whitney Freya is an expert in Inspired Living, providing practical tools and practices that free your mind from limitations and scarcity to create more in your life that lights you up from the inside out. She is the author of the new book *Rise Above, Free Your Mind One Brush Stroke at a Time* (available on amazon.com) Learn more at **WhitneyFreya.com.**

Becoming Whole Again: My Journey through Trauma into Passion and Purpose

BY SHIRLEY ARCHER

BROKEN

Some days, my greatest accomplishment has been getting out of bed. You may think that's not impressive. And, when you learn I've written best-selling books, won numerous national and international awards, graduated from Stanford, Harvard and Georgetown Universities and am a licensed attorney in the top three toughest jurisdictions, you may wonder, why is getting out of bed a singular achievement?

It is, and here's why: Because I had to talk myself out of wanting to die. I had to pick up my bruised and broken body and tell myself, I *can* do this. I can get up, get dressed, and get on with my day; I remind myself that every minute of life is worth living, simply because this is my life. And, as my Japanese mom often taught me, if an experience isn't good or happy, it's an experience from which you can learn. So, learn. Learn the lesson, grow, become a better, stronger person. Make a better life.

That is the challenge *and the gift* that life gives each of us.

Why was I broken?

When I was 16, I was awoken from my sleep by a strong man sitting on my back smothering me with a pillow. I fought to breathe. He grabbed my left arm and pulled it behind my back, tearing ligaments. I feared he would kill me. His friend told him to stop. He turned me over and tore off my Mickey Mouse t-shirt. I kicked furiously, fighting for dear life. They laughed.

"She's a fighter," one said. They laughed. One held me down as the other raped me, sitting on me, saying something like "Bitch, bitch, you know you like it." I wanted to kill him, literally, with my own hands. I have never felt such a primal fury. *I. Wanted. To. Kill. Him.*

They left. Suddenly, I was home alone again; it was quiet. They wore masks, too cowardly to even let me see their faces. They left a rope behind. Were they planning to tie me up? I grabbed my comforter like a cape around my shoulders and ran after them. Nuts, right? What was I going to do if I caught them? I saw them getting in a car on the corner and drive away. I strained to see the license plate but could not read it. The red grill of the tail lights is still burned in my memory. My mom called the police, but I was too traumatized to talk and would *not* let anyone touch me. My mom told the landlord I had been raped. We moved.

I had PTSD and panic attacks for years.

At the time of my attack, I was number one in my high school class and a varsity cheerleader. After the attack, I went on to be a runner-up to Homecoming Queen and go to Stanford University. I earned my master's degree at Harvard and my law degree at Georgetown. I'm a member of New York, Washington, DC, and California bar associations. My career choices became a way of doing my best and seeking the most challenging path, more as a way of armoring myself against a world that would hurt me, rather than as a means of self-expression or realization of my passions. But ultimately, this path of fear did not serve me...I could no longer run from the truth of what needed to be addressed.

Then at age 29, I had a major health crisis. I became sick while working as an associate at a large New York City law firm and could not recover. Bronchitis expanded to sinusitis, then to walking pneumonia, pleurisy, and chronic asthma. I wheezed so badly at times I couldn't speak. I saw multiple specialists but could not restore my health. I would be well for a few days, then become sick again. My immune system was completely depleted. Chronic fatigue syndrome (CFS) was the eventual diagnosis. Doctors told me there was nothing they could do to help me and that I may never feel better.

HEALER, HEAL THYSELF

Finally, a light bulb went on for me. This was my first epiphany. I realized I had been passively sitting, waiting for the doctor to write a magical "cure" on his prescription pad. And, all along, *no one could heal me but myself.* This realization alone empowered me. I got it—the answer was not in the prescription pad; *it was in me.* I refused to accept that I may never feel better. And, I fully embraced that it was *on me* to create my energetic and vibrant health. I began researching and learning everything I could about illness and health.

At about the same time, my regular doctor diagnosed my depression. I would wake up in the morning and start crying at the breakfast table. While "clinical depression" was not immediately evident to me, it was fairly obvious to a professional. He referred me to a therapist. At long last, I participated in group therapy for my assault, panic attacks and PTSD. This was the most powerful healing for my rape experience. Sharing with other women who had also survived horrors—some beaten by spouses, some incest survivors, some addicts in rehab, from wealthy to low income, white to women of color—provided tremendous strength by realizing we were not alone. In that rare place where we could speak openly of things no person ever wants to hear and that society doesn't want us to tell, we could lick our wounds and heal. And, as I rehabilitated from my trauma, I began to see myself *not* as a victim of a horrific crime—because, let us never forget that rape is a horrible crime of degradation and power—but rather as a proud survivor... an incredibly strong survivor.

I took baby steps to rebuild my health and my life one day at a time. If I pushed too hard, or tried too much, I would relapse. I learned patience—a very difficult lesson for me. I learned that I could not "will myself" well. What I needed was to listen to and respect not only the needs of my weakened body but also the needs of my neglected heart—my inner spirit, my soul. Because I had suffered extreme grief, terror, rage and betrayal, I had learned to silence my emotional voice because to listen felt overwhelming. I learned I could take my emotions one step, one breath, one moment at a time. I needed to put the broken bits of myself back together, like a vase that had shattered, that needed to be reconstructed slowly so that each piece would go back in the correct place. I needed to become whole again.

This is when yoga saved me.

I learned yoga as a child. My grandmother had been a wealthy, eclectic, bohemian woman in the 1930s when she attended University of Southern California and had studied Eastern philosophy and practiced yoga. In the 1940s when my father was a child, she had taken him to alternative healers to learn yoga to help with his asthma and severe allergies. From this legacy, they both taught me various poses for calm, for digestion, and for fun–headstand being my favorite.

As an attorney in New York City, I took yoga classes from great instructors but was never consistent in my practice.

But, during my healing, I experienced a second epiphany: *I needed to rebuild my mind-body connection.* Many trauma survivors go "out of body" when their bodies are no longer a safe place to be. When I was assaulted, my experience was that I somehow watched from the ceiling. My spirit had escaped. I learned this is common. I had further injured myself over the years due to this disconnect, surviving a near fatal car crash. Regardless of how modern Western medicine refused to acknowledge the role of the mind-body connection at the time of my illness, I knew intuitively that embodiment was critical to my healing. To get back in touch with my body's self-healing wisdom, I consciously worked on becoming embodied, repeating consciously to myself, *I am here, I am safe*, and awakening my sensation of touch.

To become whole again, yoga became an important part of my life—not simply physical yoga postures but an integrated yoga lifestyle. Each day, breathing deeply, being present, feeling energy rise in my body, reassured me. Pranayama breathing practices calmed and grounded me and helped me restore balance. Meditation was at first simply a way to quiet my mind, but over time it became a connection with the Divine. Philosophical principles, like non-violence or right thinking, became tools to evaluate and consider life choices.

I chose to dedicate my life to uplifting others through sharing information about how to create abundant health. I worked at the Stanford University Prevention Research Center as a health educator, fitness trainer, yoga and Pilates instructor, and briefly, as Associate Director of the Health Promotion Research Center. I wrote 15 books, authored thousands of magazine articles, and traveled worldwide educating instructors and the public about tools to promote health, not simply fight disease. I believe each person has the power to manifest personal health and happiness and I want to help release that inner power.

And, that brings me back to yoga—an ancient practice of healing and a philosophy of living. Today I'm also a meditation teacher. Meditation is the practice that lights my life.

My mother is Japanese; she was born in 1938 and grew up in Japan during World War II and the American occupation. As a six-year-old, she experienced a life-changing event. As city sirens blared warning of the approach of an American air raid, she and her mother were caught in the open—the worst possible scenario. Most others hid in caves or other shelters. Older men served as unofficial city guardians as every fit able-bodied Japanese man was serving in the war effort. One of these elderly men waved at the child who would become my mother and the woman who was her mother to lie in tall grass to hide from passing planes. He lay on top of the girl to protect her. The gunners in the plane shot bullets—*rat, tat, tat, tat, tat, tat, tat*—at the ground as one so often sees in movies. After the planes passed, the man did not arise. The girl's face was crushed into the cold ground beneath her. The woman began screaming and crying. The girl felt the man's body lifted from her. Before her mother could shield her eyes, she saw his limp, lifeless, bloody body. He had died so that she may live.

At that moment, my mom learned that the time between life and death can be an instant. The only way she could repay a stranger who had made the ultimate sacrifice for her was to appreciate her gift of life itself and to live a good and happy life. She taught that lesson to me, since he too had made my life possible. Our choice is *never* a life with problems versus a life without problems. The choice is always the life you have or no life at all.

My mom taught me that it is up to each one of us to use our power to dig deep within and create a good, happy and healthy life with the tools and circumstances that we have. She fostered a sense of hope inside of me that was essential to my willingness to heal trauma and shift my vibration.

Meditation and yoga bring me to this truth daily. My life is perfectly imperfect. It is certainly not without drama or suffering, but it is authentic and filled with grief and joy, frustration and peace. I *love* my life and the people in it from the depths of my heart. If I compared myself to branded images and personas we see daily, I would feel inadequate, but asana practice reminds me to celebrate what my body can do—whatever it can do. Meditation practice connects me with the powerful truth that I am not simply flesh and bones. I, like all beings on the planet, embody a divine gift of life. This is sacred.

Every day, it is *my passion to get out of bed* and create a great day for myself, my family and my clients. It's my passion to serve others—to use whatever skills, knowledge and experience I have to help you live a vibrantly happy, energetic and healthy life—it's such a privilege to share this truth with you! It's my mission to offer information and tools to empower you to experience the joyful, healthy and radiant life you deserve. It's my heartfelt wish that we grow and stand in the light together—like I did with my support group sisters—that we share our stories to empower and heal each other and that we create like-minded community for the betterment of all.

Special Gift

LOVING KINDNESS MINDFULNESS MEDITATION

In this 10 minute guided meditation, Shirley leads you through an introduction to loving kindness. This meditation opens your heart to self-love, acceptance, self-compassion, kindness and self-care. Studies show that practicing loving-kindness meditation regularly and progressing through loving kindness for the self and to others has profound self-healing benefits, strengthening the immune system and increasing positive feelings.

Get access here: **http://bit.ly/2UWzEQg**

Shirley Archer is known for her passion for inspiring people to want to be fit, happy and healthy and for energizing them to achieve transformations that they had not thought possible. She's a mindful living coach, meditation teacher, best-selling author of 15 books and an award-winning trainer who has motivated and educated people worldwide through personal appearances, TV, blogs, over one thousand magazine articles and books, translated into several languages.

Shirley focuses her expertise, based on 30 years of experience, to help busy people eliminate overwhelm so that they have the clarity they need to tick everything off the to-do list and achieve vibrant health and happiness. Shirley's teachings draw on her background blending East Asian holistic values from her Japanese mom [augmented by her master's degree from Harvard University in East Asian Studies and time spent living in Japan] and her love of Western science and logic from her American dad. The result: her coaching changes the way clients perceive daily stresses, so they can embody their own power and realize wellness goals.

Her self-healing journey from trauma and illness began after her initial career as a high-powered attorney in New York City was stalled by Chronic Fatigue Syndrome. Overcoming illness and depression after doctors gave up and told her she may never feel well again, [Shirley refused to believe that!] inspired her 15-year career at the Stanford Prevention Research Center at the Stanford University School of Medicine and her role as a health educator, master yoga and Pilates teacher and wellness coach.

Happily married to a Swiss man and step-mom of three children, you can find Shirley hiking with her beloved German Shepherd, Cheyenne, either on beautiful Swiss trails or in sunny California, speaking at conferences worldwide, and being featured in various high-profile media including USA Today, The Washington Post, Oprah.com, Fitness, Shape and cnn.com. Learn more at **www.shirleyarcher.com**.

Evolution of the Soul—
Alchemy on the Mat

BY DANA DAMARA

Before I started this intimate relationship with my yoga mat, I was Vice President of Marketing for a data communications company. Yes, before I was thirty, I sat at a mahogany desk that looked out over the city of Mission Valley, California. I made a ton of money and hated every second. My soul was dying and I couldn't figure out why.

And then one day, I stepped into the yoga room with my friend Angie who owned Luna Notte in Pt. Loma. She took me to the Iyengar Yoga Center in San Diego. The teacher was timeless and beautiful, and I was bored out of my mind. The class was so slow and I never broke a sweat, not once. Savasana came around, and all I could hear was the clock ticking. At the end of class I thought, what a waste of time.

About three odd years later I was working on yachts in the middle of the ocean and yoga came up again. My room was big enough for a yoga mat, not Billie Blanks and my Tae Bo moves.

Fast forward four or five years later, and I was pregnant with my first baby. About eight months into the pregnancy, I couldn't run on the treadmill, or cycle, or mountain climb. Shiva Rea and her first prenatal yoga video became my best friend.

But the real yoga started the second I looked at my daughter on October 16, 2002 around 1:30 p.m. in the afternoon. The day she was born took my breath away, and my yoga practice began. My life went from a whirlwind of self-centered activity, to middle-of-the-night feedings, slow afternoons, and days that were not my own.

I was going down a road I never thought I would travel; I was a parent.

When my daughter was one, I attended my first yoga teacher training in Hood River, Oregon with Stephanie Adams. I remember feeling terrified of standing up in front of everyone to lead a portion of the class. Extreme nausea set in after I led my portion. I wanted to run, to quit, to go home, but I had eight weeks of this training and there was no refund.

About a month after I graduated, I was in a hot yoga class, in Ustrasana, Camel Pose. I was sweating and then I started crying. I couldn't believe it! Why was I crying? How embarrassing! I immediately shut down and went to Child's Pose because I didn't want anyone to see me crying. I had no idea where that emotion had come from.

I stayed away from Camel Pose for quite a while.

I started teaching prenatal yoga and led classes at Club Green Meadows until my youngest was about eight months old. Yes, I taught my entire pregnancy, right up until two days before Ava was born. About three weeks after she was born, I was back in the yoga room, two-year-old in tow, newborn in the Baby Bjorn. If you couldn't take the distraction, you had no business in my class. My career as a yoga teacher had just begun and it ran along the trajectory of my daughters' lives. They went everywhere with me. They would either play in the child-care or hang out with me in the yoga room.

I decided to open a yoga studio in Vancouver, Washington after leaving the tennis club, and what a journey that was. Ava would play in her Pack 'n Play while we painted the walls, and Bella would run around organizing things. They were almost one and three when we opened the doors of Satsang Yoga. Those were pretty crazy times.

The studio was an incredible success, and once it was open for a year, I wrote and led my first yoga teacher training. I was told it was another stream of income that was necessary for survival as a yoga studio owner. It took me nine months to write that program. In the writing and then presenting the section on Chakras and the Energy Body was when I woke up to the "real yoga."

It all made sense to me. All the layers, the density, the light, the prophetic sayings in classes, all the philosophy, the Sutra threads, all began to make sense. The battle of Arjun and Krishna, the infinite stories of Ganesh and Shiva, the "seat of the soul," the "higher realms," the Sanskrit; the pain in the body, dis-ease, conscious living...all of it. It was like this huge spotlight turned on, and it blinded me for a minute. I had been trying to hit the snooze button on my life for several years, and the Gods said, "No more! Wake up! You have work to do!"

It got a little painful there for a while. The path I was going on began to shift, like cracks in an earthquake. Life got crystal clear and things dropped away. My heart was in the driver seat, and I was on the road to radically changing my life.

Painful didn't begin to describe it actually.

"The yoga" for me became my life. The synchronization of breath and movement had become my daily mantra. Yoga soothed me, it made me strong, and it healed my heart. We really are layers of density, and yoga stripped away all the illusion so the light inside could shine. I had studied and practiced for years, and it was all finally integrating into my cells. I was living my yoga, which was at sometimes lovely and sometimes painful. But the chaos was gone. The indecision was muted. Clarity was the only option. Conscious decisions the only way. Up-leveling my awareness, the only option. Yoga became the path that will never end because the path to the soul is truly infinite.

So I teach and play from there. They say that wisdom doesn't come from learning or reading but from being. This practice of yoga has definitely reinforced that. It's like the learning needs to physically make its way into your body, and the mind must categorize it, until the heart can assimilate it and alchemize it into love, and finally the energetic and spiritual body aligns it with "all that is." Sounds ridiculously prophetic, but it's true.

After graduating from yoga teacher training, some people wait to teach. They wait to share their knowledge or assimilated wisdom. They think they "don't know enough to teach." As an initiator, which I am, I'm here to tell you that that's an excuse, an excuse to not use your voice. If you have completed yoga teacher training, you can teach. You are enough to teach, to share, and to impart your wisdom. Your message may vary over the years, but you're always ready to share what you know, when and how you know it.

I've been sharing this knowledge as I know it since the day I received my first certificate. It's changed a bit over the years, but the core message has always been the same.

When you move your body, you awaken the soul. Strong body, clear mind, open heart. Everything moves from there. Everything. Every decision, every judgment, every relationship—it all comes from your breath and how you show up on your mat. I tell people to observe their habits the second they step on the mat; it directly correlates to what's going on inside, every single time.

When I stepped on my mat the first time, I was anxious, annoyed, overly ambitious, and distracting myself from the pain that lived inside. I was callously (and unconsciously) building protective armor around my heart, while charging forward into my life…which, for the most part, is fine, but not if you're moving from a place that is injured, neglected, or motivated by fear.

This practice is not for the faint of heart. It's for love and peace Warriors who see the unsettled world we live in and think they want to help people. Most yogis, after practicing for a while, recognize that they are not here just to "help people" but to support, love, cherish, and adore themselves through this practice. I mean, we are all *one*, after all.

These teachers are the change makers and the thought leaders. Yes, seemingly, we're going out to make a difference, but honestly, the gaze is internal. We take self-inquiry and self-observation to heart—literally and figuratively. And then we share, knowing we're not perfect but that we are instead imperfectly perfect. Or maybe it's perfectly imperfect, I can't remember which one.

I started out sharing this practice on a cold gym floor with overhead lights that didn't have a dimmer switch.

And then I shared it with pregnant mommas in a hospital conference room where I showed up an hour early to move tables, light candles, and dim the lights.

I opened my studio so I could bring the community together. I shared this love with prenatal mommas, new mommas, kids, and all the regular folk who lived nearby.

I woke up while I owned that studio, and it all fell apart. My community supported me when my life came crumbing down, when my yoga kicked in.

I sold that studio and high-tailed it to San Francisco, where all my teachers were. I planned to learn something more from them.

In three months, I was sharing this practice alongside those teachers. I couldn't believe it. Who was I to sit on that stage at Yoga Tree Castro and use my voice? My dear friend who is an amazing musician said to me, "Dana, you really need to start seeing yourself as others see you. An amazing beacon of light, love and wisdom. Step into it already and stop avoiding it."

We all need initiators in our life.

I was teaching in a room that held 150 bodies to capacity and I still remember teaching to five. I would cry every day driving back to Marin, knowing I lost money that day. But my heart knew I was meant to be there. My heart just knew, so I kept going and eventually my voice got stronger and my classes grew to a comfortable capacity. I was flexing my muscles of self-love and self-worth. I was there to prove a point, to prove that I could make it teaching yoga. I was there to prove that I didn't need a "real job" that yoga *was* my real job, because it was my passion.

In between all that I rewrote and rewrote my 200-hour program; wrote and shared a yoga program for teens called Youth and Girls Elevate; and wrote and shared multiple "advanced" yoga and mindfulness programs for my 500-hour training program. I also authored two books, co-authored four books, wrote for several magazines, and stepped on the stage of many conferences to talk about yoga and why it's important. Behind all that was one motivation…to love.

Just love.

To love my past, to love my present, and to love the unknown of my future. To love my kids, to love my ex-husband, and to love myself. In all the shifts and changes, in all the transformation and relocation, I didn't take a break to rest or learn more, I learned as I went…as is life. It doesn't stop; we are ever-evolving beings, and this yoga thing, it shifts us. It pushes us. It elevates us, and it knocks us down. It meets us where we're at, and it brings us to our knees.

Here are some takeaways from this practice that still offer me fruit every day that I get to wake up and step on my mat:

- Practice and all will come, although it may not show up exactly how you thought.
- When you breathe, your body, mind, soul, and heart all align—but you've got to breathe deeply.
- Don't wait to be perfect to share your gifts; there's no such thing as perfect. And practice doesn't make perfect; it only makes for more practice.
- "Be present" isn't just a saying, it's a necessary tool for authentic living.

Wherever you are on this path, I invite you to answer the following:

1. How do you use the power of your awareness?
2. What's your biggest trigger and why? How does it show up in your life now?
3. What's your greatest gift and how do you share it?

4. Who did you uplift today and who will you uplift tomorrow?
5. How are you using your platform and your voice as a yoga teacher?
6. What are the nuggets from your greatest challenges?
7. Who can you still forgive?

It's not about the sequencing.
It's not about the technique.
It's not about who you studied with and for how long.
It's not about your playlist or the outfits you wear.
It's not about your ability to look epic in a pose or how many followers you have.

But instead how you make people feel. How you show up in difficult situations. How you unconditionally love. And how you see yourself as a synchronized spiritual being living a human experience.

That is the practice. The life-long practice.

Special Gift

13 Moon Mystic Program—One Month Free!

Join Dana Damara every month, in the comfort of your own home, for New and Full Moon practices, meditation, and sacred ritual using oils and crystals, to connect you deeper to your truth and alignment with the Moon and Her cycles!

Visit **www.13moonmystic.com** and **USE THIS CODE: PRACTICE**

Dana Damara is a Master Teacher and healer with Shaman roots. She began her yoga journey almost 20 years ago working with prenatal women and new mothers and running her own successful yoga studio in the NW. Today, she spends her time writing books, running Embody Truth Yoga School, creating Youth and Girls Elevate (a yoga program for middle and high school adolescents), facilitating Moon Circles, and leading workshops, trainings and retreats around the world.

Dana Damara is a mother, author, coach, teacher of teachers, speaker, and servant of the heart. She dabbles in crystal therapy, essential oils, Tarot and Astrology readings, and Reiki healing. She is an activist for women of all ages and her programs support feminine embodiment, self-love, sisterhood, sacred ceremony and ritual, and offer a safe space for exploration and curiosity. Dana's essence is scented with truth and natural leadership. She has an intuitive ability to tap into the elemental connection between women, magic, and power.

Dana is based in Southern California and regularly traverses the planet, offering her wealth of knowledge and breadth of wisdom through a deeply spiritual and physically rigorous vinyasa practice. When she's not leading one of her fiery Moon Mystic Classes, she may be facilitating a retreat, hosting a Moon Circle, empowering her clients, creating an inseparable tribe with her Embody Truth Teacher Training program, or simply observing her daughters as they navigate their own karmic path.

In her quest for personal evolution, she has written two books: *Oms from the Mat, Oms from the Heart,* and is co-author of *The New Feminine Evolutionary*.

Her greatest teachers are her two daughters, her family, Byron Katie, Seane Corn, Louise Hay, Shiva Rea, Michael Beckwith, Janet Stone, and every student that has ever walked into her class. Learn more at **danadamara.com**.

I Stopped and Time Stood Still

BY NICOLE DEAVILLA

Let me begin by saying that I have a most loving and supportive family. So, I was surprised, very surprised to find samskaras, *(deeply rooted tendencies/thought patterns) within me of being unsupported. How I discovered this was nothing short of a miraculous unfolding. On a bright and sunny day...*

...I was at my desk. Working hard—or so it felt. Actually, I was working frantically and anxiously. I was coming up short financially—again. Then suddenly, I stopped everything I was doing. I stopped everything I was thinking. I stopped my fraught thoughts and overwrought movements, my frenetic activity. My thoughts were transfixed.

Time stood still.

In that beautiful moment of complete stillness, a realization enveloped me. I was hit with the dawning realization that my actions were counter to my reality. My inner voice guided me to look at my surroundings, near and far and with great clarity to see: Where I was. What surrounded me. What I had obtained. What I had been given. Who was in my life. Not as an act of gratitude, or appreciation, but rather as an act of lifting a veil of delusion—a fiction of lack and need.

In yoga we speak of *maya* or delusion as many veils that, one by one, obscure our full vision of truth, or reality. The thicker our veils, the deeper our delusion. Moments of clarity, when we experience the veils pulled aside, are gifts from heaven, and each moment lasts as long as it needs to last, as though time stands still.

Everything in the room was in clear focus. Everything outside the windows was, too. This clarity extended beyond what my physical eyes could see. This realization was a body, mind, and emotional experience. In that moment, I felt fully supported well beyond the basic needs of humanity.

Why had I been feeling differently?

Moments before, I had felt myself in a familiar state of being while working on finances and feeling the stress and pressure of making it all work. Yes, I had bills to pay. Yes, my cash flow had ebbs as well as flows. I was sick and tired of that feeling. This time, sick and tired of it enough to shake myself out of the fog of delusion.

There had to be a reason I was stuck in this rut. The answer came in that moment, when time stood still. I also perceived in that moment that there was nothing I had done wrong, nothing I could have done differently, nothing...except I could have changed my subconscious beliefs, had I known that was where the issued lied. The issue wasn't about learning more, being more clever, working harder or getting that lucky break.

Instinctively, I knew what to do—I'd been meditating for years and I had experience lifting veils. I'd done it for myself, my clients, and my students. I also knew that the veils could oh so easily fall back down, distorting my clarity and blocking the light of the moment. I vowed to overcome this maya.

I knew some of the work would be relatively easy, now that this moment of clarity had been given to me. I also knew that veils come in layers. Some layers are light and easily removed. Others are heavy and sticky and familiar. Others still are surprising and unfamiliar and we deny that they are ours.

I resolved to set to work immediately and diligently, taking whatever it would take to clear the veils, release any karma, scrub off samskaras, and get out of this particular rut of delusion that was hounding me.

I figured it would be easiest to let go of those layers that I had absorbed from the people around me and today's culture. They didn't really belong to me and weren't a part of who I felt I was or how I came into this world. These layers laid at the periphery of my subconscious. The first step was to identity them. As my mind went forward and backward through time like a runaway train, culling out phrases, thoughts, and beliefs that I did not consciously hold, I plucked them and laid them bare to examine.

I saw the insidious hold these beliefs had on my subconscious mind. I was simultaneously surprised that they were entrenched within me... and they felt all too familiar. Through this journey of reliving old feelings, stories, and experiences, one word kept appearing: Support. Or, rather, the *lack* of support.

My father did not pay child *support*.

My managers did not *support* me...

I knew I had found a key.

Support.

I knew I needed to call upon the help of my guru, Paramhansa Yogananda, and my paramgurus who came before him. With fervent prayer I waited to feel their guiding presence. Then I peered into my subconscious and mentally and meditatively sought those ideas and beliefs deep within me that were not true, yet were stuck to me like velcro. I asked that they be transmuted into the belief and experience of being *fully supported.*

Over the coming days, weeks, months, and, yes, couple of years, I consistently dug deeper. The results were paying off. My mind was calmer, I was less reactive and my circumstances were evolving and changing. Finances grew easier, somehow, though I wasn't "doing" anything differently.

Being experienced with teaching and how to work dynamically with affirmations, I knew that I couldn't just *think* my way out of this. I had to change my actions and thought patterns—and put a new recording into my subconscious mind. I created a "feeling affirmation meditation" that I used before going to sleep at night and upon waking in the morning. I took the time to feel the experience throughout my entire body.

I knew my transformation process needed to be experiential. I had to feel these affirmations in my body and get my emotions involved. I developed a connection with the divine feminine energy of the earth and the divine masculine energy of the sun, drawing them from below and above me. Then I would merge them within my heart chakra, one of the seven key energy centers in our body. From there I would offer the energy, the experience, the feeling up through my *sushumna*, the passageway between our energy centers, and to the point between the eyebrows, wherein lies the sixth chakra of insight.

Over time, I modified and changed my practice as needed. As each veil was lifted, I'd either modify it or create a new affirmation-meditation. Ahh... the feeling was so incredible as each veil was lifted and removed!

This practice I speak of is my yoga. Whether I am meditating or on the mat or going about my day, yoga is what propels me.

After much progress and fewer veils, I would still find myself getting quite stuck. I would pray and meditate, hoping to find the answer, make the transformation. I kept hearing the same missive over and over again: "And then you will die."

> *I thought I had lifted that heavy veil from my past lives...*
> *Why did it keep coming back?*

I finally realized that it wasn't enough to just let it go. To understand it and affirm my way out of it in the opposite direction wasn't enough. I needed to meditate deeper and longer to reach the samskaras. I had to *fight* it—out loud and vigorously, too. This was the veil or group of veils that were the heaviest.

And, I will be honest...they are still not completely gone. I have wrestled them to the floor. I have pushed them to the side so that I can move forward. They linger and claw at me from time to time, in hopes that I will sit back and rest, and let go of "deeper, longer, thirsty, guru-given meditation"* so that they can rise again.

I made it to the next level by realizing how much support I had received and continue to receive in my life. I needed to fully embrace and acknowledge with deep gratitude that I have always been supported. I was a bit of a wild child in some ways, and I was taken care of in all of my adventures by family, friends, the universe and, last but not least, God.

I rarely talk about such matters, let alone write about them for a chapter in a book. However, if my experiences can be helpful for others to grow and transform their own lives, I will share them.

(**Samadhi* a poem by Paramhansa Yogananda)

I began sharing my meditation-affirmation.

What does all of this have to do with yoga practice, with doing a downward facing dog, or even sitting to meditate? *Everything.* The goal of yoga practice is union. When opposites like hot and cold and supported and unsupported no longer have a grip on us and are merged as equal, neither good nor bad, they do not pull at us and disturb our peace or steal our energy.

The Ananda Yoga® affirmation for downward facing dog, is "Calmness radiates from every fiber of my being." When we are experiencing union, we radiate calmness. We radiate calmness in all circumstances. We experience our true blissful nature. Oh! How I love to be in the blissful state!

People often think that if we get rid of the pull of opposites in life, then life will be boring. However, quite the contrary happens. Life doesn't become dull. In fact, when we master the opposites—our own personal demons—life becomes so much more deeply rich.

Just as I can recall the vivid colors, the singing birds, the beauty around me, in that moment when time stood still, my relationships now are richer, my energy is richer, my experiences are richer and I am richer.

The more I am richly supported, the more rich my experience of bliss grows.

Being an internationally recognized yoga therapist, best-selling author and published researcher wasn't enough for **Nicole DeAvilla** who helped launch the International Association of Yoga Therapists Educational Standards and helped write the National Standards for Prenatal Yoga Teacher Training.

Nicole has a deep passion for coaching and launching leaders whether they are yoga professionals, political leaders, moms, authors or CEO's, so they can influence, heal and help a new generation to thrive and soar to new heights.

Nicole's strength lies in her uncanny ability to get at your root issues, whether health, wealth, or spiritual, and help you affect the momentum and change you desire. She guides you to harmoniously live a modern lifestyle, aligning your values with your work so that you can heal, thrive, and manifest that which is most meaningful to you.

With over 35 years as a yoga professional and business owner, Nicole's focus on Social Media began in 2012 when she launched her best-selling book, *The 2-Minute Yoga Solution FAST and EASY Stress and Back Pain Relief for ANYONE at ANYTIME* which helped propel her onto TV, online and in print.

Her social media adventures include working with the social media team at the Ricki Lake Show and Vanity Fair. As the Social Media Coordinator for 30 Seconds Mobile, she helped launch documentary film makers, authors and coaches via weekly Twitter Chats.

She is still a sought-after yoga therapist who can read your body, physically and energetically and apply the wisdom of yoga and the best practices of science in practical ways that work for you and your lifestyle. Because of her ability to quickly recognize solutions for her clients, she offers body audits, mental and emotional audits and chakra energy audits to set you on your personalized path to greater vitality, productivity and joy filled days.

Learn more at **the2minuteyogasolution.com**.

Special Gift

Now you can enjoy a Move, Breathe, Center, Manifest guided experience once only available to Nicole DeAvilla's private clients. Click here to receive your audio recording of "You are Supported, Held, Nurtured and Loved". Start practicing today, so you too can receive wisdom from your yoga practice as you listen to Nicole's voice guiding and supporting you.

http://the2minuteyogasolution.com/free-support-meditation

Listening to the Silence

BY STEPH RITZ

Thud! My head pops off the pillow as the walls rattle from the loud thunk against my bedroom door.

Focus! Where am I? Oh right, Gramma's cottage. Gramma!

I scramble out of bed to find Gramma Rose on the floor with half of her face drooping. *She's having another stroke after being released yesterday from the hospital—after already having two strokes!*

Gramma says in utter disbelief, "This can't be happening, this isn't supposed to be happening!" She says it over and over like a wish fulfilling mantra if she says it enough times maybe it'll become true.

It's been maybe two minutes since I was startled awake. My thoughts are racing. *What am I supposed to do? Focus Steph! She can't fall asleep. She has to stay awake. And aware! How do I get her off the floor? She's supposed to have both her knees replaced next month. Half her body is numb. The hospital is an hour away. Every minute counts. It's snowing, and must've snowed a lot last night. We're in the middle of nowhere. 9-1-1 is too far, would take too long to get here. What am I supposed to do?*

With the knowledge of levers and pulleys (thanks science teachers!), I manage to pry her off the floor, and get her safely seated with support on each side. I move as fast as I can—getting dressed, running to her room for clothes, and grab both of our boots on the way back. With the chore of getting dressed to keep her busy, I feel Gramma Rose is safe to be alone while I figure out what to do next.

As soon as I walk outside, I am hit by a different kind of overwhelm: sensory deprivation.

There's a stunning shimmering white monochrome blanket muffling all sound and obscuring all details of the land. The silence seems deafening. Every detail of the landscape is blanketed by two feet of snow that has fallen overnight. Nothing looks familiar.

For a moment, I can't hear anything. I can't even hear my own breath, as my brain refuses to process sound.

Eventually I begin to hear what my eyes see—snowflakes landing on two feet of freshly fallen snowdrifts still slightly blue with the dawning of the day. The flakes are giant—as large as your thumb print! I can actually see the crystalline structure of each quarter-sized floating frozen droplet, each one so beautifully and uniquely different from the next.

I stand transfixed.

My breathing steadies.

Time stands still.

A few moments and that's when I hear it—a message from the silence. *Push broom, pitchfork, shovel, GO!* With crystal clear clarity I knew what had to be done, and I knew I had to be fast about it...

I grab the push broom and hurriedly clear the fluffy feet of accumulated snow off the top of Gramma's car, jam the pitchfork in the front of the yard just before the drop-off, pull the car over the frozen ground up close to the cottage until the bumper dings against the pitchfork, (yeah, I've never driven in snow before), and shovel my way to the front door. I straddle Gramma Rose from behind so I become a human wheelchair, supporting her 200-pound 4'11" frame on my forearms, and manually moving her numb right side forward from my ultra-wide leg squat position (Goddess Pose) as we head to the car.

Gramma has to stay awake on the drive to the hospital. But how can I keep her thinking? Get her talking!

Gramma Rose, still with half her face sagging, starts sharing stories she doesn't want to take to the grave with her. More than anything, Gramma's stories give me perspective and understanding into the ancestral knowledge flowing through my veins. She asks me to have compassion for my cousins—

shares stories of how crazy their mom, my aunt, was even as a child truly believed she was switched at birth and was actually a princess. (*Stephie, turn right up there.*) She tells me where to find the hidden news articles detailing the abuse my cousins endured. (*Turn left here.*) She asked me to make sure the great-grandkids got something from her because they weren't written into the current version of the will, maybe something collectible they could hopefully one day give to their great-grandchildren. (*We'll be getting off at this next exit, Stephie.*)

How is it, that when faced with death, Gramma can think about how to stretch her love seven generations into the future?

For my first time ever driving in the snow and dealing with a blizzard, the journey is surprisingly smooth and we arrive in under an hour. I am so freaked out that I actually park the car and human wheelchair-goddess-walk Gramma inside, forgetting I could drive right up to the Emergency door. The medical folks act fast, really fast, and the next few hours become a blur of phone calls, pacing hospital corridors, and waiting oh-so-patiently. Once Gram is settled into a room, it's time for me to head back to her cottage.

It's only when I step outside into the blue night that I see the giant pile of snow that's fallen. *The drifts are taller than me now! It looks like two more fresh feet of snow fell on top of last night's storm!* I do a full 360° donut as I pull into the gas station. *Whoops!* Since I'm still facing the way I was going, I decide to go about my business like nothing happened. *Tra-la-la. Slick, Steph...*

When I merge onto the highway, it is a complete whiteout. Traffic goes maybe 5 mph and it is a scary crawl back to Gramma's cottage. With white knuckles, I tortuously follow the red taillights of the car in front of me in a long parade of nervous drivers inching along.

The country roads on the second half of the drive aren't all that bad and I manage to make it a mile from the cottage before I round a turn too fast and slide into a ditch. *Seriously?! Seriously Steph?! Come on!* I collapse my head on the steering wheel in utter disbelief. When I look up moments later, I'm staring at the tail end of a pickup truck—a hunter happened to see me go into the ditch and came to help me! Finally, I make it back to Gramma's cottage, totally drained.

When I look back, it's still hard to believe either of us survived that day.

Two decades later, a yogi friend told me it was the yogic practice of *Drishti, or the art of focusing beyond ordinary sensing*, is what helped me do what needed to be done to save Gramma Rose's life back when I was an 18-year-old kid.

Thank goodness I got my driver's license exactly one month before I would need it to save Gramma's life. Thank goodness I followed the deep calling I felt to go up to Gramma's cottage days ahead of schedule, as no one knew Gramma was being released early from the hospital. Thank goodness my mom supported me in taking a gap year between high school and college so I could be available. Good golly, life is interesting sometimes.

The blizzard that blew in Gramma Rose's third stroke left around five feet of snow, the pitchfork stayed in the ground until the spring thaw, and Gramma gained me as a sidekick for the next eleven years.

After that fateful day, I became Grandma Rose's voice. Gramma lost her short-term memory and often mixed up her words, the strokes fried half her vision in each eye, and her autoimmune disease made recovery a never-ending road.

Learning how loud silence can be was the spark that guided me into a lifelong journey of inquiry and exploration.

Did you know that SILENT and LISTEN are spelled using the same letters? I spent a lot of time listening to Gramma Rose's silence. I'd watch her rub her sore wrist, and silently add it to the list of things to bring up next doctor's appointment. I'd secretly set her up to win the battle to find the right words by embedding them into the conversation before she would need to say it. I'd massage her feet so I could check her skin tone and swelling levels.

Gramma Rose spoke clearly without saying anything. No one wants to be assessed; yet everyone wants to be touched and loved. And love is a universal language that does not require words—it just takes focus to hear what's not being said. While I might have been her voice, she was my song. Often, I think back to my time with Gramma as the pauses of being present—the focused breaths during tumultuous times that easily and effortlessly took me beyond the edge of what I was capable of handling.

Where you focus is a choice.

You can choose to show up with an open heart, clear mind, and determined spirit any time you want. Choose to take discovering your soul to the next level in every decision of every moment for every day to come...You get to choose. You always have a choice.

When you're writing for others, here is what I ask of you: love what you do and the people you help. Be completely confident in what you teach and know to be true. You don't have to be ready—you just have to say *yes* when opportunity knocks.

The practice of Drishti definitely influences how my fingers fly over the keyboard, tippity-tapping my heart message into words.

When did I first see myself as a writer? It wasn't when I was first published, or even after my fourth book project. It wasn't when my words were printed in 500,000 magazines around the world. It wasn't after negotiating half a billion in contracts, or even when I watched the world change when made-up words became accepted terms to describe things that had never existed before. It was only after hearing a woman say she'd gone home and packed her bags after I told my story from the stage—my story had given her the strength to leave an abusive relationship. If I could do it, so could she.

This is my eleventh book project—and sometimes I still don't consider myself a writer.

What I wish for you is to see how silence can influence the way your message flows through your fingertips, guiding you to get in touch with the wisdom you want to share so your community can receive the insights that come through you.

As you move forward with sharing your heart message with the world, I ask you to trust the practice of Drishti. Listening to the silence is a crucial part of the creation process.

How do you write from the depths of your soul?

You write by listening from truth and honesty, with mutual respect for who you are *and* the person you know you'll become. You write from your heart message, letting ancestral knowledge flow through you, bringing a depth of wisdom to the surface for others to touch and feel. And you write by listening to the silence.

Steph Ritz is a visual and verbal communication expert, who guides you to develop your brand presence with crystal clear websites and cutting-edge marketing strategy. As a writing coach, website designer, and portrait photographer, Steph has gained a reputation for turning what you're saying into what you meant to say. She's helped clients grow their radio audience to well over 200,000 listeners, get their documentary into a billion homes, and design websites known to convert millions of dollars for her clients.

When her parents passed away a few years apart, suddenly Steph was the only person left alive who knew the stories behind world-famous paintings. She stepped up to the task of fulfilling her parents' dying wish to see her famous step-dad's autobiography published. Together with the publisher, Steph turned the text into a stunning coffee table book, *Stanley Meltzoff: Picture Maker*, which delves into the stories behind art that changed the world—fully integrated with an online marketing system that still stands more than a decade after its design.

Having graduated Suma Cum Laude with degrees in Education and Writing, Steph pursued a career as a ghostwriter after her first book. Working with influential world leaders to shift industry standards, billions of lives have been impacted by her work. She teaches weekly online writing classes at **stephritz.com/workshops** and offers group retreats in the giant California redwoods.

Steph Ritz is the founder of *Writing That Converts* and author whose (non-ghostwritten) books include *Books That Sell You, Stories that Change the World,* and *Pioneering the Path to Prosperity*.

Learn more at **stephritz.com.**

Special Gift

Set yourself up to succeed with proper positioning stories for you, your products, and your brand using Steph Ritz's Proven Content Creation Strategies.

Bring more clients into conversation with you through your website, blogs, videos, articles, scripts, and books as you voice your passions with stories that change the world.

Learn More at **stephritz.com/practice**.

Yoga Saved—and Keeps Saving—My Life

BY MARCY SNODGRASS

Yoga saved my life. I know that sounds quite dramatic, but I feel like it's true. I'd had open heart surgery at the age of twenty-three due to a rare disease. Doctors said that I would continue to have surgeries and be on medications for the rest of my life. But I knew there had to be a better way. So I decided to start yoga.

I started with a video because there were no studios where I lived. I would slide that tape in the VCR and do my yoga! I could see differences in my body within just a couple of weeks. But I could also feel the changes in my mind and in my emotional capacity. Nobody really knew, but I struggled emotionally due to the steroids and immunosuppressants I was on. Yoga allowed me to begin to work through those emotions, and then work through the physical issues, too. Along with the yoga, I added a change in nutrition. I went from having whatever I wanted to healthy food only. Then to organic healthy food. Then plant-based organic food. And then juicing. I was dealing with an inflammation issue in the body and I realized that my nutrition, my yoga practice, and the body work that I received all worked together for my wellness.

It took about five years, but by using yoga, better nutrition and body work, I was able to come off of the medications they said I would be on the rest of my life. I was able to avoid the heart surgeries that they said I would continue to need.

It's now been more than seven years since I've been off of all of the medications, and I feel amazing. A key part of this has been my yoga practice; it was the catalyst that changed things for my health. Now, I love the way my body and mind feel, and my outlook on life is much better.

I travel a lot for my job, and sometimes it can be a challenge to keep up my yoga practice. The first year that I started doing yoga, I traveled 34 weeks out of the year. So I decided to take a yoga class in every city that I visited. It taught me alot because I was exposed to many different styles and teachers. It boosted my practice quickly and I learned which styles of yoga I preferred. I learned what not to do, and I learned what to do. And I got the bug to teach, because my passion is educating others.

I soon realized that I wanted to share yoga with the world. But this year of travel was all about my self-care, which is something that I believe in so firmly and so strongly that it has to be number one. I've always needed a lot of self-care, and it was definitely lacking in my life until I found yoga. My practice really helped me to learn how to love myself.

During that year of travel, I did my first headstand at a studio in Cincinnati. I wasn't too far along in my yoga journey, and the teacher walked me right through a headstand, where there was no pressure on my neck and everything felt amazing. All of a sudden I lifted up into headstand using my core. After class, I thought, "Did I really do that?" It gave me the confidence that I needed to really deepen into my practice. As a type A personality—a control freak and a perfectionist—I wanted to compete and do the best yoga that I could do. I could barely bend over forward when I started doing yoga, and so I wanted to push myself and push myself. But, as those wise teachers tell us, if you back off of your practice a little bit, you'll find that it blossoms and goes further much more quickly.

Eventually, after about a year of practicing yoga, I realized that I needed to back off and not push to 110 percent. What would happen if I tried 80 percent? My practice started to move so quickly and I was consistently doing yoga at least four times a week. I started to see changes in my practice; I was getting stronger, my legs were getting more toned, my arms were feeling like I could actually do chaturanga, which I had thought might be on my ten-year plan. It was an amazing transformation in so many ways, and I realized that I had to share it with other people.

Now, there was no yoga studio in my town, but I've never been one to be afraid to be the first person to bring something in. In fact, I was the first person to open a spa in my town! I live in a very small conservative town, and I had to educate people on what massage therapy was. I did that right out of college and loved it. So, for ten years I was educating people on what massage therapy was and was not. We created a community of people who loved health and wellness, and now, yoga would be another tool in the belt. It would fit in. So I went to yoga teacher training, and I absolutely fell in love.

As soon as I got home, I started teaching yoga classes and sharing it with my community. Of course, now I had to educate people that this was not a religion. This was a very interesting journey in our small, conservative town, to say the least! But people were open to it. Our community started to feel like a little yogi tribe. As it grew, I became more and more excited about the possibilities of seeing people take their health into their own hands. I saw people come into class who had pain and injuries who would leave strong and healthy.

Sharing yoga really lights me up. I also love to travel. My other job, sharing essential oils with the world, allows me the business model to be able to travel. So I sold my yoga business and my juice bar business, because I wanted the freedom to educate people and train them in different ways and teach them how they could put all of this stuff together. But what happens to your yoga practice when you travel? You have to stay committed. So here are some ways that I stay committed:

1. **Get a travel yoga mat.** It's super simple and easy. I do not like using rental mats when I go into other studios. Yes, they're always available, but I'm kind of a germaphobe, so I like to take my own mat. So I have a thin travel mat, a JadeYoga mat. Manduka has a great travel mat, too. Choose whichever style you like, but have something that can easily fold up and put on top of your suitcase. I find that if I carry my yoga mat with me, I will go to class or I will roll out that yoga mat in the hotel room. The great thing is, you don't need a lot of equipment to do yoga. You don't even have to have a mat, though I like having a mat. My mat feels like home to me. So when I get on the mat, I find that my body just relaxes instantly and my mind follows. Do I take that off of the mat? Yes. But I like the space of my mat because it is a symbol to me of letting go, a symbol of re-energizing, nurturing, nourishing, and loving myself.

2. **Don't be afraid to take a ten-minute practice.** You don't always need to have an hour or more. Sometimes, when I'm traveling, I will pop my mat out of my suitcase, put it on the floor, and do 3-5 Sun A Salutations, 3-5 Sun B Salutations, a little bit of side angle triangle,

and play around a little bit. I might just do ten minutes. And then, maybe later in the day, I can do another ten minutes. As long as I've done something, I feel good about it. So, don't feel like if you can't do thirty minutes or an hour, that there's no use in doing it at all. That's simply not true. Do what you can, and be okay with that. We have so much pressure on us to meet expectations. Start letting go of what people expect from you, what you expect from yourself, and just live with deliberate decisions because it's what you want to do. The shifts in your mind and body will blow your mind.

3. **Google is your best friend when looking for a studio.** Look up the studio before you get to the city that you're going to. It's really important to plan ahead, because if you get there and then you're trying to find a place, you won't end up getting to class, at least not on time. It's easy to find whatever style of class that you like and any yoga studio in whatever city you're visiting. I like to look it up and look at their schedule, and that way I can plan the times and days I can go to class and don't let anything get in the way. Just put it on your schedule as if it's part of your work or your meeting. Schedule it in like it's a non-negotiable.

4. **Bring your yoga clothes.** If you want to go to a class, you need to always have your yoga clothes with you. And if you forget to take your yoga outfit with you, buy a new outfit. It's called retail therapy. This is how I have built up a great collection of yoga clothing. It's always fun to shop for a new yoga outfit, but if you shop at the studio, expect to pay a bit more. If you don't want to have to buy a new outfit, be prepared and pack your yoga clothes in your bag.

5. **Be vulnerable, open to the possibilities, and be a perpetual student.** Sometimes as yoga teachers, we go into a class with a teacher mindset. Instead, go into class open to the possibilities, open to learning and to being a student. I love learning, being adjusted, and seeing what the universe has to teach me. Every time that I go in with that open mindset, I find that my practice develops and that my mind is more open and clear because I allowed for vulnerable truth and new possibilities. If I am stuck on doing a pose in a certain way, I have to allow myself to let go of control and let go of my ego so I can be open to the suggestion of the teacher. When I've

done this, there's an openness in my mind and in my body that mirror each other. And then, I can bring that vulnerability and openness to my life off the mat. I am amazed how everything happening on the mat are just a reflection of what's happening off the mat in my daily life. And the way that I deal with it on the mat allows me the freedom and the knowledge to do that same work off of the mat. For instance, backbends can be very challenging for some people. I had open heart surgery, so I had a scar there and I had to work for years to find that openness because I was definitely closed off in my chest, in my upper back, and in my hips. I wanted to close everything in and protect myself. And that's what we do in life. We try to protect ourselves, and in that protection, we also cut ourselves off from possibilities of relationships and new career paths. Yet, as we work on heart openers and backbends, it starts to open up to a deeper place of vulnerability. But if you never take that chance, you miss out on all these possibilities that are there for you. So take that chance! It will blow your mind at what you might just manifest.

When I first started using essential oils and then sharing them with other people, I didn't want to be part of a multi-level marketing company. Part of me just wanted to shut down and not do it because I thought, "Oh, people are not gonna like that. They're not gonna like me." I had a deep-seated fear of people not liking me and a false belief of my own unworthiness, and so I wanted to shut that piece down. But then I decided to be vulnerable. What if some of those relationships did fall by the wayside? Were those the true friendships and relationships that I really wanted in my life? Or do I want people around me who will encourage and support me?

Because I shifted my beliefs, the possibilities and opportunities that opened up for me and my family have been unbelievable. I've made wonderful friendships and connections. Our team has touched more than 30,000 families in five years. If I hadn't opened myself up to that opportunity, I would have not only lost out personally but I would have cheated other people out of awesome experiences. Sometimes it's not just about you. So if you can get out of your own way and stop sabotaging yourself, you will find amazing things will happen.

A friend taught me this a long time ago: for every amount of trauma that we have in our life, we need an equal amount of nurturing. What does trauma look like? It can be something really simple, like someone didn't like your hair or your clothing today. Maybe our kid was teased on the playground. If the teasing goes on for five minutes, that child needs five minutes of nurturing to counteract that trauma. When a pet dies, you need nurturing to counteract that trauma.

We don't give ourselves the amount of nurturing that we need to counteract all the trauma in our lives. What does self-care look like? It might be a bubble bath, reading a book, or taking a yoga class. Personally, I find that yoga is very nurturing. Whatever it looks like for you, maybe it's getting a massage, or a mani/pedi, or going to a cabin in the woods for three days. Maybe it's going to a beach with tons of people. Maybe it's going to Vegas. Whatever self-care looks like for you, practice it daily. And when you have a really trying week, be sure to double up on that self-care.

I'm a person who tends to love a lot of things. I always want to say yes. But, I realize that saying yes is not always what I need or what's best for me. I've learned to pick and choose what I want to do because I deliberately want to do it, and because it's for my greater good. And, if it's not a heck yes, it's a no. If you have any part of your body that withdraws or contracts when you think about doing something, do not do it. Do not do it out of obligation, do not do it out of guilt, do it because you want to and you deliberately decide to do it. When you can start separating things like that—if it's not a *heck, yes!* then it's a *no*—it will put your life into a much simpler place and you will be a lot happier.

When you are in a place of overwhelm, distress, hopelessness, or desperation, it's time for a retreat. Sometimes I love going on an organized yoga retreat, and sometimes I make my own yoga retreat. This is actually one of my favorite things to do. Take three days, five days, two weeks, whatever you have the time for and can work into your schedule, maybe just a weekend, and you go someplace, you stay in a hotel, or an Airbnb, and you find a yoga studio that you love, that has plenty of classes to choose from, and create your own retreat. Do two classes a day. Maybe one is a Vinyasa class, or a hot class of something that's a little bit more vigorous and one that's more restorative or a yin class. Anything that floats your boat! Maybe you want to do two hard classes a day. Maybe you want to do two yin classes a day. Whatever it is that feeds your spirit, create your own retreat and make healthy food choices on this retreat, too. You will feel so good.

Here's an example: I was just in Nashville for two weeks, and I decided that I would do yoga every day for these two weeks. My goal was to do two classes per day for at least five days of the week. I was not really happy with the way my body had been feeling, and I had not been getting to enough yoga classes. I'd been traveling a lot and eating a lot. I had been to Hawaii, Mexico, and Vegas all within a month, so you can imagine what my body was feeling like. Well, in those two weeks, I felt stronger, more energized, relaxed, and I lost one pants size. I felt more toned, and my mind was clearer and more creative. I was able to do more in a day than I'd been able to do for a while. I was getting good sleep at night, going to bed at a decent hour, getting up early. I was naturally waking up for a 6 a.m. Ashtanga class. You know that your body is rested when you naturally wake up without having to have an alarm, and you do need to go to bed at a decent hour for that to happen.

Create your own yoga retreat, even if it's just for two days. Do this for yourself. Do it for your mind, your body, and your spirit. You will thank yourself.

So, you can see why yoga saved my life. I truly know that anytime I feel overstressed, overworked, overwhelmed or just not myself, I can get on the mat and feel rejuvenated, nourished, and strengthened in body, my mind, and spirit. When I am on my mat, I am reminded of who I am and I can live in alignment with that, because I know the world needs me. I hope that yoga will remind you, too, that you are amazing, you are fantastic, you are strong, you are fierce, you are compassionate, you are loving, you are kind, and you are enough. You *are* enough.

You are *enough*.

Marcy Snodgrass is passionate about healthy living and helping you to live your best life! After open heart surgery, and a major health journey of her own, Yoga became an integral part of her healing. She trained at Core Power Yoga in Boulder, Colorado in their Levels 1 and 2 teacher training programs. She did an additional 200-hour YRT program under Tiffany Cruikshank, in Portland, Oregon, and Aruba. Marcy has attended training workshops with Kathryn Budig, Simon Park, Shiva Rea, Amy Ippoliti, Baron Baptiste, Rachel Brathen, and Maty Ezraty.

She is a doterra Blue Diamond Wellness Advocate and travels globally to help other women entrepreneurs build their businesses. Her enthusiasm and instruction will take you places you didn't know were possible. You will feel energized, uplifted, and inspired! Learn more at **www.marcysnodgrass.com.**

Special Gift

Receive 25 of my favorite essential oil recipes and tips to de-stress and create clarity in your life.

www.marcysnodgrass.com/practicebookgift

Walking the Path of Dharma

BY ANANDA DEVIIKA' MA' A'CHARYA'

What is yoga? Is Dharma the same as yoga? In the West, yoga is identified with the asanas, or yoga postures. But yoga has lost its original meaning. Let us embark on how yoga came to the West or United States.

Swami Vivekananda came to the United States to attend the Parliament of Religions in 1893, and he brought the teachings of Vedanta and the Raja yoga. This event signifies the beginning of the bridge between the East and the West. This was the spiritual awakening in the United States, not considering the Native Indians' spiritual teachings. When Swami came, there wasn't any emphasis on the physical aspects of yoga until later in the 20th century, when the yoga asanas became popular. The physical aspect of yoga was more appealing to the majority of the population since it didn't have religious connotations.

Another wave of spiritual awakening came with Paramahansa Yogananda. He brought the teachings of Kriya Yoga. And then in the 1970s, the hippie movement was born, bringing a search for happiness through psychedelics and personal development practices. Yoga offered an alternative to the drug culture as a pathway to self-realization.

> "The Thousand Mile Journey starts with a single step."
>
> —*CONFUCIUS*

The yoga movement started with a spiritual emphasis but continued with the yoga postures and fitness through asanas. Yoga sutras of Patanjali became a Bible in yoga circles. Ashtanga Yoga was introduced by the sage Patanjali, and the asanas was the third limb of Ashtanga. India is the home of yoga, but the United States became another home for yoga. Though many traditional teachings were brought over and many gurus and teachers came to the United States, the teachings were adapted to the Western minds.

As time went on, I was undergoing my own transformation.

I was born in the Communist Yugoslavia. You might think there would be no yoga there, but to my fortune, I found a yoga teacher—the former ballerina Jasmina Puljo. She was more than eighty years old when she started teaching yoga. I was greatly inspired by her amazing physical agility and flexibility and her young spirit. I wanted to find God. I was brought up as an Orthodox Christian. As a young child my grandfather would take me to church with him. I developed a belief in God at a young age. My family worshipped the Saint protector Paraskeva, a female saint who left home and went to the desert to seek God. Once she connected with the Divine and Christ she came back to bring her knowledge to others. I remember the rituals performed by the priest in my home, the lighting of the candles, the extensive preparation to celebrate the saint. These were the sweet memories from my life there.

On the other hand, through my education, I embarked on the path of the scientific inquiry through studies in nuclear engineering and quantum theory. I was fascinated by cosmology and the place that quantum theory brought to my imaginations and expansion of my mind. I was lucky to have studied under the mentorship of two inspiring scientists, an accomplished physicist and a mathematician.

I often stayed long and late hours in my laboratory. One late night as I became tired, I laid down on the floor to rest. I was falling asleep. All of a sudden, I became panicky. Something wasn't right. I felt as if I was dying. I was floating above my body. I thought it was the end of my life. I had no idea what was happening to me. I didn't want to die. It looked like hours passed. I was still floating. I knew this was not the end, but the question was how to come back! It took all my willpower. All of a sudden, my body jerked and my mind came back to my awareness, my body still lying on the floor. I had no idea what happened to me. I thought I was crazy and kept this experience secret. But, looking back, this might have been the beginning of my spiritual awakening. I often think that some special people around me are gods with human limitations.

I completed my studies and was granted scholarship to continue postgraduate studies in West Germany, where I was initiated into the tradition of Tantra Sahaja Yoga. This was a turning point in my journey to discover the inner realm of spirituality. Three months of the intense yoga training in Germany was so transformational that I decided to go to India. This decision created a lot of turmoil in my family and in my scientific community, but I was guided by the cosmic forces to follow my heart calling. Going to India turned my life upside down. India was another universe. My life was changed forever.

Some decisions we make have a very deep karmic significance. My decision was my past life calling. The cause and effect of physics is equally relevant in all other spheres of our lives. Past and the present are interwoven.

I asked myself: What is dharma and what is religion, and is there any connection between them? Most of the religions started with the esoteric teachings that are not taught today to others.

I hope that teachings of yoga will be more fully adopted in the mainstream as a spiritual path. God is not abstract but a Divine experience, a magnetic force that nobody can resist.

Patanjali defined Yoga:

योगश्चित्तवृत्तनिरोधः ॥२॥

Yogaś citta-vrhtti-nirodhah
"Yoga is the restraint of mental modifications."

TANTRIC DEFINITION OF YOGA

Yoga comes from the root "yuinj," which means to "unify," to reunite the unit entity with the Supreme entity. This union is not like the union of sand and sugar, which when mixed can be separated again, but like the union of sugar dissolved in water which, once merged, can never be separated.

"Sam'yoga yoga ityukto jiiva'tma' Parama'tmanah."

> "According to Tantra, the unification of the *jiivátmá* with Paramátmá means *yoga*. After withdrawing the mental propensities, they are to be guided toward the Supreme Entity. Then alone will the withdrawal be final. Only by guiding these withdrawn mental propensities toward the Supreme Cognition can the total unification of the *jiivátmá* with Paramátmá be possible, and this is yoga."
>
> —SHRII SHRII ANANDAMURTI

There are some basic differences between religion and spirituality (*dharma*). However, the word "religion" in its original significance, meant the same thing as "yoga"—union with God. Religion comes from the latin "re" + "ligare" (to tie, to unite): "to unite again, to tie again to the Source." The fundamental base of all religions is yoga, the experience of God—consciousness. The founders of various religions may have had this experience and taught their closest disciples the esoteric practices by which this experience may be attained, but their later followers often did not. And gradually, as the esoteric practices were forgotten, the religion degenerated into the exoteric or purely external form of worship.

I would recommend the studies of yoga as a whole, not taking one piece and forgetting the other parts. That's like a blind man describing an elephant by touching different parts and declaring the elephant is this or that.

The human dharma is Bhagavad Dharma, the path to self-realization, our birthright to know the self, God within. Though there are many different systems of yoga, Karma, Bhakti, Jinana, and so on, the fundamental path is in the realization of God within.

As the Victorian era poet William Ernest Hanley wrote: "I am Master of my Fate: I am the Captain of my Soul," we are gifted to do the same. Each of us is gifted to follow our unique path to realize our union with Paramatma, become that eternal self, immortal and infinite.

Love is the beginning of the self and the ending of the self. It is never born and it never dies.

Avadhutiika Ananda Deviika' Ma' A'cha'rya', M.Sc., RYT (500), C-IAYT, has spent more than thirty-five years on her spiritual journey, teaching and practicing Tantra Sahaj Yoga throughout the United States and Canada. A graduate of the Technical University, Belgrade, Yugoslavia, with a master's degree in Theoretical Physics, she was inspired to further research the domain of spirituality and received initiation in 1977 in West Germany.

Ananda spent three years in Calcutta, India with her Guru and was trained to become an Acharya, a spiritual teacher. She received her Sannyas, the life stage of renunciation within the Hindu philosophy of four age-based life stages. She dedicated her life to serving as a sannyasini in the Northern Indian Tantric tradition under the guidance of her Guru Shrii Shrii Anandamurti. She served two organizations, one while her Guru was alive and another that she co-founded to continue her Guru's mission after his physical departure in 1990. Ananda Ma founded Ananda Wellness Institute of Yogic Wisdom and Ayurveda, and is a speaker, healer, and trainer of yoga teachers, yoga therapists, and acharyas.

Ananda Ma is open to all spiritual seekers who are searching for a spiritual lineage or the teachings to help them understand their own calling and search for the Divine. She helped hundreds of seekers to find their spiritual home and the teachings that changed their lives. Learn more at **www.anandayogawisdom.com.**

Special Gift

If you're a yoga teacher or someone very passionate about yoga, I'd be honored to help you expand beyond your 'on the mat' practice to create a fulfilling holistic yogic lifestyle. This lifestyle allows you to be happier, more accepting of others, more content and it can improve your health. My students get to enjoy more confidence, feel centered and empowered, and are more able to make decisions and trust their intuition. Do you want the freedom to create your dream yoga career and lifestyle? What is preventing you from manifesting your dreams? Many teachers after graduation struggle to move forward in their yoga career. Either they lack business and marketing skills or don't have the support to get out there and offer their services.

- Do you want to teach yoga classes with more confidence?
- Are you seeking clarity on your next steps to manifest your dream yoga career?
- Do you desire to develop your unique style and voice that allows you to feel empowered?
- Are you curious how you can teach students who resonate with you in your favorite niche?

This Mentorship can be your day of Independence, too!

If you're interested in exploring your vision and getting personalized recommendations from me, I invite you to apply for a complimentary **Yogini Clarity & Confidence Strategy Session.** After reviewing your application we'll let you know if your application is approved, and you'll be able to schedule your session.

Apply here now: **http://bit.ly/anandaapply**

Emotional Range

BY HOLLY BEAVERS

Dead, death, and die. These were words that I didn't use for six years. I could not bring myself to say them. I would not say them to myself and, in fact, would not say them to anyone. My mother passed away October 28, 2009, and I thought I would never be able to say she *died*. I skirted around the words. I said she passed or that she was no longer with us. I could not connect to the truth that she was gone and dead. It was grief. Core shaking, uncontrollable crying, scary grief.

My mother was put in the hospital almost a month before she died. She never came out of "being under." And I certainly I did not plan that I would have to "pull the plug" on my own mother. That was the hardest thing I have ever had to do. I was with my father and he just could not do it. He didn't ever say anything, I just knew that I would have to be the one to make the decision and tell the doctor it was time. Time for her to be out of suffering. Time for her to pass. Time for her to move on.

My mother and I were very close, but not in the way some people say their parents are their best friends. She was not that. She was not a best friend, because to me, she was a true mother. A loving caring being. And she was so much more than just a mother to me. She was someone who cared the way no one else will. We shared a unique bond. It took seven years to conceive me, and maybe that was part of it. She put a lot of effort in to get me here. And now I have found peace and joy in my mother's passing, in her death.

There is joy in who she was, who she still is for me, even if I cannot talk to her in the traditional way. She is still here for me. She is here for me in the ways of always letting me be me. She listens to me when I talk to her. She hears me when I am sad or cry. She hears me when I am joyous. Her memory is always here.

In early September 2018, my yoga practice showed me the possibility of discovering joy in my mother's passing.

Three years earlier in 2015, I went through a transformative yoga teacher training at Revolution Power Yoga in Vail, Colorado that taught me so much more than just the physical practice of yoga. Through that training and my continued practice of yoga, I have been able to heal. I have put in effort, and there has been space to grieve. I am no longer bound to my issue of not being able to say *dead, death, or die*. They are words, and they are real. I was able to forgive my father for not being able to make the decision to take her off of the hospital machines. And I was able to forgive myself for taking my mother off of life support.

Joy was always in me, yet yoga is what empowered me to actually *feel* joy and sorrow. From uncontrollable sobbing to joyous laughter and everything in between, I've experienced the full spectrum of emotions from being fully enraged, angry, full of grief, frustrated, pissed, annoyed, hurt, irritated, jealous, lonely, lost, scared, overwhelmed, stupid, worried, nervous and silly to content, comfortable, satisfied, peaceful, relieved, happy, inspired, joyful, energetic, excited, and amazed. There are so many emotions I can now feel. There are so many emotions we all can feel. And often I feel more than one thing at a time.

I can be sad at the same time as happy. I can be joyful and have sorrow as well. This is how I am still sad my mother is gone *and* I am happy in my life.

I invite in the shadow of darkness in order to find the gift of healing. Inviting in the gift of grief to contrast the gift of love is to know love and joy. Yoga has been the place where I have found the edge of suffering and holding the space so I can create healing. Physically, emotionally, and energetically yoga has been a pathway for me to invite in the range of emotions I have.

I now allow myself to acknowledge all the emotions I have and not crush out the "bad" emotions. There are no bad emotions. At times, the hard emotions like anger and grief seem bad. But they are real, and joy is real… and none of it is bad. I am also not bad for feeling how I feel. It is how I am able to be with my full range of emotions.

When I am on my mat, my life is happening right then. I am present to being on my mat and in my life. Sometimes I might not even be aware of how I am feeling. Yet when I get on my mat, emotions come up and it is a safe place for me to be and feel. There is nothing else to do, nothing to fix.

How I am on my mat is how I am in life.

While moving, flowing, and just being on my mat, I have felt grief and realized I am sad. I have felt frustrated and angry on my mat, and that means I am frustrated and angry somewhere in my life off of my mat. If I am angry at the teacher, I am angry at myself or something in my life. The teacher did not make me angry. Only I can make myself angry. And in the same way, only I can make myself happy. I can create what I want around my life to make me happy.

Have you ever been angry or frustrated at a teacher? Annoyed? Bored? It is not the teacher making you angry, or frustrated or sad or bored. You are the only person who can make yourself feel anything. You have the power to feel what you feel and then, to let yourself heal.

Yoga is an opportunity to release what needs to be let go of without judgment and to be willing to recognize our entire range of emotions. Yoga gives us emotional mastery, both on and off the mat.

I have healed after suppressing my grief by allowing the emotions to be there. And now, I have a new form of healing: Joy in healing. Healing in Joy. Abundant Joy. Of course, I still miss my mother, and I also feel her peace and her presence.

It is a blessing to feel everything you feel. You are exactly as you are meant to be, with all parts of you allowed to be there.

Yoga gives us an opportunity to see ourselves. Where we are on our mat is where we are in our life. I have found joy.

Holly Beavers has put her professional focus on health and wellness since the early 2000s and is in this world to inspire others to be the become their best selves. She is the owner of Energy Exchange that incorporates all things related to yoga, Reiki, life coaching, and writing. She has a passion for creating positive energy in the body and mind to discover wholehearted wellness in everyone.

Athletics has always been a large part of Holly's life, from running cross country and track in her younger years, rowing college crew, and growing up skiing in for vacations with family, which eventually brought her to moving to the beautiful state of Colorado from Chicago. Holly attended the University of Colorado at Boulder and graduated with a bachelor's degree in Communications in 2003. Achieving a dream and goal, she moved with her amazing husband Ryan in 2010 to the Vail Valley of Colorado. They live with their three dogs, Luna, Cowboy, and Peca and a ferocious cat named Monster.

Holly has completed more than 700 hours of Yoga Teacher Trainings and is a Master Reiki Practitioner and professional Life Coach. She is currently working on a number of writing projects, including *Try Easy,* a book about trying life with more ease and not making everything so hard.

Holly wants to inspire, heal, and help people be open to their biggest and best selves. She yearns to lead people to see that anything is possible and empower people to be for themselves in a full, loving, and complete way. She loves life, snowboarding, hiking, cooking, reading, art, and getting creative.

Learn more at **hollybeaversenergyexchange.com**.

Special Gift

Receive a 20-Minute Energy Exchange Breakthrough Session at
www.hollybeaversenergyexchange.com/bookgift

Practice: One Bartender's Journey into Presence and Compassion

BY JESSICA BELL

I've known for a long time that I have a deep desire to connect with others. The awareness of this desire became very clear to me when I began guiding yoga and discovered a genuine human connection with others taking shape. As a child, I had wonderful memories and experiences of growing up in church, and in the yoga space, I felt like I was connecting back to a community of equal mysticism and love.

Connecting to others on the mat became a place of sacred participation that eventually began weaving its way into the cracks and layers of my life. Oftentimes, it presented an opportunity to *apply* what I had been learning into a place that appeared to have much opposition—the grocery store, the workspace, the restaurant...You know, the places you go back to after you step off of your yoga mat. I've learned through each experience that contrast provides a way to create harmony and bring about radical transformation.

One of my greatest experiences, in contrast, arrived as a job bartending at a brewery.

Over a few months, I began to get to know many of the regulars and met people traveling from all over the world. Each person, with a different story of why they were in this particular part of California, was in some way seeking enjoyment. A tone of comfort, conversation, and camaraderie blended into the atmosphere of the brewery, allowing everyone to find their place within.

Meeting each new face with sincerity and true presence was quite challenging for me at first. I either wanted to stay and talk, ask more questions about their travels from New Zealand to Northern California, or move on to the next order from the couple who had been waiting patiently at the other end of the bar. These interactions provided ongoing information as well as stimulation—in an amount I wasn't accustomed to!

A *sadhana* is one's personal, individual, and spiritual effort. One might also call this a "practice." When you begin something new, you may quickly realize how much more time you will need to invest if it is something you would like to gain proficiency in. You may also come to realize that there are moments in which you feel stronger, accompanied by moments where you feel completely defeated. The awareness of this ebb and flow inside of the practice is the nectar that continues to bring you back into the alignment of yourself—that which is alive and sacred within you.

As the awareness of my true role as a bartender grew, I felt a desire to rise up and meet this new challenge of meeting and taking care of the needs of so many people. And, I also felt a sizable amount of discomfort and irritability.

I had only been bartending for about a month during the peak season of summer when the high volume of tourism had arrived. My shift began at 5 pm, and the scene I showed up to most evenings was at first chaotic and loud. Every seat at the bar was occupied. Families and children were waiting in the lounge area playing a noisy X-Files pinball game. Patrons in line at the bar were anxiously awaiting to try our craft beer for the first time...many scenes were taking place at once...so much stimulation.

I needed help integrating into this new environment, so I began repeating a mantra I had once read:

> *Peace. It does not mean to be in a place where there is no noise, trouble or hard work. It means to be in the midst of those things and still be calm in your heart.*

Saying this mantra to myself again and again around a lot of commotion allowed me to surrender to it and learn from it. Instead of wishing it would be a different environment than it actually was, I saw each disruption as a place to give my full attention to. When I felt overwhelmed at any moment, I would close my eyes, breathe in deeply through my nose, remember this mantra, and stay focused on what my next task was. And then repeat this throughout my shift.

Of course, there were some moments that took me out of this alignment, leading me to another state of mind completely. But this is what practice really is: consistently showing up in the midst of chaos to deepen the awareness of your own evolution and be an active participant in it all.

Perhaps you may be feeling as though the practice of love and awareness is far-fetched and somewhat unattainable. I sometimes doubt it myself! But that is when I come back to my practice. Some days that means moving my emotions through my body on my yoga mat or surrendering to silence and taking a day to be quiet and to be alone.

It may also mean taking a few minutes each day to ask for guidance or getting into the ocean with girlfriends to connect with a loving support system. No one practice is more important than the other, but finding healthy practices that uplift you and improve the quality of your life are important to build upon. They create stronger foundations from which you can grow.

As I showed up for each next shift, I started to notice something. My curiosity was growing for how to handle each new situation and the emotion that accompanied it. I saw each one as a stepping stone for development. My curiosity allowed me to observe, rather than react. I felt connected to my own power, something that wasn't about taking over others, but rather connecting more deeply with them. I softened in compassion while toning in tolerance.

Before true transformation can take place, some destruction must occur. A practice is an invitation to something new—a place to reset, reopen, and reconstruct what needs to be made new.

This is the art of practice. This is living yoga.

Jessica Bell is an embodiment and a meditation teacher. She invites others to explore their emotions and their bodies as a pathway to a purposeful inhabiting life: A life in union with our spirit and our spirit with God.

Growing up in two loving Christian homes, Jess has been influenced by the spirit in every direction of her life. At a young age, growing up in Florida, she discovered a deep enjoyment for choreography and hip-hop dancing. It was an expression celebrating the holy and meaningful parts of one's self.

As she got older, new forms of movement made their way into her life—swimming, rock climbing, yoga, surfing, trance dance. Along with physical movement later came stillness. It was here that writing became another important piece of her practice.

When yoga truly landed in her body, it felt like a return home. She remembers recognizing that she was being guided in deliberateness by something that was living within. A new connection to God took place in a way different from childhood Sunday church. From then, yoga and meditation became ritual.

With these new practices, came many new challenges. Life seemed to ebb and flow regularly and often appeared to be hopeless in living with sincere happiness. It is with the devotion of the practice as we show up again and again, that courage for living in purpose grows all around us.

In class, Jess guides you to drop into your spirit, be honest with your emotions and explore into your body where curiosity greets celebration.

She currently calls home in the Pacific Northwest of California, teaching yoga, co-leading women's circles, writing, and sharing meditation with others through the art of bartending.

"Create an intelligent, intentional existence and you will find deep meaning." Contact Jess at **Jessicalynnebell@gmail.com** and **www.toshayoga.com.**

Secrets of the Psoas:
How This Precious and Intelligent Muscle Can Heal Our Life as We Tend to Her With Kindness…

BY SHANTIKA BERNARD, PHD

My psoas is smart.

That sounds a bit weird, you might think, *How can a muscle be smart?* But in my experience, this is true. And on top of that I refer to my psoas as a "she". Let me explain how I got here.

If you have practiced yoga for a while, you have likely heard phrases like "strengthening the psoas" or "one of our core muscles" or "deep hip flexor." And indeed, the psoas is a long muscle that originates, on both sides of spine, from the twelfth thoracic vertebra, to the five lumbar vertebrae, fans out and flows downward through abdomen and pelvis and attaches medially to the thigh bone. It allows us to be upright, lift our legs, and walk. A functioning psoas stabilizes the spine and provides support through the trunk, forming a container for the abdominal organs.

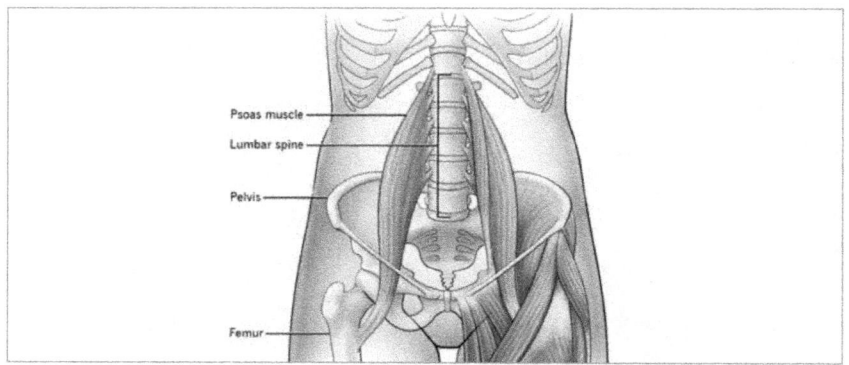

In most yoga classes, we are taught that we *have to* strengthen the psoas.

And that's what I did—through yoga, running, dancing, skiing, hiking, riding my bicycle...I considered myself the proud owner of a pair of strong psoas muscles! Yay!

In my thirties, my periods were often irregular and unpleasant, with irritability all the way to emotional roller coasters. So I did more exercise, which usually helped.

In my forties, the low back pain started. I considered it sacroiliac (SI) joint problems. I learned that I have very flexible ligaments. No big deal, just strengthen more, right?

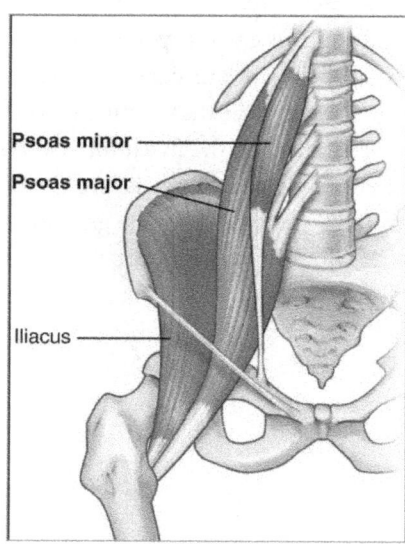

And then in my fifties, my digestion became more and more challenging, to the point where I had to make dietary changes and my emotional balance went downhill. It began to affect my relationships, my work, and my whole outlook on life and the aging process, which I had always intended to be a smooth and easy transition—*not so anymore!*

I know herbs and practice meditation, I am a somatic psychologist, and I support people in healing from trauma. I think of myself as someone who has the skills to meet emotional and physiological challenges. But somehow, none of my tools worked consistently, and I began to lose confidence in my "healer self" and my ability to be relationally present and responsive.

And then I took a teacher training in Yoga Therapy.

One of my teachers brought a chair to each of us and asked us to put our legs up and rest. Not just for three breaths, or three minutes—for twenty minutes. *Twenty minutes!*

Oh my, my old "exercise identity" thought. *How boring. Why are we doing this? I mean, literally doing nothing?*

But that *nothing* became a door, a gateway to healing in ways I didn't anticipate.

I learned to release in a way that was not available in meditation, bodywork, breathwork, or movement therapy elsewhere.

I learned to let go in the combination of *radiant breath**, allowing my weight to sink into the ground, and using what I had learned in meditation to access a sense of being supported, safe, and secure—to invite breath into the pelvic floor and to sense the softening of this muscle called *PSOAS*.

And so twenty minutes began to feel timeless as I felt my breathing relax and expand. And as this muscle began to release, images came into my mind of things long forgotten, packed away in the chambers of protection, frozen-in-time conglomerates of memory, including scents, sounds, feelings, images, and physical sensations such as contractions, trembling, and pain.

As the first surge of memories ebbed out, I had recapitulated the traumatic moments of an unnecessary and sexually intrusive surgery at age fourteen, of the birth of my first child, and of a recent fishing accident that had left me unable to walk down the stairs in my home for weeks.

I had also regained a depth of comfortable sensation and increased blood circulation in my entire abdomen that led to increased metabolism in the days after. Both my digestive and hormonal balance began to stabilize and improve in the weeks and months that followed. This was especially noticeable to my friends and family as I regained a much more positive outlook on life and my nervous system calmed down and began its repair.

I soon realized that the psoas is much more than I ever considered. It is a *magical ally* in our bodies that holds stress from early life with content that was too hard to "digest" at the time so that we could survive those intense life events. It also can "hold us together" when all else in the world seems to fail to support us.

But once we chronically over-use and over-demand the psoas' contribution—that is, by over-tightening or over-strengthening (hard exercise, intense work, or too much sitting at desks, in cars, planes, and coffee shops) and not relaxing the muscle itself and her attached supportive structures—she will have no choice but decompensate and leave us with challenging physical and emotional symptoms.

RELATING TO YOUR PSOAS—THINGS TO CONSIDER

Here are a few simple things you can do in your life to heal from what I call *psoas overload* and suggestions for how to create—or re-create—the magical supportive and loving relationship with your psoas that will nurture you, help you repair, and find your own unique intimate relationship with your psoas so that, ultimately, you can have a friend in your body that will help you heal your life.

◆ **First find ease, then learn balance, then build strength.**

Living in a culture that cherishes strength and independence and an "active lifestyle," it can easily become our main goal to focus on body shape and building strength in our yoga practice—even though that may not be what the body needs in order to heal. Trying to build strength on top of a contracted and, therefore, vulnerable muscle, calls for injury and actually deepens the core weakness and imbalance the system already experiences.

As we learn, over time and daily practice, to gently release the deep contractions and allow the underlying emotional issues to melt away and dissolve by applying some basic restorative postures and breathing practices, the somatic sensitivity in the tissues begins to return. That is the time to regain balance and build strength in an awake, secure, and receptive tissue and muscle system.

❖ The psoas is a survivor muscle.

> "The contraction of the psoas was originally designed as an intelligent response to a threat in order to protect our vital organs and to prepare us to run if need be. Today however, the threats are often more psychological in nature and more frequent than the nervous system can process."
>
> —LIZ KOCH

Moving from the deep-seated apprehension in our musculature around pelvis, spine, and legs toward a receptive and permeable pelvic integration requires that we develop a sense of safety and containment, a feeling of "owning the body" in this area.

It takes time, gentle practice, and conscious commitment to tend to ourselves with somatic awareness and kindness so we can move from the survival reaction in our sympathetic nervous system (fight, flight, freeze) to the parasympathetic response (rest, digest, repair) that allows to heal and strengthen our relationship to pelvis and spine over time and over the long term.

❖ The psoas is an emotional muscle.

The psoas holds memory for a long time due to its acquired protective and, hence, defensive nature. Emotional experiences that the psyche was not able to work through and kept guarded in an apprehensive cellular memory of the body, could often not be digested and released. With the gentle work of opening psoas hypertension, emotions can be swept to the surface where we can then consciously witness, recapitulate, accept, and release them—skills that were not available to us at a young age.

❖ The psoas connects us to the parasympathetic nervous system.

One of the big connectors between psoas and brain is the vagus nerve, a powerful messenger that can signal and "convince" the mind that there is no more danger by stopping the biological stress response of a fight, flight, or freeze mode. The vagus nerve (cranial nerve X) is a mixed nerve composed of 20 percent "efferent" fibers (sending signals from the brain to the body) and 80 percent "afferent" (sensory) fibers (carrying information from the body to the brain). Because about 80 percent of its fibers communicate parasympathetic information from the body to the brain, one could say that the state of the body in general and the psoas in particular has great impact on the state of our mind.

❖ **The psoas can facilitate personal growth and spiritual connection.**

When I teach psoas release in my yoga therapy sessions, I often observe a beautiful and deepening process of transformation and meaning-making that gives my students a sense of healing from a traumatic memory and leads them to an experience of "post-traumatic growth" and peace.

Recent studies have found that in addition to symptom reduction, yoga has demonstrated effects on personal growth, such as improvements in self-efficacy and self-confidence. Other studies have linked mindfulness practice with higher levels of positive affectivity, vitality, life satisfaction, self-esteem, optimism, autonomy, and competence.

One yoga definition of spirituality is *"the process of coming to a state of full self-actualization, or awareness, by working toward higher levels of consciousness through self-discovery".*

YOGA SNACKS FOR THE PSOAS TO DO EVERY DAY

Finally, I want to leave you with a few practical tools to try! They're bite-sized practices, like yoga snacks, for every day.

Therapeutic Asana Practices

1. Freedom pose
2. Supported bridge pose
3. One knee to chest pose

FREEDOM POSE

SUPPORTED BRIDGE POSE

ONE KNEE TO CHEST POSE

Please see my website for detailed descriptions of these practices:

- **Legs-on-chair pose**—for a psoas release after stressful events.
- **Yoga Nidra**—for stress relief, emotional support, and better sleep.
- **Constructive Rest**—for pelvic floor health.
- **Ankle rotations**—for psoas release, especially for sleep, emotional and digestive balance.

There is healing in the laying on of hands;
in the letting go of fear, in asking for help, in silence, celebration, prayer.
There is healing in speaking the truth and in keeping still,
in seeking sunlight and not shunning struggle.
Laughter and the affirmation of wholeness hold their own healing.

When the soul dances,
when the day begins in delight,
when love grows and cannot be contained,
when life flows from moment to moment,
healing happens in the space between thoughts,
and the breath before the first sung note.
Healing is a birthright and a grace.
When we dare to be open to the unknown,
when we extend ourselves in caring,
when we welcome in the vast expanse of life,
healing comes from the heart,
and blossoms from the inside out.

—DANNA FAULDS

Shantika S. Bernard, PhD, LMT, Yoga Therapist (RYT 500), is a passionate teacher, dancer, bodyworker, and somatic trauma therapist. As a certified Rosen Method Practitioner and inspired by her studies of Somatic Psychology and Pre- and Postnatal Psychology, she specializes in somatic integration, especially after trauma and loss, and the reconnection with the physical and emotional aspects  of health that have been compromised, dissociated, or lost over the course of stressful and traumatic life events.

Shantika recently completed her comprehensive training as a Yoga Therapist at Ajna Yoga in Victoria, BC, and is working on certification by the International Association of Yoga Therapists (IAYT) in 2019. She holds a license as Naturopathic Doctor (ND) in Germany and has been teaching Reiki Healing Arts in the tradition of Usui Shiki Ryoho for more than thirty years.

She works in private practice in Half Moon Bay, California; Portland, Oregon and Hawaii and offers individual sessions and groups in Yoga Therapy, Rosen Method Bodywork, Family Constellation, Inner Child Work, Sandtray, and DreamTending.

Shantika's work is attentive, gentle, intuitive, and deeply inspired by the recognition that we all heal best when we are truly listened to, within a safe environment that allows us to feel supported and respected as we unfold naturally.

Upcoming events include "A Woman's Time: A Yoga Therapy & Healing Retreat for Women in Transition"; "Yoga Therapy and Reiki: Recovery & Repair"; "Recovery and Resilience: Healing and Post-Traumatic Growth"; and "The heART of Reiki and Yoga: A Creative Meditation Retreat." For more information on these events or more suggestions on healing your magical psoas, visit **www.soul-tending.com**.

Special Gift

A Journey to Your Psoas:
A deeply restorative Yoga meditation for rest and repair

www.soul-tending.com

Tantra Is *Me*

BY LARA BRIGHTSIDE

"Tension is who you think you should be.
Relaxation is who you are."

—CHINESE PROVERB

I say this Chinese proverb near the start of every class that I teach and I remind myself of it when I'm practicing, and most especially, when I choose to hop into a fiery, hot, power yoga session.

For me, yoga is about guiding my body, mind, and soul to that still point of relaxation because then—and only then—do I walk back into the world as the truest me I can be in that moment, on that day.

Me...
With less tension in my body.
Without being anxiety-driven.
Carrying less stress.

Me...
Feeling totally, completely relaxed, having remembered and fallen back in love with life—again.
Ready to create, live, and act from this heart-centered place.

I used to believe that I was my truest self when I was fired up, tense, highly ambitious, and intensely active.

Most examples of successful people we see in the world embody these traits, like a modern-day hustler or a boxer who has geared up every ounce of his being to launch into the ring and fight for his victory.

Thankfully, it was my own driven attitude that pushed me to take my yoga journey a big step further and become a teacher.

A few years ago, my boyfriend (now husband) and I journeyed to the Shri Kali Ashram in South Goa, India. It turned into four exquisitely beautiful months where together we discovered the astounding power of relaxation through traditional Tantra yoga.

I'm going to share with you the biggest revelations I had while I was there that absolutely redefined who I am, changed how I live, how I express in the world, and how I practice yoga—forever. I hope this inspires you to deepen into our constantly renewing perspectives of the connection between yoga and life.

My teacher, Bhagavan Shri Shanmukha Anantha Natha, has studied the Rg Veda for more than 40 years and unveiled a lot that I now share in my tantra yoga classes.

I learned what "Tantra" really is, which, for me, explained everything I needed to know about life. Traditional Tantra is a life science that comes from the Rg Veda. It is a way of understanding who you are at your core and what your relationship is to this finite world.

First, the response to "Who am I?" became crystal clear.

What do you say when someone says, "And who are you? What do you do?" Maybe you're like most people and you just give a simple response about what you do for work, and where you're from.

How about when someone asks you more intimate questions about your ethics and morals, or your faith and belief systems, or about your lifestyle? What do you typically say then?

What dawned on me in my yoga training is that there are over 7 billion people in the world who all have very different and unique answers to these questions. Some answers might be similar, but they are all unique to the individual.

With 7 billion different belief systems...who is right?

Isn't it the answer to this very question that's plaguing the whole world?

Can we possibly establish a commonality between all 7 billion beliefs? Let's examine.

What I learned in my study at this very traditional Tantra yoga school is that the strongest commonality between people comes from the Rg Veda, the oldest text known to the human race. The Rg Veda is written in Sanskrit, which is the mother language of not only India, but all languages, including Latin.

The Rg Veda describes the monistic life science using symbology, like mathematical equations, to describe a view of our relationship to the finite world as an expression of the infinite consciousness.

According to Tantra science, monistic means "reality is a unified whole." In other words, it means that all existence can be described by a single concept or system. Traditional Tantric concepts that are from the Rg Veda are in *all* cultures and religions.

By studying the Rg Veda and traditional Tantra science, I not only gained a clear understanding of who I am but also found that common thread I was looking for between all faiths and life philosophies.

I gained a whole new perspective on consciousness.

On the surface or in the contemporary understanding of the word, it's about being aware of ourselves, our surroundings, our thoughts, and the way we direct our energy.

People talk about having a higher consciousness, being more self-aware or more aware in general, and about how awareness is an important first step to transformation.

According to Tantra yogic science, a truer definition of consciousness is far too vast to fully comprehend in this finite existence, and that mental awareness is different from consciousness. Tantric science wants us to think of consciousness as space...as vast as the cosmos!

In Tantra, we call this *the Brahman*, but it also has many names.

The Brahman explains how we live in a finite world and that there are limitations to this current existence, but that consciousness is infinite as it stretches beyond this finite world and it's impossible for us to fully grasp with our minds.

Brahman says that the finite world is created *from* divine infinite consciousness, of divine infinite consciousness, and that it is not different than divine infinite consciousness; this is the monistic, or Tantric view.

There are Tantric principles in all religions. For example in Christianity, it is said, "We are created in the image of God, for God to express, and we are the likeness of Him." The Bible opens with, "In the beginning there was the word, and the word was with God."

Science tells us that everything started from the Big Bang where all this matter blasted out to create our Universe.

According to Tantric science, the first sound was OM, and OM resonated into different levels and manifested into form. Everything was created from this sound and energy, therefore, OM is the mother sound that vibrates into matter. Everything has a frequency, a vibration.

Let's not forget to mention Einstein and E=mc2.

Everything truly is energy.

When I started to look at myself and my life from this perspective in a really deep and profound way, I fully realized that I'm not different than anyone else. We are all the same. And we truly are *one*.

I discovered that my purpose is no different than anyone else's on this earth: to express as my pure, Divine Self—as the divine consciousness that I AM.

You are Divine! Everyone and everything is Divine!

My teacher, Bhagavan, would say how infinite consciousness is horny! It wants to see all different, beautiful forms of itself!

Traditional Tantra is about removing false identities and expressing from a place of love. Essentially, Tantra is *love*.

Now yoga for me is Tantra, and Tantra is yoga.

I practice yoga to clear and clean off the dirt that's piled up on my body, mind, and spirit, to drop fears, filters, and conditioning, and return to my true, relaxed nature that honors the Divine and expresses beautifully as a human person who flows with LOVE in the world.

Tantra sees you as much more than just a set of muscles and bones.

Happiness isn't about how far you can stretch; it's about enjoying yourself.

For me, yoga is about total freedom. And Tantra yoga has taught me to live in relaxed wholeness, rather than in tension and fear.

Relaxation is who I am. It's who I aim to re-become each time I visit my mat.

Tantra is *me*.

Lara Brightside combines her voice and intuitive guidance with the ancient essence of yoga to transform pain and struggle into peace, love, and happiness. She is a traditionally educated Tantra yoga teacher who studied with Bhagavan Shanmukha Anantha Natha in Goa, India at Shri Kali Ashram. She's also a vocalist with a lion heart from which to sing; many can't believe such a big voice can come from such a little body!

Lara is an intuitive marketer working with some of the top personal development experts in the world. She spends most of her waking hours seeing that "people release struggle and self-realize how truly bright their life really is."

Through LivingBrightside, Lara, and her husband, Kevin Heidt, partner with global leaders and conscious businesses to cultivate happiness, health, and positive growth for their audiences and clients through bright ideas, magical marketing, and high-vibe execution.

To learn more about LivingBrightside or to contact them about your project, visit **www.livingbrightside.com.**

Coming Home into the Arms of Joy

BY ADRIANA BUENAVENTURA

I had a happy childhood and vivid memories of deep joy. I remember lying in bed after a long day of playing games and having fun like any happy child does, a wave of bliss washing over me so overwhelming that it was hard to hold my tears of joy. It was a feeling of warm and tender yet lively and dynamic, wanting to expand itself. I found myself surprisingly immersed in the depth of a swelling heart, pulsating this effortless joyful presence that had at this point taken over my entire being. I simply allowed it to allocate and be. My heart was filled with gratitude. From what I remember, I was relaxed, open-hearted and present in the moment. Deep inside I recognized this safe presence. It was familiar, like meeting with a loved friend after years of separation—or like coming back home after a long trip. This experience imprinted in me the knowing that there was something bigger than myself—a higher power, a magnificent presence alive within me. Without realizing it, this experience of connection to bliss became my point of reference when I most needed it.

As life happened, experiences like this one—for some reason—faded away. A few years later, while I was a young teenager, I was emotionally and sexually abused by a trusted adult and family friend. I suffered complex trauma for several years, well into adulthood. During those years, I felt easily overwhelmed, anxious, and fearful. I felt disconnected from the joy that fed my soul and was left empty inside—no life, no deep joy, just lots of sadness and sorrow. I was no longer at home within myself. I felt helpless, imprisoned, disempowered, and, at times, even embarrassed. However, my warrior-like spirit and the deep knowing that there was something bigger than myself kept me afloat.

After the abuse ended, my entire life became an incessant quest to free myself from the unwanted anxiety in my body and to recover the connection to the joy that fed my soul. I tried various holistic modalities such as Reiki healing, visualization, and guided meditation techniques and read self-help books. Each of these modalities was somewhat helpful. Then I came onto the path of yoga.

One day, during my yoga teacher training, a strong emotion came over me. It was the first time after so many years that I heard loud and clear my soul crying desperately: Take me home. The abuse was replayed like in a movie screen that was difficult to avoid. Even though painful, somehow it was also a relief. I had no choice but to face all the pain that had been suppressed in my body, now expressing itself in my tears, and I didn't understand that this was the first step in my coming home. Yoga postures led me into to a deeper meditation practice that has now become my go-to any time I find myself straying from home.

The deep sadness is gone now, but there are occasional days when difficult emotions arise and anxiety wants to take over. Some days, a part of me seems to retreat into fear, into the known darkness of the past.

But now, I know how to get out of that place and return to joy and come back home. I sit to meditate. I show up to the reunion of joy.

The journey is long with many steps. For some of us who have had trauma when we were younger, we may need someone next to us to help us navigate as we try out different healing modalities. There is nothing wrong with this. In fact, it is an amazing aspect of being a human, the fact that we are helped by mutually calming our nervous systems with other human beings.

Wouldn't it be nice that you could feel safe in the presence of the utmost peace when something seems to "go wrong" in your life?

I want to invite you to look into your life and think of a moment when you felt alive inside—in the flow. It can show up as a feeling of oneness with nature or the universe, while contemplating the ocean or the stars. It can be felt when we hold a baby, or when we simply forget ourselves during an activity that we truly enjoy. If you are still looking for that moment, think of an event that ended well. Sometimes, we can also hear a persistent voice that tells us to "go home" and stay permanently at home. Let this experience be your inspiration to go back home.

So, whenever you experience uncertainty about the future, anxiety, or a difficult emotion, remember the truth of your experience of aliveness. You are not your fearful racing thoughts. You are not the tightness in your chest or heart palpitations, nor the sensation in the pit of your stomach, nor any other uncomfortable sensation. These thoughts and sensations are actually here to act as a reminder that have you have drifted away from home. They are a valuable gift to set yourself free.

A calming yoga practice helps us release the unwanted sensations in the body and calms the mind in preparation for meditation. As we develop acceptance for the uncomfortable sensations, we will at some point connect with the part of us that is always still, permanent and eternal. A new door opens up allowing us to expand our sense of self. In such a state we feel in the flow. When we continuously surrender into the arms of the warmth and alive presence within, we feel untouched in the midst of life's challenges.

Paramhansa Yogananda stated that the Divine can be perceived in 8 different aspects: peace, calmness, love, joy, light, sound, power and wisdom. From my experience, as we accept what is, this facilitates surrender to happen and thus opens the door for at least any of the 8 Divine aspects to come forth. Surrender requires you to not expect a specific outcome. Surrender implies a total sense of trust that you will receive what you need at the time that you need it. It is an act of courage. If you devote yourself to a daily meditation practice, I am confident it will rejoice your being in profound ways.

When difficult emotions arise...
Choose to find the pathway back home.

Yet dark, uncomfortable, uneasy,
choose to observe what's within.
Persist. Something is awaiting to be freed.

Without judgment, let it be,
watch its ebb and flow.
Patiently wait. Let it be.
Behind the tumultuous emotions
resides a long forgotten safe place,
Remember you can surrender in its depths.

Even unclear, absent, hidden,
know that it is there,
allow your breath to smoothly take you to that space.
Once your heart is calm,
and emotions recede,
your heart will be receptive to feel.

As you watch your breath,
you surrender control.
Allow yourself to give way to its flow.

Let your longing fuel your heart,
Lift your gaze, relax,
with vehemence, ask.

Without attachment,
Simply be. Accept what you feel.
When all doubts fade away,
surrender into the greater presence within.

Forget yourself,
over and over again.
Choose to come back home,
stay there and take this uplifting presence everywhere.

> *"And in the midst of the dance of life, disease, and death,*
> *If you keep calling Him,*
> *Undepressed by His seeming silence,*
> *You will receive His answer."*
>
> —Paramhansa Yogananda

Adriana Buenaventura guides her clients to feel happier, healthier and live purposeful lives in the midst of life's challenges. She supports those who struggle with anxiety to calm their minds, get clarity, and find the courage to make choices that bring fulfillment to their lives.

An industrial engineer by profession, Adriana discovered the power of yoga and mindfulness in her own wellness journey and found her life's purpose, becoming an internationally certified yoga therapist and mindfulness mentor. Her clients also benefit from her life and nutrition coaching.

An Ananda Yoga® Teacher and Yoga Therapist, and a long time meditator, she has worked with various healing techniques including those from Raja Yoga and Ayurveda in her own life. Adriana draws on her inspiring journey recovering from emotional and physical trauma to help others recover and thrive. Her understanding and compassion for those who have experienced suffering in any form is complemented by her extensive experience with meditation and yoga through which she helps her clients free themselves from their body reactions and come back to their calmness within.

Adriana supports people both in-person and online and helps them make the necessary life changes needed to attain their fullest potential. Her peaceful and joyful demeanor as well as her healing from trauma inspires her clients to be the very best with their families, at work, and with themselves. She is also fluent in both English and Spanish. Learn more at **www.uniquesplendor.com**

Special Gift

BEING IN THE NOW: A CALMING YOGA PRACTICE

Experience a grounding yoga practice to help you be in the present and release anxiety. As you tune into your body, accumulated tension will release, your nervous system will calm down, and your body and mind will feel calmer. Calmness-inducing yoga postures and breathing techniques coupled with affirmations will uplift your spirit. This video gift includes approximately 30 minutes of gentle yoga and 5 minutes of guided visualization.

www.uniquesplendor.com/free-gift

Learning to Stay: A Yogic Journey to Motherhood

BY KALI CARMEL CATHIE

Like the Goddess, Yoga kind of snuck up on me, and asked me to stay. Whatever it threw at me, or dug up from within me, the invitation was to *stay with it*, and *breathe through it*. Even when "it" was a diagnosis of infertility, yoga promised that *staying with it* would move the energy of fear and resistance through my body and teach me to hear a deeper wisdom.

When I look back at my youth into my twenties, I could declare it as time epically wasted. If I were still in blaming mode, I would lay it on the drunken hummingbird living inside of me. She was looking for a different me in a different reality, not believing she would ever be whole—unless I became a mother. Yoga would teach me to see this drunken hummingbird as my greatest teacher—a bold, brazen and mysterious goad for the kind of balance only physical health can bring.

In my early twenties, Yoga began to awaken my hummingbird, dry out her wings, and gradually encourage her to fly a different path. Transparency, honesty, deep connection, and Truth slowly became much better ideas around which to pivot. The practice of yoga was slowly seducing me from within, one mini awakening at a time. In hummingbird fashion, I fluttered back and forth between the bottle and my practice. But, with yoga, daily life began to feel better, safer, and more manageable—no matter what Truth was unfolding in the world we were living in.

Yoga's "Eight Limbs" offered a structure within which to climb the unpredictable and messy realm of this soul's experience as infinite potential embodied in precious human form.

Transitions, pain, and discomfort on the mat mirrored how I navigated life off the mat. The way of the yogi eventually became just a better way to live. Being present with my breath, sitting in silence, moving through asanas, keeping my body-mind clean and clear, honoring the sacred guidelines, and staying with and breathing through whatever came up taught me to respond to life more intelligently than I had been. And a confusing world started to reveal an order to the chaos.

In my thirties, a skillfulness that came from beyond me started to dance through my spontaneity. A more present hummingbird was being born within me, and she began to trade fear, nervousness, and resistance for self-love, understanding, and acceptance. I was starting to embody radical Trust as the deepest Truth was seeking to emerge.

The wisdom flowed when the dance between the intentions of my little self and the Divine Self alchemized so that *the vortex of creation that I Am* channeled an intelligence of its own. I started to receive the deep seated knowing that my little self was not in control. And in the face of uncertainty, while walking in the mystery of not knowing, and the fear of infertility, *yoga kept asking me to stay.*

So I stayed. And I breathed through the fear of not being whole while the voice of Wisdom continued to deepen.

"Om *this* is it now" became the mantra.

As my thirties disappeared and my forties loomed nearer, my cleansed hummingbird got panicky, and instead of trusting *what was it now*, I accepted government funding for two rounds of in-vitro fertilization—both of which failed to extract any eggs from my thirty-eight-year-old body. With labels like endometriosis, blocked tubes, polyps, cysts, and now sinister-looking tumors, I was labeled *infertile*. They said the only way I would get pregnant was if I did more IVF—and *this time* with donor eggs.

Yoga told me this was not my path, that it was time to *let go.*

Now yoga was asking me to *stay with* that which I did not want to believe.

Finally, after much therapy, countless negative pee sticks, the mourning of babies who never were, a million tears, utter desperation, and hours of deep inner practice around surrendering to *what is*...I found the Grace to let go.

Truly.

Completely.

I finally exhaled into radical Trust.

Yoga turned me inward where I connected to the Goddess who was living Her life as me. She guided me to ask, *"If not this, then what?"* I had become a devotee of Goddess practice. I experienced Her in everything—"Her" meaning the Feminine Face of Spirit, held by Her inseparable other half, the Divine Masculine in all It's nurturing, honoring, holding, supporting, ground-of-all-Being way.

I gave my life to Her Breath that was breathing me. I declared to the soul I had been communicating with for the past decade that I was no longer trying to control and manipulate outcomes for this physical body of mine and that I was no longer going to feed this body in the ever hopeful, preconception way I had been. If a miracle wanted to appear in my womb to be birthed healthily and joyfully unto this planet, naturally, in its own good time, I would be available for that. But I was no longer orienting my life around what *wasn't* happening. It was time to focus on what *was*.

I was finally done putting my life on hold waiting for that fairytale to happen.

Probably for the first time ever, I realized I could live for what was happening *now*. And, because I no longer had a personal agenda, whatever else was trying to emerge through this human body could now have its chance. But the true gift was that I could *be* in my body without feeling that it had failed me. I could finally appreciate it as it was without needing it to be different.

And with that, at forty-two years of age...

I let go.

No one would have noticed from the outside. Nothing immediately looked different. I didn't need to tell anyone about it. But on the inside, everything had changed. This I have come to know as the flowful, spaciousness of *Grace*. It's a subtle yet incredibly potent form of surrender to what *is*, and it is the ultimate gift of yoga.

I settled into Grace, enjoyed my body as it was, and followed the call of the Goddess to create *Sacred Feminine Wisdom Online*. This became a six-week course that honors women's menstrual cycles, the phases of the moon, the female archetypes, different faces of the Yogic Goddesses, and Lord Shiva Himself. This stretched and pulled me in every direction, but *Grace* led the way, shedding the longing and yearning I'd lived with all my life.

My sacral center was on fire. *I was finally creating.*

For the first time in my life, I was free. I was *me*. I realized I was whole. Plan B was going to be just fine. I could stay *here*, too.

And then, at forty-three, thinking I was in the early stages of menopause, I received a most unexpected gift. I was naturally—and apparently miraculously—pregnant.

I was forty-four when the imaginal realm morphed its way through the veil and birthed into physical form. The healthiest, most beautiful and wide-awake baby I'd ever seen was suddenly living in our house.

But at nine months postpartum, I found myself so utterly empty and depleted of nutrients that I couldn't think, had no energy, and worst of all, I was utterly depressed. I'd waited so long for this miracle, and now here he was, crawling around, giggling, spreading pure light and joy—and I just felt like an empty vessel of darkness.

Yoga told me to withdraw my senses and turn inward. With such a paradox at play, I recognized the work of the Goddess. Something else was also seeking to emerge into this physical realm.

Yoga asked me to listen.

And so I prayed.

I meditated.

I listened deeper.

I needed *energy*—physically, and financially.

The art of yoga now taught me how to cut a deal with the Divine.

If I stayed with it, I would find both.

A new opportunity danced in my reality. Yoga told me to leap, and the net would catch me. And it did! What was at first a traumatizing realization now spun me down an incredibly michel—and deeply purposeful—path.

There truly are no mistakes. Ever. Period.

Today I am no longer the drunken hummingbird. No longer the girl waiting on another for her life to create abundance through. No longer un-whole or infertile. No longer identifying as my profession. Now, my personal life and my business blend together as a mind coach and ambassador for *true health*—the kind of health that empowers you to live abundantly in *every* way—physically, psychologically, emotionally, spiritually, and financially.

I live in a hydrated, nutrient-rich, energized body.

I cast my vote with each dollar I spend.

I raise my son in the healthiest way possible so that which is seeking to emerge through and as him in this lifetime can do so also.

I am the Creator of my life, the container for his.

Like the spider, I spin the world in which I live out of my own womb, and then I live as the Creatrix, in *that* world sharing the gifts of my experience. I am living in a reality I intended to live all along. I didn't find it at the bottom of a bottle, or from the reassurance of another. I found it in the heart of yoga and in *the art of staying with what Is*.

At the time of this writing I am in France, sitting in a castle that looms from a cliff. My husband and baby are playing by the River Lot down below. My life has been a haphazard traverse through the painfully, beautiful chaos of a mother trying to be born. Yoga taught me to *stay* with what Is. So I stay, and from *here* I dance on the edge of my comfort zone creating abundance, purpose, meaning, and value simply by being me—whole and complete, and always with plenty of room for improvement.

Kali Carmel Cathie is a Wanderlust Certified Yoga Teacher who has been practicing yoga for nearly 20 years and meditating for around ten years. She is originally from New Zealand but calls Tahoe her Spirit home. She has a Bachelor's Degree in Psychology and is in her second decade of practicing Spiritual Hypnotherapy. Kali's spiritual teacher is Sally Kempton and much of her work with the yogic deities of the Hindu Pantheon is interlaced through all that she does.

A unique kind of life coach, Kali supports you to connect with your manifestive self using her keen intuitive sense, hypnotic and meditative tools, yoga and a knack for asking the right questions. As a distributor for Kangen water, pure and premium superfood and CBD, she is an ambassador for True Health—physically, emotionally, psychologically, spiritually, and financially. She offers spiritual guidance via the Tarot, which she has read for three decades, workshops in Hindu deity practice and other soulful arts. She is working on a book steeped in sacred feminine wisdom for daily life, due to release in 2020. Her latest passion is in hosting a podcast called 'Dear Kali, Conversations to Elevate Consciousness.'

She feels blessed to enjoy motherhood and the bumpy path of parenting, wandering in the woods, writing, traveling, connecting with inspired people, and experiencing different perspectives. And one day she will become a potter.

Kali invites you to create True Health with her. It is her prayer that as more people conscious in their approach to life become truly healthy in their body-mind, and bank account, that we may collaborate intelligently for the greater good of ALL. On an entrepreneurial level she offers personal coaching to those who join her team in creating personal sovereignty from authentic and aligned visions for a sustainable future. Learn more at **www.KaliCathie.com**.

Special Gift

Please enjoy this **free audio practice** gift for learning to stay with what is. By revisiting this guided visualization you will notice a shift in the perspective through which you have been viewing that which is uncomfortable, anxiety-provoking, or just seemingly wrong. With practice, you will connect to the deeper levels of truth within you, allowing that which is actually seeking to emerge through you at this time to do so. Even in the darkest and hardest of moments, the next level of light within you is seeking to emerge.

Use this link: **kalicathie.com/free-gift/**

Finding Home Within

BY KATHERINE FOLK CLANCY

"Fill my body, fill my spirit, fill me with the sound of AUM"

"Do you think this yellow is like school bus yellow or lemon yellow, Mama?" my three-and-a-half-year-old daughter asks as we complete the color wheel while watching an online tutorial. We have watched this tutorial at least thirty times. I have yet to see the second tutorial on color blending, because the color wheel is the one she asks to do. It is familiar, and she understands how to engage me in conversation. I will stop and look at the pencils she is holding up, compliment her selection, and choose one, and then we will color for a bit, repeating this exercise.

While we color, I think about how my practice of yoga has given me a different perspective on how to recognize my daughter's desire for connection. It has taught me about letting go of my goals and to just be present.

My daughter came into my life very late after nearly 10 years of trying for a child. My pregnancy was very difficult, and my husband's method of dealing with the grief of the past and the stress of the present was to tear the house up with the intention of rebuilding. The deconstruction reached such a frenzy that when my incredibly healthy little girl was born, I was forced to move out and my marriage was over. I left that life with little more than my daughter and the clothes on my back. Our house was unfit to live in, and even our cars had been torn apart in an attempt to fix them.

After I moved into my new apartment, the image that I carried around for months was of a sad and lonely woman pushing a rickety baby carriage while trying to find a place to live. I identified with the moment as I retold that story to friends. But as time passed, I shifted to an observer who gently let the lonely woman with an infant walk away. My yoga practice had helped me release the identification and neutralized the pain.

My path to yoga started with hatha yoga. One of my physical education module choices in eighth-grade included yoga postures. This was highly unusual for the time—more than thirty years ago. Later I would try Zen Buddhist meditation. I loved the starkness of Zen. I enjoyed the mental challenge of the readings, but I never felt the tradition penetrate. I deeply longed for it to work. My path meandered, but mostly to traditions where accumulating knowledge was the path to release suffering. And I felt that I was slowly changing over time, but a deep longing remained unsatisfied.

About a decade ago, I encountered a tradition that involves a lot of chanting. I went for a week-long retreat to learn how to teach meditation to others. I thought I would do yoga, pranayama, and meditation in addition to the class. But we also chanted. A lot. There was chanting before meals, chanting before class, chanting while waiting for latecomers, chanting before meditation, chanting after meditation. Recording of the chants were played in the kitchen and during meals, and between classes you could hear the chants. I felt like I was in a musical, but without a story, costumes, or much in the way of anything beyond the simple repetitive of saccharine phrases.

If I had known about the chants, I never would have come. I was the rare kid in church who enjoyed a well delivered sermon but hated the singing. Music was my least favorite class in school, so much so that I would volunteer to do tasks to get out of the wretched weekly hour. As a camp counselor, the only time I would actively lead singing was when we walked from one activity to the other as it kept the kids out of trouble. But at the retreat, I paused. I had enough Buddhist and yoga training to find my aversion to chanting suspect. Why was I so resistant?

I had read that chanting is a powerful and healing tool. It resonates your body even down to the cellular level and helps you regulate your breath, your hormones, and your mental focus. Chanting can be healing. As I meditated, deepened into yoga postures, and focused on the class material, I was in a unique place to be less contractive toward chanting.

So I yielded and participated, and by the end of that week a deeply powerful healing energy opened my heart. For the first time, I really began to feel and understand the power of yoga that comes when you connect the body and mind with the heart.

"Fill my body, fill my spirit, fill me with the sound of AUM."

I would love to tell you that it was shortly after that moment when I physically healed all ailments and was able to have a child. But I trudged through five more difficult years. After having my daughter, my health was very poor. With no family within hundreds of miles, I found myself to be the sole caretaker of an infant. I was unable to do yoga postures or meditate for more than a few minutes. But I was able to chant. I would chant for hours. I would chant while I drove, to put my daughter to sleep, when we woke, while I cooked, when I bathed and dressed her. This chanting carried me through a time that could have been very dark. But it was enough to shake me from identifying with the image of the woman pushing a baby carriage trying to find a place to live. Chanting kept my yoga practice alive in a way that helped me continue to uplift, transform, and neutralize my attachments.

As my daughter and I finish the yellow wedge in the color wheel, we chant as we color. And once again, I feel a little release. I let go of the attachment of needing to move onto the next tutorial and embrace the power of connection my daughter seeks—and the ever-renewing love inside of the present moment.

"Fill my body, fill my spirit, fill me with the sound of AUM."

Katherine Folk Clancy is a mother, scientist, professor, and a devoted practitioner of yoga. A lifelong yogi, she earned her meditation and yoga teacher training credentials in 2012 and began teaching meditation and yoga. In 2017, she finished the coursework for her 500-hour yoga teacher training certification. Katherine uses yoga in all aspects in her life and finds it connects her more deeply with her child, students, friends, and family. Having struggled with health issues for decades, Katherine's practice helped her regain her health and vitality, empowered her voice, balanced her approach to life, and increased her time in the company of positive and supportive people. Compelled by the deep peace and healing she has found through yoga practice, Katherine experiences joy in coaching others to optimal wellness. Learn more and contact Katherine Folk Clancy for a free wellness consult via her **Facebook page: Mind Body Wellness Coaching.**

Yoga: The Final Frontier

BY GILLIAN CONFAIR

I didn't grow up with yoga: I grew up with science fiction. J.R.R. Tolkien and Philip K. Dick crowded out copies of the X-Men on my bookshelves. My walls were lined with signed photos of actors from Buffy the Vampire Slayer and Stargate: SG-1, and I marked the days of the week by what was on the SciFi Channel.

The theme of science fiction was woven into my entire childhood: the old Star Wars movies, the new Star Trek spin-offs. It was the language of curiosity and discovery that my parents taught me from a very early age, and it peppered my speech and fundamentally shaped the way I saw the world.

Unsurprisingly, I was the weird kid in school. Spouting references from obscure TV shows doesn't make you a lot of friends at age six...or age ten... or age fifteen, and there's a vast difference between being the weird hero in a movie and being called a freak by your peers.

In those tenuous adolescent years, I used SciFi as an escape. I ran away from the bullies and the insecurity to the far-flung reaches of the universe. I watched odd alien creatures be welcomed with open arms and lauded for what made them unique. I wished I could experience that for myself—being celebrated for being me instead of singled out and ridiculed for it.

Sadly, for me, that wasn't the case. And so I escaped into the world of the fantastic every chance I got. I doubled down on my nerd enthusiasm and attended conventions and joined forums. I traveled farther away from normalcy, and in this I found a sort of peace.

Fast forward a few years later, and I found yoga. It wasn't a fantastic retreat from life but a method for finding peace *with* the world around me. I was hooked.

In my first teacher training, I learned about the yamas and the niyamas—the first steps toward enlightenment. In the niyamas, the actions toward self, there's a part called *svadhyaya*—self-study. I liken it to the moment in "The Empire Strikes Back" when Luke goes into the cave and faces nothing more or less than his own fears.

For all the fantastical realms my mind had escaped to, or that I'd dreamed up, the scariest thing I could imagine was being alone with my own thoughts. And now, I was doing just that. Being forced to face the twisted and saddened parts of me was like opening an old wound. All the patterns of negative thoughts and habits, what's called samskaras, had to be examined.

My earliest dive into the tenets of yoga forced me to confront the pain of being bullied. It made me look at all of the patterns I'd developed as a defense against the hurt. I had to dig up the root of my low self-worth, of escaping, and of defensiveness. And deep at the heart of these patterns were the early memories of being laughed at and bullied for being different.

And like a shell around all that pain was science fiction. As I dredged up the old shit, the difficult memories and darkest parts, I saw this continuous thread of fantasy and escapism. My first reaction was to blame the tools of my self-preservation. I told myself it was time to put away childish things.

I started to fall out of love with science fiction. It was devastating and embarrassing: this part of me I'd invested so much of my life in and had now deemed frivolous or unimportant. This pillar of my identity became something to hide under the rug. I tucked away the comic books behind my row of yoga texts and decided that SciFi was a phase I'd moved beyond.

Then I studied yoga more. I dove into it—thousands of hours, dozens of books, and a handful of teacher trainings. And the more I studied, the more I realized the lessons of yoga were at the heart of all of that SciFi I'd loved growing up:

- Prana, the energy that unites all things, was the Force in Star Wars.
- Ishvara pranidhana, the concept of surrendering to the divine, is at the heart of Star Trek's great mission to explore the vast universe.
- Those samsakaras from my own self-study were time loops from TV shows like the "X Files."
- A higher calling wasn't just your dharma, it meant you were the Chosen One.

So if all of these concepts were at the heart of what I loved, why did I feel so embarrassed by it now? That was my ego, those old samskaras and fear of being laughed at or called a freak rearing its ugly head. And so I turned back inward. Only this time, I didn't think of it like the cave in Star Wars. I didn't use a metaphor from a book or a movie. I used my yoga; my practices of meditation, and compassion, and non-reaction. I saw the old wounds and didn't blame what had made me different, or even the people who had singled me out for those differences. I embraced them as teachers. I pulled the part of me that was strange out of the shadows. I dusted off my comic book collection and proudly put it next to my copy of the Yoga Sutras.

Sri Swami Satchidananda once wrote,

> *"To get to the point of complete dedication, many different routes are available: hundreds of paths, religions, and philosophies, all with one ultimate goal. It is immaterial what we do to achieve it as long as we achieve it."*

A character in my favorite show, "Farscape," once said,

"What is unique is always valuable."

My path has been odd and circuitous, but it got me to where I am today. More importantly, it helped me to discover *who* I am, and honor it as unique.

The most powerful thing I can say is this: Choose the path that makes the most sense for you. Find the one that clicks, no matter how strange it seems from the outside. Because the only way to embody these concepts of yoga is by embracing the person they're meant to inform—ourselves.

Gillian Confair, E-RYT 500, has two great passions in life: yoga and science fiction. She pursues both with the same commitment and finds the same joy, curiosity, and excitement in learning more about the great unknown both in outer space and inner space. The first she pursues through reading and watching all things SciFi, and the second she explores through the practice of yoga. She com-  bines these two passions with her video series, SciFi & the Sutras, and in her classes.

In 2013 Gillian created The Average Yogi, a website welcoming all yogis to the practice, regardless of age, shape, size, or ability. Through humor and honesty, Gillian offers space for exploration and self-love, both on the mat and off. Her goal is simple: Come as you are, and the practice will meet you there. She has learned that embracing what makes you unique can set you free, and she is honored to support others in their journey of self-discovery. Her enthusiasm extends to anatomy, alignment, and yogic philosophy and shapes the way she teaches yoga.

Gillian leads yoga classes, workshops, and teacher trainings in the San Francisco Bay Area. Through a combination of challenging and unique flows, her classes get you out of your head and into your body. The goal is to leave worries at the door and plant seeds of positive thought to carry throughout the day. Come to her class prepared to move and sweat. Leave feeling uplifted, energized, and more positively connected to the world around you.

Gillian lives in San Francisco with her husband and their expanding collection of SciFi memorabilia. Her teaching schedule, upcoming workshops, retreats, and trainings can all be found at **TheAverageYogi.com.**

Chef Yoga: The Power of a 10-Minute Daily Practice

BY LAUREN D'AGOSTINO

Five more minutes...

I'm practically staring at the clock as I move through the kitchen, waiting for the back door to open.

Five more minutes until my prep chef comes in, and then I can take a break from prepping produce from the farm for our house-made veggie burgers. The seasonal veggie burger has been selling out every other day—which is so great—but also means more production for me and my team.

I really shouldn't take a break today. I'm running behind on my prep list and there is still so much to do. It's already well after lunch...

But if I don't take this ten-minute yoga pause, I'll be running behind in my self-care. And I've learned, the hard way of course, that even ten blissful minutes of self-care makes all the difference in the world for me. This daily ritual, much like my morning ritual, has become non-negotiable. But it wasn't always like that.

It's October and the fall harvest is abundant and strong. We've been so busy this month opening the cafe and are working long hours, but we hardly notice. We are having so much fun getting to know each other and meeting our new customers. We knew the first few months of business would be filled with long days and tests of patience, so we made a commitment as a team to prioritize our physical, emotional, and spiritual health. A pact to check-in with each other and put our health first so we can be 100 percent invested in our mission to bring delicious plant-based food to our community.

When I feel energized and mentally clear, my body feels strong and capable. I could start the work day with a full battery, physically and mentally, but as the day went on my body started to feel sore and tense. The standing and repetitive motions of working in a kitchen cause my mental capacity to drain and my creative juices to congeal. And honestly, I didn't sit down much in the afternoons because I was afraid I wouldn't be able to get back up!

When I was working a second job, nearly full-time, as a waitress in the evenings a few years ago, I had to be ready to serve, even after I'd finished my work in the bakery kitchen. I had to recover and recharge quickly for the fast paced and physically strenuous demands of the restaurant.

I had to lean on yoga.

I discovered inverted poses and hip opening poses that gave me hours of energy. I depended on back bends and downward dog to reverse the effects of gravity and standing on the hard kitchen floor all day. When I'd finally get home after a sixteen-hour day, seated poses and heart openers were a saving grace. And slipping into savasana was not always easy because of the mental stimulation from the restaurant. So I relied on a diffuser with dōTERRA essential oil blends Serenity and Vetiver to take me into delicious sleep before I had wake up and repeat the process.

I've learned that what's really important for me is to stay relaxed and focused on self-care and staying well. So the way that I show up for my physical, mental, and spiritual health is by taking ten-minute yoga pauses when my prep chef comes in after lunch.

I sneak away to the office where I keep a yoga mat and my favorite dōTERRA essential oil blends for chefs and spend ten beautiful minutes working through my afternoon ritual. I turn the lights down and begin my practice by massaging the soothing blend oil into my feet, knees, neck, and lower back. While my body absorbs the oils I focus on my breath for a few minutes and breathe in the energizing and uplifting aroma of wild orange and peppermint. And, with about seven minutes to spare, I begin a yoga sequence to recirculate the blood and energize my body for a productive rest of the day. Usually it's a few sun salutations, followed by some juicy hip openers, finished off with heart openers, which are great to counteract my posture from the morning. I sign off on my practice with a few mindful breaths and a moment of gratitude before reaching for my socks and getting ready to go back to the kitchen.

My team has come to expect that I take a ten-minute yoga pause every afternoon, and if I don't, they nearly force me into the office to recharge. It is so much more pleasant to do my work in a body that feel strong, capable, and in flow. I feel such relief after I complete my afternoon ritual that I cannot imagine going a day without it. Learning to focus on and respond to the cues from my body to take a break, or even just a pause, has been life changing.

A few years ago, I had bronchitis for five months because I was overworked, overtired, and was not making time to take care of myself. How's that for a hard lesson learned? It was the worst I've ever felt, and I sometimes can't believe that I let myself stay that ill for so many months. I stayed so sick because I wasn't stopping, or even slowing down, to let my body rest and recover. I was moving so fast and working so much that I couldn't breathe—so of course bronchitis would manifest. Now, my daily yoga pause is how I nourish myself—every day, taking just ten minutes to check in with my body, mind, and soul.

I invite you to ask yourself if it time for you to create some new self-care habits, so that you can truly optimize your energy and flow in the world. If so, grab some essential oils, dim the lighting or go outside, and move your body—or rather, let your body move you! When I quiet my mind and become truly present, I find that my body starts to move *exactly* how it needs to. My muscles feel like they are getting massaged from the inside out, and I feel an incredible sense of relief in my being.

Freestyle yoga works great for shorter practices. Using basic yoga poses will drop me into the present moment so I can really let my body guide me. When I feel like my form needs correction I'll pop into my local studio for a live class with an instructor to check in and be led through more of a healing sequence. It always brings me a deeper connection and reminds me of how transformative and important a regular yoga practice and yoga community are.

I'm a huge fan of virtual or at-home yoga practices, too, because I can do them on my own time. Even if I only have five minutes, I can find a class that fits into my schedule. Sometimes I need an intensive reset so I'll do a thirty-day yoga challenge or boot-camp to get back on track. What works for me one month may not work for me the next month, and that's okay. I used to feel guilty for not showing up for my practice like I had in the past, but I now realize that my yoga has simply taken on a different form. Instead of a twenty- to thirty-minute sequence in the evenings, it may be a few sun salutations in the morning to prepare for my day—but this still counts!

Allow your yoga practice to evolve with you.

However your yoga practice looks right now is how it is supposed to be. It's not always a cute Lululemon outfit or an expensive yoga mat at the chic neighborhood studio. Sometimes it's jeans, non-slip clogs, and a space in my kitchen. But the outcome is always the same: I return back to center, recirculate the blood, and savor whatever time I've made to meet myself face to face on my mat.

Lauren D'Agostino is a Plant-Based Chef and Lifestyle Coach using plants and doTERRA essential oils as powerful medicine and self-love as a catalyst for lasting lifestyle change. She makes natural health approachable, easy, and simple by encouraging her clients to connect to their intuition as it relates to dietary and lifestyle choices. Inspired by her work as a vegan chef, the global  consciousness shift and her own transition into living a natural life, she is guiding others to lead a more plant centered lifestyle both on and off the plate. Learn more at **lifewellloved.me.**

Planting Seeds for New Beginnings

BY JANE DEL PIERO

Girls compete with each other, but...women empower one another. I could feel the vibrations beginning to reformat my cells as my true nature was shifting into my core. Twenty-one days of full yoga immersion while living in the ashram was moving me away from patterns and behaviors that no longer worked for me as an empowered woman. Seed by seed, the vibration rippled out from deep within the spinning vortices of each chakra.

I was raised to be competitive: compete in school, be the smartest, compete in skiing, volleyball, basketball, softball, track and field, and soccer...

The competitor was born inside of me, and this athletic, redheaded Taurus loved it. I would get such a rush out of people cheering and screaming their support, Go Big Red Go Big Red. It was intoxicating.

I was the goalie on my local soccer team, and I was a natural athlete. Show me how to do a sport and with time I will excel at it. My childhood soccer team was undefeated; we won for years and years, in fact, no one scored a goal on me for five years. I had my name printed in the newspaper more times than I could count and became the ultimate competitive female, lettering in every varsity sport and always driving myself to be on the starting team.

Growing up in Telluride, Colorado, my father taught me to ski at two years old and it became my zen meditation to ski in the beautiful mountains of the San Juans.

I ski every day of the season no matter the conditions or the weather, and it lights my heart with joy. Some days I cry while skiing; other times, I laugh, as the sacred space on the mountain heals my emotions.

My drive to ski and be in amazing shape has at times been hard on my body, and I've paid the price in dealing with broken ankles and torn ligaments.

Years later, I've used that drive, powerful self-esteem, and competitive nature to create a successful private healing practice, travel the world, provide healing treatments to rockstars, work for Hollywood producers and manifest an amazing life. Until...

CRASH!

On October 2, 2016, in the Newark Airport on my way to Rishikesh, India for Yoga Teacher Training, I slipped and fell slamming my butt hard on the marble floor. It was the worst fourteen hours of my life! I had severe pain in my lower back and my legs that would lock up in spasms as I tried to sardine myself into the tiny airplane seat.

It was a spiritual kick in the ass, a wake-up call to pull myself into my heart, into my center and find my true happiness. A painful reminder every day of how my ego and my endless drive—at any cost—had finally caught up to me.

Yoga reminded me of my true purpose and my true nature—who I really was other than the scholar and athlete who made my family proud. The life-changing practice of daily yoga, mudras, mantra, and meditation helped me realize that yoga wasn't about competing to be in the best pretzel shapes and handstands but about honoring and illuminating the light that resides within.

Yoga wasn't a quick fix. In fact, it's been years and years of seeping into my bones, my heart, my mind, and my soul, polishing up the woman within so I can empower others.

By paying close attention to the alignment of my body, my awareness of my physical body has been finely tuned. I've become more observant of the postures and various activities I participate in and am able to identify what is beneficial or detrimental to me. This increased awareness has assisted me in analyzing each and every action I take. I now eat with full awareness of how the food I consume affects me internally and affects my energy.

The yogic practice of Asanas and Pranayama has had a powerful cleansing and releasing effect on my body, mind, and emotions. After completing my daily practice, I find myself in a more relaxed and calm state of mind. In the past, I had a very short temper, as do many competitive people, but my daily practice has changed my temperament. Now, I rarely get angry. I am sensitive and have to work daily on my energy field and check in constantly to discern what is mine and what isn't. When I get a yes, I examine my emotions and allow my body time to process. If i get a no, I say return to sender.

Sadhana is a relationship with myself that I invest in and commit to daily. Sadhana requires daily discipline and an attitude of openness to the universal self that shows up and leads you to the mastery of yourself. Japa is the meditative reputation of a mantra or divine name. This is vibrational atonement for my heart and soul.

My Sadhana incorporates the chanting of the *Bija Mantras, the Sounds of the Chakras.* The Bija Mantras are mono-syllable seed sounds used as tools for the expansion and broadening of one's mind by harnessing the power of sound vibrations. When the Bija Mantras are said aloud, they activate the chakras to purify and balance the mind and body. Resonating with the energy of the chakras, when chanting the Bija Mantras helps me focus on the instinctive awareness of my body's needs.

These mantras were developed to create balance and harmony in the human body, mind, and soul. Everything in the Universe is in a state of vibration, and every part of our body has a specific rhythm and pulse. When all of our systems are balanced and in tune with each other, we experience perfect harmony and health. When our energy centers are imbalanced, our body will gravitate toward mental, physical, or emotional dis-ease. Sound therapy is an effective way to heal and rejuvenate ourselves, as every cell in our body is mainly composed of water which makes them excellent sound resonators.

Mantra is a Sanskrit word made up of two syllables: "man" (mind) and "tra" (liberate). Thus, in its most literal translation the word *mantra* means "to liberate one's mind." In Sanskrit, a "seed" is called "Bija." The word *mantra*, when translated, by virtue of its practical use, relates to a sound that can "create transformation."

Jane Del Piero is a medicine woman, modern-day shaman, acupuncturist, nutritionist, sound healer, and Ascension and Soul Path Transformational Guide who has worked internationally for over 15 years. Jane is the owner of LuvLight Alternative health care in beautiful Telluride, Colorado, where she has had a private acupuncture, herbal medicine, shamanic healing, sound heal-

ing, and distance healing Theta and radical forgiveness practice for 13 years. She spent many years studying with various healers and shamans and completed a 13-year apprenticeship with Mayan traditional healer Beatrice Waight. Jane worked in the music industry for 17 years, providing healing services to touring musicians. Helping clients heal everyday aches and pains,

Jane dives deeper, facilitating a personal journey of stepping into power and truth by relinquishing self-doubts, limiting beliefs and fears, and by releasing old patterns and behaviors that no longer serve. She guides and supports individuals who have chosen to do the work necessary to tap into amazing health, vitality, power, personally, professionally, and spiritually. Jane is a co-host of The Wild Women's Circle in Telluride and creator of Sacred Hoop, a monthly shamanic and ceremonial class. Jane is a Kundalini yoga instructor trained in Rishikesh India at the Shiva Tattva Ashram and a Tantra yoga instructor trained at The White Durga Tiger School in Quito, Ecuador. Jane co-hosts Sacred Hoop retreats worldwide, including retreats in Machu Picchu and Telluride, and Rishikesh India Yoga Teacher Training. For more information email **jane@luvlight.net.**

The Next Right Thing

BY BANTON DYER

My path toward yoga started because I wanted to beat people up. As a child, I had been beaten and chased, and I felt a lot of fear. I wanted my fear gone, and I thought the only way was to be big, mean, and tough. I saw martial arts as a way to become the biggest, meanest, toughest person. But, unbeknown to me, martial arts was my first "next right thing" toward my spiritual quest. My first sense of spirituality came to me through the classical Chinese martial arts.

I was sixteen, angry, and had low self-esteem. I thought I needed to become powerful to defend myself. But, what I got was standing meditation, *sangha* (spiritual camaraderie), a code of ethics, and a new direction in life.

I fell in love with martial arts through the practice, through the repetition, the realization, the being in the moment, and the expression of my soul through the movement. If you are not in the moment, you get hit. You learn. You are brought back to the present moment. In the present moment, you learn to let go of worry.

Martial arts gave my mind and soul a positive direction. It also gave me honor and helped me develop a sense of reverence that I had never experienced before in my life. I gradually embraced the spiritual aspects because of the experience of letting go. It was not intentional. It was by accident. It was a byproduct of wanting to "beat people up."

It was through the training that I developed a sense of being able to be in the moment and let go of what was going to happen later in the day or tomorrow. And that practice, over a prolonged period of time, at least got me to the point of not reacting to all of my *samskaras* deeply rooted in the subconscious old anger, old fears. Back then, I still had these intense angry, fearful emotions. But, through the practice, I got to where I didn't have to physically act upon them. The code of ethics that comes with the classical martial arts was a big part of what I was absorbing. This is very similar to the yoga practices of *yama* and *niyamas* (the do's and don'ts of yoga).

A major component of my practice was the standing meditations. The practice is what enables you to be on fire yet learn not to react, to just stand in the moment of both the pain and the ecstasy and to relax. To be able to meditate in a painful, stressful environment—even a battlefield—conditioning you to relax in all sorts of situations.

Chinese martial artists aren't made, they are forged.

Martial arts did make me tougher and stronger, but it did nothing to alleviate my fears and rage. It enabled me to stick to a code of ethics of not reacting to my fears toward others in a violent manner. I was off to a good start. The steady practice of standing meditations particularly helped me not react to certain emotions by not reacting to the physical pain of the martial arts practice.

Martial arts practice was the first time that I ever felt an experience of self-nurturing. It allowed me to be able to experience my own sense of being. As time went on, I experienced deeper levels of self-awareness. Later, in yoga, I was able to experience the next stage, which for me was feeling self-compassion.

"We will love you, until you can love yourself."

My martial arts practice helped immensely in connecting me to a spiritual life. However, I was still emotionally depleted from a life of chaos. I was suicidal. My life was one self-destructive act after another.

Eventually, my lifelong relationship with drugs and alcohol caught up with me. The memory of the tough love I experienced from the people whom my dad introduced me to during his recovery, when I was twelve, helped me to move to my next step. I needed that sense of family and direction.

In my recovery program, I found spiritual tools. Applying those tools to my life eventually led me to develop an experiential sense of God. Before this, I never had the feeling that someone else had my back. Believing in God and feeling supported didn't come easily.

The first thing I remember is that I was furious with God, or the Higher Power, as I wasn't even sure if I believed. I had a mentor who mentioned that was good; you can't be mad at something that you don't believe exists. What I got out of it was having different tools to work on recovery, not necessarily believing in them but using them brought me a sense of God—or something or someone—having my back. Eventually I had that feeling of presence or awareness in my life.

I look back now on my experience during that time period as Karma Yoga (the yoga of spiritual action). The tools we used worked if you did the practices, working hard to make amends and face your fears. They don't work if you don't do them. The goal is to become self-less. To be more interested in helping others than interested in your own personal problems.

My feelings of being stuck and the dysfunctional thoughts and actions continued. I had become aware of my *samskaras,* but they were so big that I was afraid and didn't know how to address them. My next best step was psychotherapy and counseling.

I got into counseling because I was still rageful, unhappy and felt self-hatred and unworthiness. I was left alone for many days and weeks as a child, and the pain from the isolation was unbearable. This created my deepest *samskaras* of this lifetime. I was also beaten and molested numerous times and told frequently that I was useless, stupid, ugly, and fat even though I was none of those things. As painful as that was, the abandonment and isolation I experienced were far more painful. One therapist said that the worst thing you can do to a prisoner is to put him in solitary confinement. These words broke my denial that my childhood had any resemblance to normalcy. Knowing this helped me to break through and take my best next step.

Working with many therapists over the years enabled me to at least be willing to look at my deep emotional scars, feel them, and begin to heal them.

Besides the extreme emotional pain I felt, my body, though fit, was racked with physical pain due to the numerous beatings and by intense martial arts training. Though strong and agile, my core wasn't able to support me, giving rise to back pain along with other pain from old injuries and broken bones. Acute back pain sent me to yoga.

Later it was the consistent practice of yoga and the practices beyond the asanas or postures that took me further and helped me go deeper into emotional, physical, and spiritual transformation.

God only knows when I began to practice yoga. It was a while before I become serious about adding another practice, as I still maintained a martial arts practice and was hesitant to add more to my daily routine. But I started to see a similarity in martial arts and yoga. I also was able to see and experience the depth of yoga once I made the commitment to a regular practice, as well.

It wasn't until I had a consistent practice that I could understand what other yoga practitioners had been talking about. Fortunately, I found compassion through yoga, and experiencing self-compassion was mind-blowing! Yoga has opened me up to a deeper sense of spirituality through practicing *ahimsa* (non-violence, compassion). More than one of my yoga teachers and mentors saw the need for me to focus on *ahimsa* for my own well-being, because I was always so hard on myself.

So I did. After a couple of months, I began to have some breakthroughs. I saw how I was being cruel to myself. Then I saw myself mentally and emotionally beating up on myself, and then again I saw myself beating up on myself for beating up on myself. Once I was able to see this spiral clearly, I was able to begin to practice letting go of it. I could then use my yoga techniques to help let go of the judgment that led me to be emotionally violent with myself.

In a yoga teacher training, I learned that every trauma and stressful moment that I had was probably still embedded in my tissues and nervous system. Wow. No wonder I still had a lot of work cut out for me.

Through the various practices of yoga—asana, pranayama, and dhyana (yogic meditations)—I no longer need to prove myself to others and I care for myself better. I am also more aware of when I am getting out of balance being too *rajasitic* (passion) or *tamsic* (lethargy). I find that I experience *satva* (true balance) when I am traveling from one of those to the other. That is that one moment when I can experience true serenity.

For someone like me who had so much self-hatred, my key yoga practice has continued to be *ahimsa*. This has been an extremely powerful practice.

A psychic energy worker once told me that when I came down here in this life I picked a path that was either going to kill me or change me through a radical crash course in spirituality. That really resonated with me.

I am fortunate to have found the right next thing. It's enabled me to not only stay alive but also to thrive.

Banton Dyer is sought after for his hard core, yet heart-centered guidance, and is known for helping you find healthy ways to cultivate your focus and vitality.

Relying on his background in yoga therapy, physical training, and martial arts, Banton supports you to transform your life as you become the healthy vibrant individual you know you can become.

Over the past 35 years, Banton has worked with people of various backgrounds, from people on their last dollar all the way to billionaires. His clients have come to expect nothing but the highest level of care and compassion from him, even when he is challenging them to take their next best step in difficult times.

Whether your challenges are in board rooms, at home or on the street, Banton knows how to get to the heart of your concerns and apply a personalized and well-honed approach to helping you be successful.

His strength lies in having overcome life's most challenging situations himself and the ability to empathetically help others to overcome overwhelming trials in their lives. He has a deep passion for helping people find their own way to physical and emotional restoration, no matter how busy or difficult their life, so that they can experience the joy of being supported in what they love or desire to do most. Contact Banton at **bantondyer@yahoo.com.**

Ako ang Tulay: I Am the Bridge

BY JEAN EDRADA

It was my mama who took me to my first yoga class almost ten years ago, a time in my life that was plagued with anxiety, depression, confusion, insecurity, and feelings of unworthiness. It was in these classes that I first experienced bliss, feeling a sense of ease, peace, and presence wash over my whole body, my whole being. One of my favorite asanas was bridge pose: feet rooting into the earth, head firmly grounded, shoulders hugging toward each other, heart opening and reaching toward the sky. In bridge pose I found a physical embodiment of something I had always been drawn to without any conscious understanding of why.

My yoga practice became the space where I would allow myself to discover who and where I was coming from. It was the time that I would allow myself to recover deep memories of the past and envision incredible dreams of the future. It was as if I could meet myself over and over again, entering one end of the bridge and coming out on the other side more myself.

At age twenty-one, the most important thing to me was discovering, defining, collecting and creating a sense of self with purpose and passion. In 2014, I received my 200-hour certificate and began teaching and managing a studio in Chicago. I spent almost all of my time immersed in the practice and in the community. I was growing into myself—but also growing distant from the people who had brought me into the world—my parents.

We'd always had a deeply complex relationship. The age difference between myself and my parents was almost the same between myself and my youngest sister.

In August 2015, I moved across the country with my partner to start a new life and to pursue graduate studies. Two weeks after I moved, on my first day of school, my mama was diagnosed with Stage 4 colon cancer. When I flew back home, I asked her if she wanted me to move back. She answered, "No, *anak* (child). I want you to live your life." So I chose to stay in California.

In April 2016, my maternal grandfather died from a heart attack. I flew home for his memorial service, and the night before my flight to California, my papa was rushed to the emergency room and was diagnosed with Glioblastoma Multiforme, a severe form of brain cancer. I stayed for a few weeks after his surgery. Again, I asked my parents if they thought I should move back home, and again they said, "No, *anak*. We want you to live your life."

So I did.

I went back to my own life, to a bubble I had created, far away from the realities of my parents' diseases. In April 2017, while my family and I were visiting family in San Diego, my maternal grandmother died after two weeks in hospice care. She died exactly a year after my papa's diagnosis.

The bridges between us were both burning and building at the same time.

My mama's cancer metastasized to her liver and bones and, by the time she celebrated her forty-eighth birthday, she knew her time was approaching. She left this world that August, four days before my birthday. In December, I moved back to California to become my papa's main caregiver. I witnessed the deterioration of his health, both because of his cancer and because of a broken heart. He passed in 2018, seven months after his wife. Since then, I have become the caregiver of my sisters, and we have become each other's mama and papa.

It is with this incredible loss that I have been initiated into the path of the warrior. I have been built, burned down, resurrected, demolished, and rebuilt...again and again. Each manifestation of the bridge has become more resilient, built from the wisdom of the one that came before and the fortitude of the one after.

To acknowledge and accept this path is to be both the vehicle that moves on the bridge and to be the bridge itself.

I recognize this bridge as my body—built from the flesh and blood and the hopes and dreams of my ancestors. Every layer holds the memories, stories, and traumas of the people who came before me.

One particular memory of my childhood has resurfaced again and again: I am carried across a bridge made out of wooden planks and ropes. My mama and papa take turns holding me as they walk from our province to a hot spring. That bridge, as simple and as wobbly as it seemed, carried many people across.

I recognize that being a bridge is an incredible privilege and responsibility—and I am ready. The losses I have experienced have enabled me to gain a wealth of gratitude, reverence, passion, and purpose in this life. I know that there is no way I am leaving this Earth without having erected many bridges for others. I am the bridge that helps others to build and walk across their own bridge.

The bridge I am building is called Movement and Medicine. It's a bridge between people and plant medicine, bridging the gap between cannabis as a therapeutic means of play and as a tool of healing. It bridges the gap between those who have access to this resource of healing, community, health, and wealth and those who don't. It bridges the gap between those who are part of yoga, meditation, and spiritual communities and those who feel invisible, unseen, and unaccepted in those spaces. It is a bridge for all different expressions of life to walk on the path toward healing and well-being. It is a bridge for all people who seek to embody their most authentic, holiest, and highest selves.

Thank you, papa, for carrying me on your back on that bridge so many years ago. Thank you, mama, for taking my hand on that day and leading me across the bridge into yoga—and into my deepest truth.

I am this bridge.

Ako ang Tulay.

Jean Edrada is a yoga practitioner, community organizer, educator and the creator of Movement and Medicine. Serving and impacting communities across various ages, backgrounds and cultures in Chicagoland, the Bay Area, and Los Angeles for more than a decade, Jean understands the importance of a resilient body, mind, and spirit. She has been practicing yoga for  eight years and received her 200-hour RYT in Chicago in 2014. She regularly collaborates with and supports platforms such as Gabriela Chicago, Tree Femme Collective, and Equity First Alliance as well as local non-profit and youth organizations.

Jean's work provides guided explorations of yoga, movement, and meditation integrated with a therapeutic relationship with plant medicine, specifically with cannabis. The transformative framework of Movement and Medicine is grounded in Jean's own stories of overcoming trauma, especially the recent deaths of both parents from cancer before the age of fifty. Through transmuting chaos to consciousness, Jean has developed a deep reverence for cultivating space for the body's primordial wisdom to be happy, healthy, and whole. Her mission is to create safe and sacred opportunities to explore one's own internal world and how we relate to and move through a complex and complicated external world.

As a first-generation immigrant, as an able-bodied woman of color, and now as a parental guardian to her three young sisters, Jean has seen the enormous impact of inequality on the bodies, minds, and spirits of communities of color, on those with mental health issues, on the poor, and on other disenfranchised communities. She envisions a world in which people of different colors, shapes, sizes, abilities, challenges, conditions, and expressions of life have equitable access to resources and spaces for healing. Jean believes in an embodied spiritual practice and strives to empower the individual on their journey to the highest self. Learn more at **www.MovementandMedicine.com**.

Elevated Connection: A Gateway to Healing

BY JENNIFER FARNHOLZ

Transformation. I'm drawn to this word. To me, transformation represents an outlook on life and how we perceive what is going on in the moment. I have found within my personal teachings that with awareness and compassion we begin to *live* in a transformative state, or *flow* state, not fighting the experience, just witnessing it and allowing the moments to teach and guide us.

Yoga has been the common thread that ties my experiences and my challenges together in a mosaic of pain, creativity, struggle, growth, connection, and love. Each component is beautiful and critical to my unique journey toward finding my inner light center, my passions, and, ultimately, connecting continuously back to myself.

Each person's life contains a constant tide pool of pain and lessons learned. It comes in and takes over for a period of time, then releases its hold, allowing for insight and the discovery of lovely hidden treasures—when we are able to open ourselves up to the ebb and flow.

My past emotional pain, which I now call "echoes of lessons I am in the process of re-learning," is a constant teacher. As a girl, I was curious and sensitive; I was called over-sensitive. I was exposed to violence and felt vulnerable, which can change a person in a powerful way. I feel the struggles and challenges of others in my heart and mind, and this has also paved the way for me to learn about my true calling. I have found incredible insight and been guided toward my natural ability to teach, grow, and explore constantly with many bumps along my life's journey. These bumps lead me along a path toward Elevated Connection.

This tale of healing and connecting began to unfold on the physical level when I was eleven, out of nowhere, I became incredibly ill. It seemed my body was, for unknown reasons, eating away at my muscular tissue. The doctors and specialists were unable to figure out how best to help my body fight the infection. I remember lying awake at night with the inner knowing that my body was fighting for life. I was put on trial medications, and I was lucky. I survived. However it was the starting point for a lifelong journey of physical struggle as well as a beginning of learning about self-healing.

My beautiful and miraculous body is my constant inner guru, for she is gloriously powerful and resilient, as well as sensitive in many ways. Oddly, our society often sees sensitivity as a negative thing. But my sensitivity has been my superpower throughout much of my life and has guided me to heal myself and others.

Each of our gifts and curses has a way of showing us what and who we truly are. It is always our choice how we choose to look at them.

After being released from the hospital I began a lifelong mission to connect to my body and mind in a deep and meaningful way. From the medicine that saved my life, I developed hormonal imbalances that plagued my body since age eleven, I formed growths in my uterus and surrounding area. These growths made it challenging for many parts of my body to function properly. I remember one doctor telling me in my early teens that I would most likely never be able to carry a healthy child to term. I developed late in my teens and very quickly realized with the sudden growth spurt I suffered horrible pain every month; when I started to menstruate I would bleed for 25 to 28 days, I developed hormonal sclerosis of the spine, forcing me to quit sports because of the agony of moving too quickly. I was terrified, and I lived in fear of the future, at war with my body mentally and physically.

But I was also resourceful and determined to learn how to heal myself. Over time, the realization sunk in that doctors could only do so much. Synchronistically, the world of yoga magically appeared in my life. The first yoga class I took was a game changer for me. I began asking questions and using my inquisitive mind to map out how these movements and poses were allowing me to feel stable and balanced in my body—something I hadn't felt for months! I was enthralled with the way I felt and the way my body responded to this movement.

Each and every yoga pose I learned became a unique chart that steered my body away from pain and into the awareness of opening, and releasing into an endless container of self-love. My mind became calm and contemplative instead of reactive and overwhelmed. Little by little, I began to love and trust my body again.

Then, while I was still a teen, something happened that haunted me for years and still brings up moments of struggle and inner shame. I was raped by someone I trusted. This took such a toll on my emotional state that I retreated from certain elements of my life—yoga included. Today, I stand strong in knowing that it was not my fault and that I had no idea I would be treated like that. I share this part of my story to witness my own fear that I feel coming up while at the same time intuitively knowing that I must share this part of my story. If it has the opportunity to give another the courage to open up to feelings and release that pain, to relinquish them from being a victim then there is beauty in the sharing.

I felt shame and deep loneliness for a time, but I also learned to reach out for help and to talk to professionals who could guide me through the process of forgiving myself and the other person, releasing my fear, and eventually coming back to loving myself once again.

I grew strong in mind and body. I began my first of many yoga teacher training programs. The years of daily practice connected me to a deep desire to help others. I began teaching yoga and practicing massage therapy as my first of many modalities of body healing. I was in my element—healing, teaching, and coaching others filled me with such inner joy. I felt strong and confident in myself and my skills at such an early age. I was ready to take on life with both hands!

It's funny how life sometimes puts a pin in our aspirations. As I was learning and getting ready to travel and teach abroad, I began to develop allergic symptoms towards everything I touched. Dust, perfume, grass, animals, even certain types of fabric would send me into a full-on bout of itching frenzy. At night I tied my hands up with socks to prevent scarring. There was no discernible reason why this started happening, and, after a year of tests and high doses of prednisone, my doctors had no idea how to help me. I felt helpless and completely out of my element. I dove deeper into my yoga practice and started learning more about meditation and visualization. This helped me, and over months and months, I finally felt able to control my body's automatic need to itch.

For days I would feel itchy but would use my mind to switch off the desire to itch. This small repeated victory helped me greatly as I made it a personal mission to solve this issue. I went to see an incredible naturopath, who helped guide me back toward acknowledging and stepping into my personal healing power. It was our first visit and, within minutes, she checked my skin, tongue, and eyes. She was horrified no one had thought to look at my liver. It seems my liver had been fighting its own personal battle. Since eleven, my liver had been trying to rejuvenate from the side effects of the medication that was given to save my life. My liver tissue had been slowing dying, so by seventeen years old I began to go into a state of cirrhosis. My liver was functioning at 30 percent, and my skin was trying to shed toxins. It was another long fourteen months of being itchy, feeling repulsive, and being ridiculed by people who didn't understand. But, with time and patience, my body began to heal.

This was a powerful lesson to learn:
Our bodies are always working toward healing.

It may at times seem like the body is working against you, but when I changed my perspective, the realization I came to was that my body was diligently working *for* me every day without fail. I just needed to learn how to listen to the unique language of the body and create space by giving the body what it needed to heal itself. With help from my naturopath, guidance from my yoga teachers, and a strict daily regime geared toward healing every cell in my body, in two years I was able to move forward in my life.

After that experience, I took on the world; training for triathlons, completing Ironman Canada and several half Ironmans. I traveled for months, teaching and growing from the experiences—learning to surf in South America, rock climbing, and scuba diving in Thailand, Vietnam and Greece. I would stretch daily and connect the breath and body. Meditation was part of my daily healing and reconnection with myself. Back home I started two businesses that were geared toward teaching yoga and helping others on their healing from the inside out.

However, a crucial piece in my own puzzle was missing: I was lacking balance. I came face to face with the lesson of the statement or the word NO. I came into a time in my life that was a true test of finding out what inner strength and self-love really meant.

My lesson at this time was my first real attraction to another, and I leapt into a romantic relationship that threw me so far off course I found that gradually—and so slowly—I no longer knew or recognized who I was. My inner guide screamed in warning, yet my mind made excuses. I struggled to prove to my partner that I could live up to the expectations to be the perfect lover, business owner, confidant, money saver, and that I could feign happiness so no one could see the pain and anguish I was in. Receiving the miraculous news I was pregnant, beyond all belief that it was possible, I struggled and felt like I was emotionally and mentally drowning. Feeling like I had no way to get to the surface for a gulp of air. This new reality literally struck me full on in the face as I was shaken out of my state of denial. It left my head spinning and my heart dragging three miles behind me.

I had lost all contact with my former self, my family, and my friends. Even my meditations and visualizations were filled with nightmares and thoughts of not being good enough, how silly and stupid I was, how I had to work harder, be better and prove to this person that I deserved love. Why did this love hurt so much? I had fear in my life like I had never experienced before, fear of the truth, fear of the unknown, fear that maybe I wasn't good enough.

Breath in...Breath out...slowly I found I my way back to my yoga practice and, in secret, I would meditate as I began to clearly see the lessons this phase of my life was teaching me. The first lesson was the realization that there are pieces of the self that can never be taken away by another. I just needed to trust they were there and find those inner wise and compassionate conversations that would steer me toward self-love again.

For me, Kundalini Yoga will always hold a special place in my heart because it guided me through the fog of injustice and victimhood I was trapped in. I was so fearful of taking that step into class. I look back on that fear now and realize with fresh eyes that I was fearful of the change—even positive change terrified me. For years, I had lived in a low-grade state of fear. I had isolated my emotional self, choosing to not feel at all instead of the daily anguish and pain I was living in. And I didn't know, what would happen to me when I started to feel again?

With gentle and continuous steps back toward my yoga and meditation practice, I gained the courage to leave that relationship and started to re-establish healthy boundaries in my life. I no longer allowed another person's voice, thoughts, actions, or even looks to control me. This fundamental lesson taught me that I always had a choice. It wasn't an easy choice, at least not for me, but when I chose to see that person's actions as just a representation of how they treat themselves, I could release the hurt and move forward from letting the words or actions have any effect on me at all. The story of the abuse, struggle, and challenges became my personal teachings for true empowerment. I stand proud in the fact that I was able to get out of a situation that brought me to my knees. My body and mind had felt like it had all but collapsed under the immense pressure of that situation, with the Kundalini energy building and clearing away the rubble, my breath was all I needed to start thinking clearly and slowing rebuilding.

Yoga is miraculous in that it does not control; it has no limits. It is open space within the body and mind for both the individual and also the connection between each of us. Yoga is just one form of this, that pure connection is where I truly believe deep healing begins. When we connect with ourselves, we learn to love unconditionally and stand strong in who we are. And then that inner love spreads outward at such a velocity it expands beyond what we can comprehend. We begin to see the world with compassion and a depth of understanding that cannot be gained through fear and resistance.

The true power of yoga is something that each person connects with differently. However, in my very core, I have come to realize this: I move my body to reconnect my mind and ignite my spirit of the breath. This is what connection yoga is to me...transformation toward loving myself, and through me I love all who are on their own unique path of inner realization.

Jennifer Farnholz teaches and guides clients along their unique journey of re-connecting to their life and in doing so helps to create an abundance of energy and confidence that reflects in all aspects of living their empowered life with eyes wide open. Her laid-back manner and joy-filled perspective infuses her many teachings and allows her to connect in a very deep and personal way with clients.

She offers a unique and specialized blend of yoga, meditation, mind/body nutritional coaching, water and energetic realignment of the chakras, body healing modalities, counseling, breath work and visualization. She has combined all these teachings into a powerful and result driven program that is catered to the individuals needs and aspirations.

Jennifer is a lover of life and its many twists and turns. She absolutely adores working with groups of people, focusing on the opportunity to witness the common struggles within a shared story that we all can relate to and together begin to heal through the courage of sharing. Transforming hurt into unseen blessings and valuable lessons that no longer isolate, instead they build us up to form a truly elevated connected community. Making this dream into a reality she has taught seminars, workshops and retreats throughout Canada and around the world over the last 17 years.

Jennifer is beyond grateful for having a body/mind and spirit that grows stronger and wiser with each passing year, finding true inner love for herself and extending that love to those around her.

Learn more at **elevatedconnections.ca.** To join in the growing conversation about how to heal and grow from physical, mental, and emotional trauma please visit our **FaceBook group: Elevated Connection Hub** at **https://bit.ly/2pWkixH.**

My Break-Up with Yoga and Healing a Broken Heart

BY SHARON FORTIER

My story with Yoga is a common one, yet not a story commonly told. If you are holding this book in your hands and flipped to this page, welcome friend. I am honored to share my story with you.

Long ago I stumbled upon a book about Yoga. It was the late 1980s, and I was in college. The book looked silly at first as it was very much from the '60s. Suddenly, I was wrapped in that magic that happens in a bookstore, when a book picks you, and off I went to begin a long adventure that would shape my life and my relationship with yoga.

The book presented a twenty-eight-day yoga plan, and I was committed to it. This commitment opened up the space in my life, like an invitation, for yoga to flow into all aspects of my experience. For years I pursued teachers and workshops that brought me to a place of confidence in my skill as a practitioner and teacher. I began to teach and soon opened my own studio.

I devoted myself and my time to making this studio a place where people could come to find healing and community. My reward for this commitment and service was a profound connection to the energy that is yoga. I felt as if the teachings were flowing through me—not coming from my training or from my ego mind but from a place much greater.

Sounds amazing right? It was. However, one pitfall about amazing and enlightening experiences is that we try to hold onto them, recreate them over and over again. Suddenly something that occurred because you learned to surrender causes you to keep striving to reach that place again. Instead of an invitation, there is a command, an expectation.

There's a principle of yoga called *Aparigraha*, which I was taught meant non-grasping, but it is also translated as non-attachment or non-possessiveness. In my ego's desire to claim this experience as mine, I created a separation between me and my beloved: yoga.

From this place of separation, I began to look around me and see what I perceived as the adulteration of yoga. I admit that this comes from a place of judgment. Only from separation can we judge. But judge I did. I judged goat yoga, I judged yoga at the brewery, I judged yoga while hanging from the ceiling. Each judgment drove me further and further away from that place of union—away from the surrender to yoga's flow through me.

My teacher was a purist. She had trained with gurus in India and held yoga as a vocation, not a business. I felt privileged and entitled to judge. After all, *I was doing yoga right, I had a superior teacher.*

Regardless, the magic was gone. I finally gave up striving, but not by surrendering. I just simply gave up and walked away, all the while believing the problem was "out there" rather than inside of me. I blamed my separation on the "other" that was taking *my yoga* and changing it—distorting it.

I felt betrayed and abandoned. I not only lost the connection, I lost my confidence. I tried teaching a couple of times, and the loss of connection made me feel as if I was an impostor. I withdrew and became angry. As I pulled away, I closed down parts of me that identified with yoga. It was lonely.

After years in this place of separation, I found myself on a path toward healing. The voice that called me back to myself was the voice of the Priestess path and the rising of the Divine Feminine. This isn't the path for everyone, but on this path I learned to surrender into the knowing that I am already whole and deserving of love, even if I have judged. I learned to have compassion for myself and others for exactly where and who we are in this moment. I learned to expand into a place that knows that the only separation, competition, and comparison that exists is within my own perception.

Having unearthed these truths from within, I have come around full circle. I find myself back in the embrace of my yogic practices. Only this time, I feel that my vessel has been crystallized by this experience. Now I am able to resonate and amplify the energy of yoga rather than trying to contain it.

It turns out, I did have a superior teacher. *It is called life.* How do we learn if not through failing? How do we recognize the light if not for the contrast of darkness? How do we teach if we do not first learn the hardest lessons?

In separation, we learn the joy of coming back into the fold.

I place this piece here as an offering to you. Whatever your journey holds, in this moment, I will sit with you in your separation and in your pain. I have been to that place and made it to the other side. I am holding the door open for you to find your way back to whatever it is that you have lost. I invite you to relax, release the effort, and allow the flow of life to return you to a deeper sense of connection.

The Divine light and shadow that is within me bows to the Divine light and shadow that is within you.

Namaste.

Sharon Fortier is a daughter, mother, wife, teacher, seeker, and massage therapist. For 23 years, Sharon has been working with people as a massage therapist and energy healer. This vocation has brought her deep appreciation for the art of service to humanity and the honor of being present with others in their pain, be it physical or emotional.

After earning a bachelor's degree in Natural Resources Management and Engineering from the University of Connecticut, Sharon attended Connecticut Center for Massage Therapy. Over the next several years she participated in workshops in various modalities of bodywork and began her study of yoga with her beloved teacher, Marilyn Mariani. As a complement to this, Sharon studied Reiki and Transformational Energy Healing.

Through working with her own shadows of fear and pain, Sharon has developed empathy and compassion that she employs in her Life's Work. It is these personal experiences that informs her work and deepens her capacity to hold space for those struggling with physical pain, loss, addiction, anxiety, and depression.

Sharon is studying in a Priestess training program through Priestess Presence in lineage of the 13 Moon Mystery School and pursuing certification as a life coach. Coupling these skills with the knowledge acquired during her career as a bodyworker and yoga instructor, Sharon plans to offer self-care coaching to adolescents and adults for coping with life's challenges. Contact Sharon at **apathinward@att.net.**

A Deeper Truth:
Trusting the Wisdom of the Body

BY PAUL GEMME

I began yoga late in life as a way of reclaiming my body after years of physical trauma and neglect. Physical liabilities prevented me from hitting the gym, yet I needed a way to build strength and flexibility so I chose yoga. I was physically active for most of my life with outdoor pursuits such as hiking, kayaking, and camping. Yet sadly, arthritis, fused vertebrae, and age began to take its toll on my body. It was with some reluctance and fear that I carved out a minimal amount of time during my week to begin a yoga practice.

Even though I began my practice with restorative yoga, I found it difficult to manage even the simplest of poses. My Happy Baby looked more like a Disgruntled Old Man, but I found that I was improving as time went on. So I increased my practice from one day a week to eventually three to four days a week in the studio and a daily practice at home. I added a couple of gentle yoga classes and a somatic yoga class as well as continuing my restorative practice. In addition, I made a few other lifestyle changes, including switching to a plant-based diet that dropped my cholesterol levels over fifty points and my weight by forty pounds. I felt like I was well on my way to reclaiming my health.

However, during this time, I received some devastating news; my sister Jacquie, was diagnosed with terminal lung cancer.

Here was a woman who never smoked, had walked across the entire United States on a peace march, lived as a Buddhist nun for twelve years, and devoted her entire life to helping others with her incredible strength, spirit, and energy.

One of my favorite memories is when we traveled together, along with my twelve-year-old daughter, to Japan for the dedication of a peace pagoda. Jacquie, having lived in Japan for several years while she was helping to build a pagoda, took us on a guided tour through the country, connecting with her old friends and contacts to secure housing for us at Buddhist temples along the way. It was an incredible ten-day experience.

After living in Japan, Jacquie moved back to the United States and after prayer, meditation, and deep soul searching, she decided to give up her robes and continue with her education. She earned her master's degree and worked as a trauma therapist while living in upstate New York. She continued working full-time while receiving treatment for her cancer.

Jacquie and I have always shared a common bond through the healing modalities. In 1985, I entered into recovery after years of addiction and alcohol abuse. I eventually began working as a substance abuse counselor and developed a serious interest working with men and men's issues and eventually working for a non-profit organization to help urban youth.

I became actively involved with a statewide men's organization COMEGA.ORG (CT Men's Gathering) and continue as an organizing committee member, to design and manage two weekend retreats each year. I also "sit circle" with two separate closed men's groups to work on my own healing and have been doing this for more than thirty years. I mention this because when I began this yoga practice, I wasn't prepared to discover this part of me that felt so incomplete.

It was in retirement that I began yoga with the intention to reclaim my body. Little did I know it would be the conduit to take me home to myself at a deep, profound level. My understanding of the mind-body connection became a more grounded and meaningful experience.

After my sister disclosed her awareness of her terminal cancer, I believed I had accepted her diagnosis. But then I began to notice, even with all the yoga I was doing, that I was developing new physical pain in my body. The discomfort seemed to be intensifying. It hit a crescendo when I visited Jacquie and she disclosed to me a potential time frame for her death. Her treatment was designed to provide her with more time, but if it wasn't successful, she could go within a matter of a few months. She continued working full-time while receiving treatment for her cancer.

Several weeks earlier, Jacquie had shocked me by asking me to build her a casket. She wanted a "green burial" so the casket needed to be biodegradable with no metal screws or hinges. She knew I had the skills to accomplish this, since I ran a boat-building shop in my work with youth.

My sister was living her death consciously with transparency and grace.

I, on the other hand, thinking I was living her impending death openly and consciously while processing it with my men's group, was actually withholding my deepest grief—and it was manifesting in my body. I felt resistance to building the casket. My mind was telling me, "If I don't build the casket, she won't die." However, my body began speaking a Truth to me that I couldn't ignore. I wish I could say I recognized this truth right away, but I didn't. I experienced several long weeks of physical pain and difficulty with my breathing.

The moment when Jacquie disclosed her death time-line literally took my breath away. For several weeks, my breathing was labored. I began manifesting a serious body pain that wouldn't leave. I started modifying my yoga practice to compensate for the pain or I would skip yoga all together.

One day in a somatic yoga class when I was in a heart-opening pose, I began to sob. The more I relaxed into the pose, the more grief I was able to release. It allowed me to drop into the profound understanding and reality of my sister's death and significance of my loss. It also triggered past trauma and the betrayals I had been storing up in my body for years.

My yoga instructor made sure my fellow yogis didn't try to "fix" me. She placed her hand on my back, gave me permission to cry and provided a safe container to release my grief. I felt all my muscles relax and the pain in my body dissolving. My breath began to return to me and my pain dissipated over the next several days.

I see my daily yoga practice through new eyes now. Yoga speaks truth to me if I allow myself to listen.

My mind can tell stories of denial, but my body wisdom knows the truth. Yoga is helping me to process life in new way, and it helps me to let go of that which I used to unknowingly hold onto. It provides a place of understanding and knowing that more will be revealed as my breath settles in my body.

Paul Gemme worked in the field of addiction recovery for over seventeen years. In the late 1990s, he was instrumental in designing and implementing a two-week, overnight, rites-of-passage camp for six and seventh graders at Rowe Camp and Conference Center in the Massachusetts Berkshires. He and his wife, Maureen, directed the camp for five years. Paul is also an avid woodworker, and his creative energy and passion for woodwork-

ing led him to birthing African and Native American style drums and flutes and facilitating drum building workshops teaching others to build their own drums.

During this time, he spent many summers in the Berkshires conducting rites of passage and coming of age rituals and ceremonies. He partnered with Return to the Fire, a men's organization to facilitate father-son canoe trips on the Allagash and Penobscot Rivers in Maine, and in 2007 he paddled 200 miles by canoe down the Pelly River through the wilderness of the Yukon Territory. He has spent a life of adventure, designing workshops and teaching others along the way.

Paul's desire to continue working with young adults came to fruition when he was offered a position managing a boat-building shop for a non-profit young development organization in Hartford, Connecticut. There he taught boat and cedar strip canoe building, life skills, and job readiness training. While there, he developed a nature program with the support of National Geographic—called "Science on the River". Youth trapped snapping turtles on the Connecticut River and employed a "Critter Cam" to the turtles' carapace, gathering data for the National Geographic Society.

Paul has been actively involved in men's work since 1985. He currently belongs to two men's groups. He has been an active participant and organizer for the Connecticut Men's Gathering (COMEGA.org) since 1996.

In retirement, Paul continues to explore all that life has to offer. His more recent interests include vegetable gardening, growing dahlias, vegetarian cooking, and yoga. His adventures on the road involve touring on his Honda Goldwing Motorcycle. Paul and Maureen enjoy visiting the country by motorcycle and have been across the United States and into Canada multiple times. He loves taking photos of barns while out on his motorcycle and has a photo blog on Facebook called "Barns along the Way" with more than 20,000 followers.

As a morning practice, Paul meditates for 30 to 45 minutes and spends daily time on the yoga mat at home. He attends yoga class three to four times a week, at Journey of Yoga studio in Simsbury, Connecticut. Learn more at **facebook.com/barnsalongtheway.**

Yoga: A Pathway to Inner Peace

BY JULIANNE GILLESPIE

Yoga is software for the soul, and is a journey that combines breath work with body work. This union of the mind, body, and soul gives us a feeling of bliss and is a pathway to mindfulness and inner peace. It allows for a connection that supports us to live in the present moment, rather than focusing on the past or future. When you can be more present in your daily life and stop giving away your power and energy to things that drain you (things that have happened in the past or worrying about what might happen in the future), you have the ability to live in a *flow* state of *being*. This happens when you quiet your mind and all of the chatter (which is typically created as a result of our never-ending to-do lists, as well as our technology). For example, your smart phone is connected to your email and to your Facebook which is connected to your friends and their videos and on and on. It is a never-ending loop of technology that draws you in and, as a result, you can get sucked in for hours and it is so draining on your energy. Setting healthy boundaries around your technology and everything else that you do is the key to inner peace. *Make technology work for you, not against you.*

THE SOLO YOGA JOURNEY

There is no such thing as perfection in yoga, it is simply a *practice* and a personal journey that offers us a chance to see where we may be comparing ourselves with our neighbor while on the mat. Yoga can also bring awareness to any self-judgment we have around what poses we can or cannot do; this is all just part of the learning and comes with practice. Breathing and feeling into your senses is the key to deepening in to your yoga. Practice the poses that feel good for you and follow your bliss!

EXPANDING YOUR AWARENESS

When you can connect your mind, body, and soul through yoga, mindfulness, or meditation, you see things from a different perspective. As your awareness expands, you may be able to see the bigger picture, as if you were on the top of a mountain looking down. This flow state allows you to connect to your *inner guidance,* or intuition. Once you stop looking outside of yourself for answers and instead turn inwards, you will become more aware of what is *really* happening. Then you can look *as an observer would, without judgment,* to see what is really going on. Once you identify the issue, you have the ability to take action and make appropriate changes in your life without getting trapped in an emotional whirlwind.

LET YOUR EMOTIONS FLOW

By *feeling and releasing* any stifled or suppressed emotions, you have the ability to heal yourself and open up your heart to more love. These suppressed emotions can be held in different parts of your body as a result of times when you were not speaking up for yourself or taking care of yourself. Yin yoga is a wonderful practice that helps to release emotions from the body. It is much slower, and each pose is held for longer periods. It is one of my favorite practices, because it is so easy to incorporate mindfulness in the stillness of the poses. Try adding essential oils for further mind body integration and connection through your breath with aromatherapy yoga.

CHAKRAS: THE WHEELS OF LIGHT

There are seven main *chakras,* or energy centers, in the body which run from the base of the spine to the top of the head. When these energy centers are out of balance, we can become physically ill. Yoga is a wonderful way to balance your chakras, quiet your mind, and become aware of what is happening in your body. I have discovered that my body can recharge (just like a battery) when I practice yoga and mindfulness meditation.

Other benefits of yoga include improved flexibility and range of motion, enhanced immune function, greater endurance, better balance, and increased strength and muscle tone. The integration of the mind and body brings calmness and clarity, even in the midst of chaos. It teaches you to *let go* and be in the present moment in this *expanded state of consciousness.*

SELF-CARE: MEDICINE FOR YOUR SOUL

As a partner in an accounting firm, I endured years of stressful tax seasons that have become much more bearable since I started practicing extreme self-care. By putting my needs first and holding steady in that commitment, I now flow through stressful situations with ease and grace. This can be true for anyone in any stressful profession, because it's is all about how we breathe! Vitality starts with an awareness of your breath. By focusing on your breath, taking breaks, and listening to your body, you can get out of your head, become more present, and discover a deeper sense of self-worth. Walking in nature is also very helpful for balancing our energy, as we can draw up the energy from the earth to support us in feeling grounded, centered and connected.

FOCUSED HARMONY

With the union of the mind, body, and spirit through yoga, you can experience more freedom and life becomes more joyful. In this state of unity and harmony, you can experience increased health, happiness, and peace through balance, restoration, and connection within yourself.

When I set an intention at the start of each practice, I am more focused, have more clarity, and can fully recharge. This awareness results in more *presence,* or mindfulness. Sometimes I will use a mantra to help me focus.

Yoga inversions are helpful for relaxation, balance, building confidence, feeling energized, increased immunity, and to prevent illness and reverse blood flow in the body and improve circulation. Twisting poses are good for detoxification of the body. My most recent discovery is Viparita Karani or Legs-Up-The-Wall Pose, which I find to be a great way to stop mental chatter. Try unplugging from technology and plugging into the wall instead! Be gentle on yourself as you reprogram your life with yoga for more well-being, presence, and happiness.

Julianne J. Gillespie is a Certified Public Accountant (CPA) and partner at Simione Macca & Larrow LLP. Throughout her career of more than thirty years, she has built her practice based on the foundation of relationships and serves her clients with the ultimate goal of seeking to do what is best for each client. She graduated from the University of Connecticut with a Bachelor of Science  degree in Accounting and has provided accounting, auditing, consulting, and tax services to a wide variety of industries, including clients in architecture, engineering, construction, real estate, insurance, manufacturing, printing, and not-for-profit.

In addition to her work in accounting and auditing, Julie advocates for her clients by supporting them with tax planning and projections and guiding them through tax audit representation with the Internal Revenue Service and State of Connecticut. She has also assisted clients with financial reporting, accounting and cost controls, systems, business planning, mergers and acquisitions, financing, and cash flow analysis, playing a critical role by acting as a catalyst for her clients to navigate their businesses, especially through times of change.

Julie is certified in Reiki 1, is a certified Law of Attraction Basic Practitioner, and is a Numerology Academy certified practitioner. She is also a member of the American Institute of Certified Public Accountants and the Connecticut Society of Certified Public Accountants, where she served on several committees over the years including the Federal Tax, Community Service, and Continuing Education Committees. She served a three-year term as a member of the National PCPS Technical Issues Committee, which monitors technical issues and developments in accounting, auditing, professional ethics, peer review, and governmental accounting that could have significant effect on closely held companies, not-for-profit organizations, government, and the CPAs who service them. She also served on the Professional Issues Task Force. Julie enjoys collaborating and networking with the expanding world marketplace through MSI Global Alliance, an international network of more than 250 legal and accounting firm connections in more than 100 countries.

A founding member of Women's Wellness Fund at Middlesex Hospital, Julie is actively involved in the Women's Business Alliance of Middlesex Chamber. She enjoys giving back to the community by being actively involved in causes close to her heart through volunteer opportunities that support animals, the environment, and healthcare. Most of all, Julie enjoys spending time with her family and Chinese crested dog, Isadora. Learn more at **www.juliannejoy.me.**

The Sweetness of Peace

BY HEATHER GREAVES

Following a yogic lifestyle, I experienced deep peace. Yet right around the thirty-year mark, a low-level anxiety surfaced and wouldn't go away. I was perplexed. My biggest question was, "What has caused this anxiety and how can it go away?"

Our life's journey brings us through time, from a dependent baby to an interdependent youth and then to an independent young adult. We may think we are totally self-sufficient, but in reality aren't we always dependent on each other and on nature for growth and support?

A book by Richard Hittleman introduced me to yoga. Some basic practices, philosophy and principles of yoga were explained and I breathed it all in with much relief. The seven-week step-by-step course for rejuvenation became my empowering companion. I practiced yoga poses daily and in earnest. After all, there was the promise that a few minutes of yoga every day could make a big difference.

Years later I would become fascinated with meditation, the inner aspect of yoga. Meditation instructors teach and students practice according to their own understanding. The meditation practice brought me so much peace. The repetition of the words, "I am a peaceful soul" was effective. With great enthusiasm, I regularly arose at 4 a.m. and practiced sitting to meditate for 45 minutes.

Over time, drawn by the sweetness of peace, I practiced less and less asana and more and more meditation, study, and self-reflection. Time passed and I suddenly felt unwell; quite light headed, actually, and my mental state was affected. I began feeling anxious. Friends and family were concerned. One friend suggested I start to include a physical yoga practice like the Sun Salute to be grounded in my body to reduce the light-headedness and anxiety.

That suggestion worked. I felt more alive in my body. On advice from a health professional, I stopped using my imagination to go way up above the earth in order to separate myself from the pushes and pulls of the world and to spread light around the earth. The surprising changes in my health signaled that there was a whole lot more occurring with yoga and meditation than I understood.

Later through Ayurveda, the sister science of yoga, I would discover how to move energies in my body mind toward balance, modifying lifestyle, sleep, diet, meditation, and postures. My sense of well-being and vitality improved as knowledge of my own body increased and I appreciated my body temple more and more. A whole new world dancing with qualities such as temperature, texture, moisture, and weight came alive within and around me and I unconsciously embraced interdependence. The sun, water, and air that nourished the body were like ever-giving parents.

Yoga philosophy purports we are multidimensional beings consisting of the physical, energy, psycho-emotional, intuitive/witness, and bliss bodies (*koshas*). How were these five bodies affected as I practiced yoga? What challenges were obvious and what benefits would I claim?

Reflecting on the journey, I can see how I first learned to care for the physical body and the energy body with yoga and Ayurveda. Through the ethics of yoga, the psycho-emotional body was nurtured as kindness grew. All styles of yoga, for example Bhakti and Kundalini, have suggestions for a harmonious relationship with self, others, and nature. A code of conduct for living in community is also evident in faith-based organizations and indigenous communities, an affirmation of the importance of relationships.

As I write this, I identify those feelings of sweet peace that came with meditation as the last of the five bodies—the Bliss body. The intuitive aspect or the witness did receive care as well. How did I develop the witness? When did I become conscious of working with or living as the observer?

Up to a point, I had practiced just one form of meditation. A time came when it felt necessary to explore another type. I decided to practice mindfulness meditation. The book *Peace Is Every Step* by Zen Master Thich Nhat Hanh became my guide, and I became a disciple.

I had read that yogis say those who are aware of every breath become masters. And how amazing that this meditation practice aligned with this way of being. The idea that there was a meditation practice of being aware of the in-breath and the out-breath and cultivating loving kindness appealed to me. What I didn't know was that this practice would nurture a compassionate witness and quell the anxiety that caused me distress.

This low-grade anxiety showed up everywhere. One day as I drove along at my own pace I looked in the rear view mirror. I saw the cars behind me and for the first time really noticed my response to the cars. I witnessed feeling anxious and also the thought that I might be preventing other drivers from moving ahead at a faster pace. I consciously and slowly breathed in and breathed out quite a few times.

It was the beginning of bearing witness to a feeling that is different from being consumed by a feeling and emotion. I had caught myself in the act of call and response. The call was anxiety, and I responded with self-sabotaging thoughts.

I was definitely concerned and even frustrated about entertaining this type of "I am less than" belief in my subconscious. Why couldn't I drive in peace? There was no one signaling I should move out of the way, no horn blowing or lights flashing. Still, I recognized that I felt threatened when there was no threat, and this way of being didn't sit well with me.

Months passed, and the times I became aware that my body was breathing itself increased. Then something miraculous happened. Again while driving I came to a stop and observed myself watching the cars in the rear view mirror. And this time there was a different thought, a precious thought: *I have a right to be here.* This was the claim that rose up from within. It was a *wow* moment, a blessed moment, a shift.

The door opened to ease and a sense of freedom, and I walked through. Anxiety still called on me. My response was different. My first response and now an automatic response is to be right there with the breath, feeling her move in my body—the in-breath and the out-breath. And because of a formal daily practice, that expansion in the body to receive the breath can be felt lower in the body. I can relax the abdomen so it receives the breath.

When the body senses a trace of a threat and automatically responds with an increased heart rate, my first response to that call is to go home to the breath, greet the situation with an "I see you" inner smile that melts tension as quickly as what can sometimes be described as a whiff...sometimes.

Of course, there are incidents of anxiety or surprise where greater clarity is necessary. In those cases I want to understand not only the circumstances but myself better. I want to know what is important to me in that situation. The question no longer is "Why am I anxious and how can it go away?" Instead, the cause for reflection is, "What is it I need in this situation and how can it be satisfied?"

I love that the philosophy of yoga offers evergreen solutions to the modern mind. And I love that when anxiety calls, I have a response.

Special Gift

A 16-minute audio guided journey with music "Breathing through the Storms" that moves awareness systematically through the body, then connects you to your breathing and inner landscape with sounds of the ocean. You practice using your breath as a resource to hold you steady through emotional and physical storms.

Listen here: **www.yogatogo.com/imi.php**

Heather Greaves shares how to remain connected with one's inner calm and to enjoy waves of freedom well into the autumn of life. As a Yoga Therapist, she guides you through stages to claim a mindset to live the life you want, see with increasing clarity, and experience more ease in your unique body.

Over the past four decades as a yoga and meditation teacher, Heather has shared strategies for rejuvenation with people from all walks of life. As a trainer of yoga teachers, she especially assists those in caring professions add more therapeutic skills to their toolkit. Twenty years ago she initiated a yoga program at a resource center for people living with cancer and now serves as adviser to its expanding yoga program. She also facilitates yoga retreats where participants create community, play and win together.

Heather has a deep passion for inspiring others to self-reflect and follow their inner guide, anchoring this individuality to heritage and community. This fosters appreciation for the interconnectedness of human beings. Learn more at **www.yogatogo.com.**

Healing Through Stillness

BY KEVIN HEIDT

Ayurveda, rich in various, techniques, traditions, and philosophies, has always been a practice that supports one's ability to self-heal, self-correct, and self-regulate the body, mind, and soul.

Every move, every breath, every realized intention shifts us further from the current understanding of who we think we are and closer to the intentions of divine consciousness expressing through us. Healing through Ayurveda practices such as yoga, pranayama, meditation, and conscious decision making truly makes life beautiful. Most anyone with a regular practice can attest to how such actions have improved their life and enriched it with meaning.

But how can alternate nostril breathing, chanting praises, performing asanas, or—taking no action at all—help you heal?

What are you actually healing *from*?

And what can you do to improve the potency of your practice so you continue to unfold into newer versions of yourself less affected by past trauma and become better prepared to receive and respond to the uncertainties of life?

It's possible that the answers to these questions—and to further questions we have yet to realize—can be found through the ground-breaking work of Biodynamic Craniosacral Therapists.

Biodynamic Craniosacral Techniques come from Osteopathy, which is a modern medical practice whose core principles dovetail those of Ayurveda.

Here we understand the body functions in wholeness as a complete unit; the body possesses self-correcting and self-regulatory mechanisms; and structure and function are reciprocally interrelated.

Through the exploratory work of osteopathic physician Dr. William Sutherland in the early 1900s, *Primary Respiration* was discovered. Primary Respiration is a full body unified field moving in a rhythmic tidal motion. Originating to the mid-line of the body between the cranium and the sacrum, Primary Respiration expands out from the midlife to beyond the physical boundary of the body then contracts back inwards to the mid-line. Like a river with different currents, Primary Respiration moves in a tidal fashion, with a varying degree of frequencies, depth, and healing potential.

It is important to note that Primary Respiration is a regulating function ever present in all living beings whether a practitioner is palpating for it or not. Right now as you read this words, Primary Respiration is working like an Inner Physician, intelligently seeking out the best plan for self-healing and self-correction so that you can have the best opportunity to live your best life.

To be human means you live a dynamic life. The diversity of these dynamics come from how you interact with an ever-changing environment and ever-changing circumstances. We experience all shades of love, kindness, stresses, disease, toxins, and varying levels of trauma.

The more physically, mentally and emotionally healthy you are, the more internal resources you have available to support the unfoldment of health. This is because the potency of Primary Respiration is strengthened by the available internal resources. The greater the potency of Primary Respiration, the easier it is for the body to dissipate and release dis-ease from within.

Occasionally we face overwhelming situations or a series of events that are too intense for the body to process. Such traumas manifest into dense physical and energetic fulcrums in the body. These fulcrums affect us on a day-to-day basis and alter how we approach situations and navigate the world around us. Only when the right environment and the right resources are available can the Primary Respiration begin to resolve these internal fulcrums.

In Craniosacral Therapy, the practitioner feels and watches the Primary Respiration of the patient as it *ebbs and flows* through its tidal movement. When the right environment is achieved, the patient will feel safe and comfortable to the point where Primary Respiration shifts into what is known as a *still point,* or dynamic stillness. In a still point, the patient drops into a safe place where resources can be relocated from immediate stresses to internal fulcrums that have been locked deep in the body. In a still point, the tidal flow of Primary Respiration is no longer present but there is a new sensation of life. It is a sense of inquisitive intelligence and healing potential that is reorganizing the body's field through strengthening our support aspects and chipping away at those unwanted energetic dark spaces of condensed, trapped trauma.

As a practitioner, experiencing someone amidst a still point has been the most humanizing and humbling experience of my life.

To witness an internal intelligence that is always present, yet rarely experienced, truly speaks to the unlimited potential of our divine consciousness. Within each and every one of us lay sensational opportunities yet to be realized until made available through the evolution of our species.

I see Craniosacral techniques not as a therapy but as sensational communication between two sentient beings. The most effective practitioners are those who are highly receptive to their environment through what is known as their Felt Sense. A developed Felt Sense consciously receives information from the environment through their own unified field. We call this establishing a practitioner presence. By cultivating a practitioner presence you are able to feel Primary Respiration in another person as well as in yourself. Essentially, this is a meditation of discovering deeper understanding of what it *feels* like to be alive through cultivating a deeper relationship with your awareness.

Traditional Tantra and Ayurveda teaches us that life is ours to enjoy, that the act of living is the act of self-unfoldment and self-discovery. The world is a place for us to express and gain a deeper understanding of our divine nature and learn that consciousness is not only ourselves but literally everything around us. The practices of Tantra also remind us that we are not a sum of our experiences but the true essence of Divine Energy playing here in a physical reality, a reality that has its challenges and can lead us away from our conscious connection to the divine. In terms of Craniosacral Therapy, reality is a dynamic environment that can hinder the internal unfoldment process of the original matrix.

Simply knowing, by truly owning the fact that there is no limit to what it feels like to be alive, is the first step to manifesting your own internal resources and supporting the function of Primary Respiration inside of you.

When you meditate, do so with dynamic stillness. See that the sensations of your life become more important than your thoughts, and that the intelligence of the original matrix expresses in every cell while correcting and redefining who you are on a cellular and energetic level.

When you move and flow in a yoga class, know and understand that you are creating an internal environment conducive to self-healing and self-regulation and rich in healing resources. Just by having the strength to walk into the studio, you are making a better environment for a better you.

And one of my favorites, when you lie in Savasana...release. Let the feeling of being safe flow over you to the point where just drop down deep and all boundaries disappear. This, my yogi friend, is resting in a still point rich in healing intelligence.

The greatest of life's experiences come from the blossoming of sensational openness. You have the opportunity to continually discover new meanings and new understandings to what it *feels* like to be alive. The deeper the relationship with yourself, the deeper and richer your relationships will be with others and the world around you.

Kevin Heidt is a traditional Tantra yoga teacher and a natural and intuitive therapist with a focus on Craniosacral Therapy. Through his teaching and therapy, he combines the modern and ancient understandings of the human body to provide people with experiences that leave them in awe and in tune with their complete and perfect nature. Kevin shares the ancient understanding of yoga based on study with his teacher Bhagavan Shanmukha Anantha Natha of Shri Kali Ashram. Kevin spends most of his waking hours being "a friend" and seeing that his clients, students, and friends "feel brand new!"

Through LivingBrightside, Kevin, and his wife, Lara Brightside, partner with global leaders and conscious businesses to cultivate happiness, health, and positive growth for their audiences and clients through bright ideas, magical marketing, and high-vibe execution.

To learn more about LivingBrightside or to contact them about your project, visit **www.livingbrightside.com.**

One Downward Dog at a Time

BY DEBBIE HOWARD

Yoga is a very old and dear friend of mine. Our relationship dates back nearly 50 years, to when I was 16 years old. It was 1969, and yoga was considered a bit weird, but somehow I came across Richard Hittleman's *Introduction to Yoga* and it resonated with me. I used his book to teach myself the physical positions and even inspired a few friends along the way.

I may have been initially attracted for a very simple reason: our family was going through a divorce, and I was seeking to find my balance amidst all the turmoil that was going on. In addition to having raging teenage hormones, I was grappling with losing all that was familiar and safe to me.

> *Little did I know at the time that I would be making a friend for life—a friend who would help me through thick and thin.*

Like all good friendships, yoga has always been there for me. Even if I may have lapsed and been inactive for a while, when I start again it is as though we have lost no time at all. The comfort is immediate. The trust is inherent.

Yoga helped me again in 1981, when as a young career woman I experienced anxiety and stress so intense it manifested itself in chest pains. After visits with two heart specialists and lots of expensive tests, I was diagnosed with mitral valve prolapse, as well as a much rarer heart condition known as WPW Syndrome. Fortunately, neither of these conditions is life-threatening, but it was scary to learn about, especially since I knew my paternal grandmother had suffered with heart problems. The doctor wanted me to start taking beta blockers, a way of blocking the parasympathetic nervous system so I wouldn't get so worked up.

On the other hand, the thought of taking *any* medication for the rest of my life was unacceptable to me (since I was only 27 at the time), especially if it wasn't life-threatening. I decided to address my problems the hard way. This was the point in my life where I gave up smoking (for the first time), and I also learned some new relaxation techniques that I could do on my own, as well as re-engaging with yoga classes. I got my racing heartbeat under control and have never taken medication.

Yoga helped me again in menopause, when my world was spinning and nothing seemed to give me peace. I tried various natural supplements, but nothing worked as well as refocusing myself on yoga as a way to find my way through in an emotionally balanced way. I hired a private instructor and gained some new techniques. Again, yoga did not fail me.

As helpful as yoga was during these times (and I experienced dramatic lifestyle improvement both times), the time in my life that yoga was the *most* beneficial to me (so far) was when I was caregiving for my mom, when she was diagnosed with Stage IV lung cancer. I served as her caregiver from afar (from Tokyo, Japan, where I had lived and worked for two decades), coming back and forth to support her on several rounds of chemotherapy. Then I served as her live-in caregiver for the last six months of her life.

During this time, my world was turned upside down, and the challenges and emotional roller coaster of caregiving—let alone the inevitability of losing my mom—sent me scrambling for ways to cope. I realized early on that if I didn't find a way to practice self-care, I would not make it. I also realized it was important for *me* to take care of myself first, so I could in turn be there for my mom. I developed a program that allowed me to get the exercise and mindspace I needed. Doing yoga stretches was an important part of my program, even if I only did one downward dog a day.

In fact, I found the very act of rolling out my mat and doing that one downward dog to be a clear symbolic gesture to my self-care. I also learned it helped me get started, and often I would do *more* than just one downward dog, just because it felt so good to stretch.

At night, I used an audio "yoga relaxation exercise" to end my busy day. I rarely made it all the way to the end. Rather, it helped me to clear my mind and just float off to sleep, leaving all my fears and concerns with the universe.

In my work with family caregivers, I recommend self-care that includes not only physical activity such as yoga postures, but also meditation, both of which work very well to support emotional balance in spite of the heavy demands experienced. Even when time is scarce, setting aside a moment for yourself is the best policy.

For me, yoga is a long-term, reliable friend I can count on no matter what. It is a touchstone, a comfort, and a positive therapeutic reality.

Yoga—especially the downward dog position (even if it is only *one*)—has become a symbol for me of doing something positive that is just for me. It is an action I can take to get myself back to a good place (if I have strayed) and to proactively keep myself in a good place on an ongoing basis.

For me, yoga is also a symbol for *active choice* in my life. There are many aspects of life that are out of your control, but one thing you can always do—no matter what—is to choose to be grounded, to be whole, and to do something you know is good for you. I like to think I'm taking life "one downward dog at a time!"

Debbie Howard thinks of yoga as a lifelong friend—one that she relied on heavily while serving as her mother's caregiver in the final stages of her battle with lung cancer. Debbie was running a Tokyo-based market research company at the time of her mother's diagnosis and spent a year traveling back and forth multiple times to help her with chemotherapy and so forth. As her mother's disease progress, Debbie moved from Tokyo back to South Carolina live in and provide 24/7 support.  She ran her business off the dining table her family had eaten at since she was in the third grade, using time zone maximization, Kinko's, Office Depot, and anything else she could to make it work.

Bringing together her professional research skills and her personal experiences, Debbie has spent the past 10 years since her mom passed away working to integrate her experiences—along with the experiences of more than 200 other caregivers—into a book. The result, called *The Caregiving Journey: Information. Guidance. Inspiration.* guides caregivers through their journeys in a straightforward, heartfelt manner, with a focus on self-care and viewing the caregiving journey overall as a transformative experience. Learn more at **www.thecaregivingjourney.com**.

Special Gift

Receive your FREE *Caregiver Resources List* at
www.thecaregivingjourney.com/caregiving-resources

The Gifts of Practice: Inspirational Meditations and Poems

BY MICHELLE KAHAN

We are all brothers and sisters in this vast ocean of love.
Accept each moment as a place of inquiry and growth along your path.
Some moments there will be suffering and sorrow;
Some moments will be filled with joy and laughter.
Both sides bring us closer to the creator and remembering who we are.

Through the physical practice of yoga, we start to create a relationship
with the body.
Listening to the needs of the body...
Let go...receive...
Through exploration of the breath we learn to quiet the chatter of the mind
and gain tools to approach life in a more balanced alignment.
By surrendering, we realize that we are already whole in body,
mind, and spirit.
There are so many gifts and reasons to step onto the practice mat and
celebrate this connection with all aspects of our being.

Sometimes the body feels joyous and light, laughter filling our days.
Sometimes the body feels sluggish and heavy, sadness or
depression dragging us down.
This duality of light and dark guides us to the middle ground.
Look in the mirror and say, "I love you, I am worthy of love and respect."
Create healthy boundaries for yourself, as they filter out through the
love of the heart.
Listening to and trusting in life, while facing challenges head on
with a belief that all is okay.
All is okay.
Surrendering, we allow life in and release what is not needed out.
Trust yourself and know that you have the power to be whoever
you wish to be.

IDENTITY

This image of who we think we are on the outside is based on an illusion.
How we look...what job we do...how good of a parent or partner we are...
Delve deeper in and you'll see that behind these masks of identity we have created is our true self.
Pure spirit and light resting in the place of being; without judgment, harsh thoughts, or desires.
Just simply being here right now; as we take in all that life is offering us in this precious moment.

Take time to appreciate the body and all that it offers us, the chance to experience, explore, and grow.
Through the practice of yoga, we honor our body through movement as we allow ourselves to express certain yoga poses.
Surrendering into shapes that feel foreign to us and letting go of self-judgment, as we breathe into the unknown.
As the practice deepens, we may notice the gifts of yoga start to extend off the mat into a way of being and living life.
We come home to our truth by loving who we are on the outside and by allowing the light of spirit to shine from the inside.

GRATITUDE

When I am drawn to my mat for practice, the outside world disappears.
Life seems so simple as I take notice of each breath.
Inhale...Exhale
The slow rhythm of the rise and fall of my chest reminds me of the present moment.
A moment filled with joy, love, and patience for life itself.
How simple life can be when we quiet the mind and take time to be with our self.
Awaiting the gifts of the daily practice to show us who we really are.

Peace flows in and through us like the wind.
We grasp to hold on but find our branches snapping.
Life is about change and letting go of the illusion that we have control of anything.
Will you find the space inside to trust the unknown and the path that is unfolding before you?
The sun shines, the clouds shroud, but through these times of clear seeing and confusion there is wisdom and learning unfolding.

LETTING GO

Why do we choose at different times of our life to struggle?
We grasp, pull, and try to control life's events or outcomes.
So much energy is put into these actions when all we need to do is let go
of the struggle and be in the beauty of life.
As the tightness of the control softens we become aware of the breath,
accepting the grace of the present moment, and receiving the gifts that
each moment bring us.
Life takes on a more ease-full way of flowing when we can just surrender to
what is and simply be.

ESSENCE OF LOVE

Allow your heart to open to love,
for this is who you are.
Take a moment to breath into the heart.
Rest into the expansion on the inhale...
and soften on the exhale.
Each step along this journey will bring you closer to
knowing who you truly are...
beyond words and time.

Michelle Kahan has been an avid seeker of poetry her whole life. She is a yoga therapist and the co-owner of Ajna Yoga, where she co-designs and writes curriculum for Ajna's Yoga Therapy College. Michelle is currently compiling her first poetry book and lives in beautiful Victoria, British Columbia. Learn more at **victoriayoga.com**.

Special Gift

Enjoy this healing meditation from Michelle.
https://youtu.be/-PnbNN6vEAY

The Purifying Fire of Open-Hearted Awareness

BY LEE KEMTER

During raging wildfires in North America, heart-wrenching scenes of deer, rabbits, squirrels, and all kinds of wildlife appeared on social media.

The animal lover in me sent prayers but tried not to look too closely. Then one day, an image vividly appeared on my computer screen. Innocent creatures were caught in the fire. No way out. No one could help them.

Experiencing the pain of others is familiar. Since childhood, I've been conditioned to believe if anyone was afraid or upset, I have the responsibility to do something to make them feel better, to take care of them.

Through a video, I was gazing into the eyes of a frightened deer. Feeling her panic, my heart collapsed with grief. A feeling of spiraling sorrow and anguish gripped me in a fraction of second.

Looking into her eyes and drowning in my emotions, my mind stopped. I suddenly became fully present with the intense feelings arising in me.

In a rush of wide-eyed revelation, I experienced that the ocean of feelings were fully mine.

And they were absolutely divine.

As tears filled my eyes, an orgasmic sense of joyful triumph and celebration shook my inner world. An expansion filled my whole body that I've never experienced before.

Why at *that* time? Why with so much pain rising up?

An inner knowing emerged that this situation was not my direct responsibility. It was not my fault. We share this beloved planet and are connected with all forms of life. The fear I saw in the deer and other animals was meant to be a trigger for compassion and open me up to a new way to help them. Not through pity or tears, but through compassionate, energetic communion with them.

Spontaneously, a process I had been developing and practicing over the past year began to unfold. Gently closing my eyes, I felt the agonizing feelings fully as they arose. They were a visceral tidal wave, but I let them surface unimpeded. Then I allowed those feelings to enter into a vast, loving space that was expanding behind my closed eyes. I let the feelings remain in that space, being accepted unconditionally as a divine expression of my humanity.

This process took a few minutes and brought me into a deep sense of calm and connection with the wildlife in the fire. My feelings of sorrow blended with love and created a serene inner space, ever expanding into gentle compassion.

My heart longed to spend time blessing and loving the animals in communion, soul to soul.

Often, I've seen a post or photo on social media that stirs my heart. Immediately, I'd reply that I was sending blessings as an expression of love to whoever was suffering. But how much time and focus did I give to that expression? Or did I move on with my day, feeling that I had met my obligation to bless another in that moment? Did I stop to see, in my body and mind, how I was affected?

With a more expanded heart, I looked back at the images of the deer, rabbits, and other animals. Purposefully, I closed my eyes and became aware of the expanding space behind my eyes.

With a quiet heart, in which the feelings of sadness and despair were now totally soothed and accepted, I could bless the animals.

This process—purposefully relaxing, and then accepting as part of me the feelings of pain and sorrow—became my way to approach social media posts and any political news or conversations that triggered uncomfortable emotions.

Profound change found its roots in me when I started feeling my way through each emotional situation rather than strategizing and thinking... getting lost in plotting and fantasizing about how to change the situation or how to get rid of my uncomfortable feelings. These coping mechanisms are strategies that humans develop to feel safe. We get distracted or flee from emotions, fight with them by resisting and getting upset, or become frozen, numbing ourselves to them.

None of that worked for me.

Instead, I changed my inner world. Compassion for myself and others took hold.

I became more aware of moments in daily life, such as during morning yoga practice, when unsettling emotions came up unexpectedly. The process I was cultivating of letting these emotions be present allowed their source, which is usually from childhood, to land in a new world of nurturing and care.

The energy can flow. My open-hearted awareness can lead the way as presence and acceptance unfurl over and over again. Positive brain patterns are created. A full breath fills my lungs and I begin to discover the Truth that the ancient scriptures speak about. I am fully divine. The capacity for sadness is part of my divine being. Profound love and compassion are there too. I have it all. All the qualities of the sacred whole.

A fresh vision for my life is emerging. Connection and care for others starts with loving compassion for all of my emotions. I value hugging, supporting, and connecting with others.

As a species we are wired for soulful connection, which is supportive and healing.

The connection with my own heart, with the animals and other human beings, is a blessing and a gift. This connection no longer causes me pain. It's a doorway, a jewel in the dark that guides me into an experience that nurtures my soul and each and every soul whom I encounter.

Judgment hurts. It feels sharp and cold. But now, feelings can arise freely without judgment. And my heart leans into the warmth of compassion and love for everything that arises.

Throughout time, fire has created an alchemical process for yogis and yoginis. May the scorching fire of the time we live in bring us to a sense of open-hearted awareness of our birthright to love all parts of ourselves.

Our sorrowful, frustrated, weary emotions can become wrapped in the loving arms of self compassion and universal love.

For **Lee Kemter,** connection is everything—a loving, healing force that she experiences in the company of people, animals, and nature. She enjoys finding out-of-the-box ways to help people find the innocent child inside.

Decades ago, she left the comfort zone of a corporate office to satisfy her inner hunger to make a contribution to people's lives in a deeply meaningful way, a choice that led her to spend five years studying and teaching at an international retreat site in India. There, she designed and taught a meditation curriculum to support hundreds of students in exploring a new and vast inner landscape in the areas of personal and spiritual growth. Today, Lee continues her studies of the priceless yogic traditions and practices, including her cherished meditation practice.

Lee is the author of *The Hidden Light*, inspirational stories of animals she trained and cared for who underwent miraculous changes, profound healing, and transformation—teaching her how she, herself, could approach life's challenges in new ways. Her online course *Mindful Pet Parenting* teaches people how to soulfully and consciously parent their dogs.

Lee dedicates herself to yogic practices and the study of the ancient wisdom traditions, and, from a place of deep optimism and trust, she enthusiastically engages with daily life as a playing field for insight, growth, and the upliftment of others. Lee is a spiritual growth and meditation mentor for those exploring and seeking the deeper dimensions and meanings in life. Connect with Lee at **leekemter.com.**

Special Gift

Lee Kemter is offering two special gifts so you can engage more deeply and completely with the practice in this chapter: a video with a detailed explanation of the practice, plus an audio recording in which Lee, herself, reads this chapter. Listening to Lee's soothing voice promotes a deeper level of assimilation, which can help you make this practice truly yours. Experience how Lee's expert guidance and gentle way can support you to move through life's complexities with calm, clarity, and confidence. Access your two gifts at **www.leekemter.com/practice.**

Trusting the Process of Change

BY JULIE KIDDOO

For as long as I can remember I have resisted change. I've carried a fear of the unknown and, at times, I've lost sleep and my appetite over it. This fear of change and of the unknown has translated into anxiety and at one point turned into deep a depression. However, yoga has given me the tools I need to shift this. And now, I am in a place of trust.

When I was seven years old, I was molested by my male babysitter. At age sixteen, I was sexually assaulted while backpacking in the Colorado Rockies. By the time I was seventeen, I was so anxious about what lay ahead of me like college and the unknown that I was hospitalized for severe depression. All these experiences have called me to question my safety and security. My tendency is to want to control change and have everything in my life be perfectly organized so that I can feel safe and secure. And yet, as I look back at my own experiences, I can see how trust was missing—a natural outcome of trauma.

When I was in college, every time a new quarter began I was a basketcase. I would cry from the overwhelm of my new workload. How was I going to fit everything in with school, my classes, my sorority, my work, and my friends? I called my mom crying for two weeks straight. At one point while I was in college my mom created a painting for me called "The Extension Cord Painting." There was a belt buckle-type object in the center with several lines painted off of it, all in a different color. Each leg represented a different aspect of my life. It was a helpful visual for me so that I could see everything that I had going on and gain a new perspective. Throughout the whole painting were streaks of brown, representing the unexpected things in life that come up that I could not control. The painting was a great tool for me to learn to trust that everything would be okay. I am so grateful for my mom's offering.

Growing up I did not go to church. I believed in a higher power but didn't know what that looked like, and I never put my trust in any sort of faith to get me through the dark times. Instead, every time I went through change, I would cry and complain about everything I feared and dreaded in my life. Then at some point, usually two to three weeks after the change took place, I would get settled into my new routine and would feel like myself again—until the next change. Finally, yoga showed up as my saving grace and gave me access to a higher power.

One thing that I have learned from my yoga practice in the past several years is that no matter what, I will be okay—whether on or off the mat. I cannot always choose the circumstances I am in, but I can choose the way I respond to them. I know that I need to be willing to be ungrounded and comfortable with the unknown so that when I do get re-grounded my roots will grow back stronger. Much like a perennial plant in a garden, I can be planted in a spot and if that spot no longer serves me I can get uprooted and transplanted to a new location that suits me better. I know that I am whole, perfect, and complete. I am safe, and I am secure. I love myself no matter what is happening.

My yoga practice has given me a wonderful gift—a process to clear negativity and acclimate to change in my life. It's allowed me to believe in something bigger, like the "Universe" as a higher power. It's allowed me to see that there is something much bigger than me at play in the world. And, when I give up control and trust in that higher power, things always seem to work out!

Throughout the past eleven years on my yoga mat, I have come to believe in God as my higher power and when I remember to ask Him for whatever it is I want, I can experience more ease, more grace, and trust the process versus trying to fix it or force an outcome.

My yoga teacher Baron Baptiste says that in the face of fear, we have three choices: we can run, we can stay and struggle, or we can stay and relax. This is our central nervous system's automatic response to fear: fight, flight, or freeze. My tendency is to stay and struggle. I know that whatever I resist will persist, and the longer I stay and fight the process I will keep getting the same results but keep expecting a different outcome. However, when I remember to pray, use my breath, and get on my yoga mat to move some energy, I have a choice as to how I respond. I cannot always control the circumstances, but I am completely responsible for my own responses to them.

When I use the tools that yoga offers me to transform anxiety, I am yet again restored. I trust that everything is okay. I trust that there is good in the world and I am renewed. I trust in myself, in the community around me, and in my faith that I can endure whatever change is coming my way.

Julie Kiddoo lives west of Vail, Colorado with her husband Tom, their two children, Charlie and Catie, and their golden retriever, Nala. Julie owns Revolution Power Yoga, a Baptiste Affiliate yoga studio located in Avon, Colorado. She has completed more than 1,000 hours of training with Baptiste Yoga, is a LifeForce Yoga Level 1 practitioner, and is a teacher and a leader of yoga, influencing hundreds of lives on and off the mat.

Julie recently published a memoir, *Bye-Polar*, sharing her struggles with severe depression and the healing she found along the way. Through a tremendous amount of courage and support, she found her path to wellness. Yoga, meditation, self-inquiry, community, and a willingness to come apart in order to rebuild anew have helped her grow and thrive. In addition to being on her mat, Julie loves spending time in nature, writing, skiing, and on road trips with her family and having fun with family and friends. Learn more at **revolutionpoweryoga.com**.

Daring to Trust that a Phoenix Will Rise

BY CARINA LIEU

I am the first of my seven children born in America. My mom instilled high hopes for me to "do better" than my older siblings and parents could. I internalized this expectation in my effort in school. So when failure hit, it felt like watching all parts of me crumble. Oprah once said, "Failure is just life trying to move us in another direction." When I was 28-years-old, I went through an extremely difficult phase. Many spiritual friends I made at the time talked about the Saturn's Return, this astrological cycle that occurs every seven years and forces us to look deeply into the decisions made leading up to that point and adjust our actions to more fully align with our intuition. When I found myself broke, with low self-esteem, and afraid—literally the opposite of how I saw my future self then—I saw Saturn's Return as an opportunity to surrender and truly listen to my instincts. I did not want to travel down the same road for years to come. Einstein once said, "The definition of insanity is doing the same thing over and over again, but expecting different results." I did not want to be a laughing stock. I wanted to change. And I proceeded to do so from the inside.

If you are reading my story, know that my journey lasted me another seven years and if you are wondering, I do not regret it. In fact, I implore you to try it when you undoubtedly reach this unshakable feeling where you know you must change and the only person you need permission from is yourself. Don't shy away from it. Lean into it and listen.

It took a long time, but today, I am more clear about why I left my past behind and confident in how I overcame it. I am forgiving. I am expecting a child. I am in a positive relationship. My yoga practice has deepened. My life isn't perfect. But I had to reach really deep inside to arrive here. I'll explain why.

When I was 22-years-old, I fell in love with a boy. He was charming, older by two years, had a master's degree, was intelligent, worldly, and mysterious. The mysterious aspect kept me intrigued. Despite the warnings, I devoted my heart singularly to him. We didn't immediately get together. After three years of being apart, I had a chance to get with him and I held onto it. The old adage I memorized as a teenager that kept me attached was, "If you love something so much, let it go. When it comes back to you, it was meant to be." He seemed bigger than any person I had met before. I craved him.

In my intuition, I knew it was unhealthy and even illogical in some ways. But I stubbornly wanted to prove that if I wanted something or someone, I could have it: the guy, the job, the credentials, the lifestyle, etc. No matter how hard or obviously wrong the relationship got, I kept my hopes up that I deserved the things I desired. After all, it was *him* and I had invested so much.

I will divulge a few of things that went wrong but ignored to illustrate the extent of my obsession. Early on in our relationship, I received an urgent call on Saturday morning from him while I lived in Oakland and he was in LA. He stated that loan sharks were after him and his life was threatened. He needed $1000 wired to him immediately or he would die. Frantically, I pulled together about $500, because I was a non-profit worker at the time, and walked into Check Cashing (for the first time) to wire money. My heart was racing and my adrenaline was high. After I wired the money, he, in an anticlimactic way, said the situation was fine. I later learned that while I was panicking, so was his best friend Don, and his older sister Ophelia. She was raising a family in Florida, but wired him her rent money! Don also contributed money too and he was the only person my boyfriend at the time repaid. Meanwhile, his sister contacted the cops and they were searching for him on conspiracy and fraud charges. All of this was so intense, my head spun. I was angry, confused, and resentful. I felt betrayed, and untrusting. I never got to resolve that feeling or story with him. Somewhere between when I broke up with him and he became homeless, I set it aside.

When I moved to LA, I reluctantly let him live with me temporarily and he offered to be the rent collector for all the tenants. Each month, we gave him our rent and assumed he had good intentions. After three months of unhappy cohabitation, I moved out quickly. Not too long after, the landlords contacted me saying that we were behind on three months of rent. I showed them my check book proving that I paid my rent. The reality was that my ex-boyfriend gambled the rent money each month. When confronted, he would bait and switch the landlords, by telling them he would get them money on a certain date, then send them bits, and re-convince them to give him more time. He never had any intention of paying them back and they lost about $5,400.

After that incident, I worried about his health and encouraged him to get addiction help and suggested a sober-living home. I was a student at the time, who saved a little bit from my non-profit job. On good faith, I loaned him between $300-450 to pay rent at a sober living home. And he again, gambled that. He never had any intention of paying me back. That was the last loan I ever gave him. But in the coming years, he would, out of desperation, pawn my things, my roommates' things; he would con desperate and wealthy women into paying him consultant fees while he plagiarized academic work and passed it off as his; and become homeless, so he would bum off of my car and apartment.

I don't know how I compartmentalized my life but I did. I was in a tough master's program. I cared about doing well. In my dreams, I would work hard so he could get on his feet as an actor. When he was successful, he would support me in return. I was juggling a lot of responsibilities in hopes to make a difference in the world. But I was hiding and ignoring this terribly unsafe and toxic relationship which was ever-present. It was as if I had gotten sick too and couldn't decipher if he was the problem or if I was.

When I finally graduated, I got my first 4.0. In the midst of the economic downturn of 2008, I applied for and gotten a position in Congress with the first Chinese American woman elected to office as a Field Representative, Caseworker, Domestic Violence liaison, Transportation liaison, and Constituent Mail writer. It was a great blessing to be recognized for my hard work. Yet, this position would be the experience that would drive me to break away from him, but not without one final call.

Working for Congress, the member I worked for worked tirelessly, to the point of exhaustion. I wanted to keep up and rise to the challenges. I thought, I admired her but at times I didn't want to become so vapid. I saw how the work we did left little time for reflection but we were constantly going. I felt my life revolve around hers and eventually the political world which relentlessly focused on image and superficiality.

One night, I left my new apartment and he did not have the key. He walked ¼ mile to meet me to retrieve it. He was upset with me. I went home later and apologized to him. He went to bed forgiving me and for once, I thought we seemed peaceful. But the calm comes before the storm. The next morning, in a hurry to get to work, I forgot my purse at home. I realized this midday when I went to fill out the USPS Mail Forwarding/Change of Address form. I called him to provide my debit card information for the $1 charge I would need to make. At this point, he may have noticed the cash I kept in my wallet because I was moving and needed cash for buying craigslist furniture.

He decided to spend the cash in my wallet, the money in my checking account, and pawn my laptop and ipod for cash for the casino that day while I was at work. When I drove home, and I couldn't reach him, I had a horrible feeling that he was at the casino. I got to my apartment and asked the landlord to let me into my apartment. I noticed my things were missing, that my bank account was empty, and started texting him: "Why did you do that?" His response was, "You deserve it." That reply left my head spinning again and I was angry, confused, and betrayed. This time, however, I had nowhere to run to. It happened in my apartment, the one I paid rent for by myself in.

At that point, it was time to make some new decisions. I was working in a high-stress job where image was pinnacle, and I need to protect my home. My old roommate contacted me about picking up her old keys—she was an attorney—and I started to tell her something was wrong. She came over, calmed me down, and spoke assertively to the police on my behalf. I felt mute. The officer recorded everything and at the end, he said, "I've seen cases like this and if someone has an addiction, they should spend their own money, not yours."

Suddenly it clicked. I allowed someone else to take control of my life, in spite of the good I saw in him. I had stopped noticing and protecting my boundaries. It was then that I decided to allow a temporary restraining order to take effect and that nothing was going to stop me from letting this person back into my life again.

That was a frightening time. I was pushing myself at work still but I was distracted. I was disappointed that I let all of that happen for three years. I was messy. I had to spend some time uncrossing the wires in my brain to get better. I knew I had the option to push through the pain and dive deeper into work. But I was afraid that by doing so, I would come out the other a little too much like my boss.

I was able to accomplish more than I could ever have achieved alone with him, but it was time for me to search within myself for self-love and strength. As a daughter of refugees, I'd been taught to just press on, and while I appreciate and am grateful for the resilience I learned because of this, I had been in deep in denial about the abuse I underwent and enabled. Being 300 miles from home, I needed to re-establish networks for self-care.

I made a decision from then on to *never* let myself down, to follow through on decisions I made. Every morning, I hiked to Griffith Observatory. I challenged myself to travel without a map. I'd reach the top and meditate. In the afternoons and evenings, I went to as many yoga classes as I could, most of them from a Forrest yoga instructor. In her classes, I would cry. I felt myself become aware of my own body. This was where I felt my healing begin.

I fell in love with nature, and I found a fellowship that combined equity, nature, and urban planning. I would research and make real policy recommendations for increasing diversity in National Parks. I moved into a National Park, where I lived for most of a year. Meanwhile, I continued my practice and found a yoga studio less than half a mile from my office. I dedicated myself to self-study, work, and yoga.

I chose to undergo my first 200-hour YTT program with Mary Pat Murphy, a wise woman in her 70s who beamed light. She paid watchful attention to my development. Through her careful facilitation, I became close to my loving Kula, or community. My kula was made up of suburban white women who were welcoming, warm, and kind toward me. As a young woman whose social network had crumbled, their inclusiveness was exactly what I needed. They were the family I could depend on. To this day, I have a picture of all of us framed in my living room.

Yoga was a portal for me to go into, and through, so I could face my pain. When the pain felt daunting and hopeless, yoga gave me the courage to sit with the fear and transform the energy into self-knowledge. With the discipline that yoga requires, and through the yamas and niyamas, yoga became my teacher and I was able to learn about and release my mental garbage. Honestly, I had no idea that when I acquired my degree, ready to enter the real world, that I would undergo the life-changing trauma that would lead me to undergo this healing journey. I always thought that if there was a top, I was rising there and nothing would stop me. Through yoga, I saw that having *satya* (truth) and *ahimsa* (kindness) were integral for dealing with myself first and then with others. Because of my yoga practice, my professional life has slowed down, and I now choose to live authentically.

It was one of the most peaceful periods in my life, but still, I faced my own demons. A depression with frequent suicidal thoughts hit. Through an ally, I found a free therapy program at the University of Akron and started seeing a graduate student there who was gentle, understanding, and kind. She reminded me that some of the messages in my head needed a reality check. She saved my life at that time—along with yoga.

Leaving it there means possessing the self-knowledge to move on and seek new horizons. My life today is starkly different from my past, and writing this story somehow cements that truth.

I was always perceived as outgoing and confident, but the last six years have brought me on a detour to learn my truth. Yoga helped jump-start that journey, eventually therapy and a pantheist belief system came along to help.

As a freshman at UC Berkeley and coming locally from Oakland, college seemed easy and everyone in my dorm supported my activism. My second year proved to be different because never before had I felt so self-conscious and unwanted. I had a strong primary identity as a social justice activist and a role in the student organization, but no real support network. Because of this, I drowned in my expectations of myself and in the projections and expectation of others. *Why couldn't I get myself together to be the leader everyone expected me to be? Why was I failing miserably in seemingly every aspect of my life?* I needed mental health support, but did not know where to begin.

My solution was easy: Move away.

Moving to LA was hard at first. My commute by bus to school was miserable. I was close to giving up until I moved into an apartment across the street from school. I was slowly but surely learning that my happiness was within my control.

After college, I went to graduate school and earned a master's degree in Urban Planning and, within a few months, I started working for the 27th district Congressional Office.

If everything happens for a reason, my journey has not been by accident. Some days, my identity as a child of refugees creeps in and tells me this approach doesn't seem good enough. Momentarily, I live with guilt. But as I look around, my life is balanced with a clear conscience. My work is consistent with my work philosophy and ethics: I am a teacher in an urban school where I mold young minds on science.

What motivates me today is so different from what motivated me six years ago. As I continue to work on self-care, personal development, and professional growth, I remember to have patience with myself and understand that the work I do now will make a big difference later. Instead of taking shortcuts, I face my fears. Instead of going up, I am "moving down," as Jack Kornfield puts it. And this process is no cake walk. I am seeking liberation, and nothing worth having comes easily. So I wait and I have faith that one day the phoenix will rise again.

Carina Lieu is a Transportation Policy/Planning and Education professional who has worked in various levels of government and among the least served populations in education. She brings curriculum development grounded in civic engagement through working and living in the San Francisco Bay Area. She has studied dance and Mahayana Buddhism since the age of 8 and is fluent in Vietnamese and Cantonese. In  2014, she completed her 200-hour Yoga Teacher Training at Namaste Yoga in Ohio, under the watchful eye of Mary Pat Murphy. She holds a Bachelor of Arts in Ethnic Studies from UC Berkeley and a master's degree in Urban Planning from University of Southern California. Learn more at **www.carinalieu.com.**

Mother, Loss, and Coming Home to Love: A Story About Navigating the Unknown

BY ALISON LITCHFIELD

Each of us will experience a time in our lives when things fall apart and we feel like we have lost our ground. It may be through the loss of a loved one, a job, or a home or the painful ending of a relationship. When life pricks us in these ways and we are thrown into a reality that is unpredictable, how do find our ground and face the uncertainty that life presents?

When I was nineteen, my mother was diagnosed with ovarian cancer. I remember feeling numb because I didn't really want to believe she was sick. My sisters and I were together when we got the news, and we were all in disbelief of what the future may hold for us and the possibility of a life without our mother.

I drove from there to start my junior year of college in Maine, and my mother started on her healing path. We all went about our lives in as normal a fashion as we could.

Eighteen months later she passed away at home with all of us there. Spring was in full bloom. With love and devotion to our dear mother, we guided her to the other side.

The night before she left her body, I stayed by her side and held her at the threshold as her breath faded in and out. I remember feeling the terror and fear that arose in me as she danced with the other side. It was just me and her and me in the dark. Death was so near.

Though I didn't know it at the time, this was my first encounter with one of the mother archetypes in Hindu mythology called Kali. Kali represents the dark mother and is the goddess of death, darkness, and uncertainty. For many of us, this is a scary topic because as Westerners, talking about death is taboo. That night I felt the presence of this deity as I sat with her in her fragile state. It was both terrifying and radical.

In the weeks after her passing, I was heartbroken, and though I tried to go on with life as usual, underneath I questioned the meaning in everything. I found temporary refuge in nature and through the distractions of my college social life, but grief weighed on me.

About a year later I moved to Boulder, Colorado and had my first encounter with yoga. When I stepped on my yoga mat for the first time since losing her, I felt my ground. Standing on my mat, breathing in and out, and feeling my body steady gave me a sense of coming home to myself. It was good to be home. Feeling my muscles and bones and the energy as I flowed in and out of these postures gave me a glimpse of what it was to be whole and connected to something bigger. My yoga practice was like a sacred temple that I entered each day to find meaning.

Through yoga I came to understand the idea that mother represents our first connection to life and love. A mother's love is the deepest love there is, and so when I lost my own mother I felt on some level that I had lost love. In my practice I worked to feel whole again, and then when I became a mother, that need was temporarily filled with becoming a mother. As my kids grew, however, I realized that someday I would lose them, too, and that they were never really mine to begin with.

The second time Kali came to meet me was during a time when I felt stuck in the role of housewife. An inner rage arose in me that could not be contained. I felt my own mother's rage, and I knew that it was time to look this fierce goddess in the eye. She was, after all, part of me. She revealed to me the places I had repressed, the disowned parts of myself. As I began to look, it was dark and scary, but what I knew from the teachings was that if we are willing to look at our demons this energy of Kali as the divine mother will hold us there with unconditional love to help us heal those wounds. That is exactly what happened, and what I found on the other side was my first taste of freedom.

In these last six months, my oldest son hit some challenges as he came into his teenage years. He became distant and detached, and it brought up a lot of those old feelings of loss and grief in me that had been hidden. I didn't know how to reach him and felt like I failed him as a mother. I shared with a friend how much fear I had around losing him, and he gave me some very helpful advice. He said, "You have already lost him. He is a young man now and you have done your job. Now it is up to him." When I heard these words I felt compassion for myself. It allowed me to see he was not mine anymore, and never really was. The universe works in mysterious ways, because after that, divine grace descended and we have found a beautiful new mother-son relationship.

The loss of my mother has given me such a profound understanding of impermanence and the temporary nature of life. The Buddhist teachings tell us that nothing is permanent and change is inevitable. If we can accept and appreciate life for what it is, nothing will ever go wrong and we will see the beauty that already exists everywhere.

I'm eternally grateful for these teachings and for the practice of yoga, which continues to guide me back to self-love and acceptance. When we cultivate true love of self, the love that is present within radiates out to all beings, all peoples, and to Mother Earth herself. For so many years, I lived with the fear that loss meant I would lose love; I lived with my heart protected. A teacher once said, "Do your practice, all is coming." All these years of practice and I am able to access a much deeper love in and for myself. A love that is infinite and beautiful because it's a love that isn't dependent on anything outside of itself. I know how to trust and allow the divine mother to hold me when I have to navigate the unknown or the disowned parts of myself, and I can hold that for my boys as well.

Finding ground is not about finding safety and security but is really a practice of acceptance and coming home to loving ourselves fiercely and letting go over and over again into the cycles of life, loss, and love. It's not always easy and takes a courageous and open heart, but in that process, we find a deeper more profound connection to wholeness and the interconnectedness of all life.

Alison Litchfield is an ERYT 500 Yoga Instructor, Certified Rolfer of Structural Integration, and founder of Embody Radiance and Yoga School. She has been a yoga practitioner, teacher, and embodiment educator for more than 25 years. Alison came to yoga just after losing her mother at age twenty-one, and yoga gave her a place to feel at home in herself.

She fell in love with yoga and traveled to Mysore, India in 1997 to deepen her yogic studies with the founder of Ashtanga Yoga, Shri K.Pattabhi Jois. Shortly after returning the States, Alison completed Richard Freeman's first yoga teacher training in 1999 and became one of his senior teachers. A back injury led Alison to do the Rolfing 10 series, and it was so transformative that she became a Certified Rolfer of Structural Integration and started her own healing practice in 1998.

Alison has many years of study in somatic studies and the healing arts including Rolfing, Iyengar and Vinyasa flow yoga, energy work, and feminine embodiment practices. She weaves structural alignment with awareness and whole-body integration to assist students in finding optimal health and embodied living in the everyday modern world. Alison also studies natural medicine, which supports a conscious lifestyle with empowered purpose and optimal health using foods, herbs, and pioneering information that transforms surviving into thriving.

Alison does powerful one-on-one work and leads workshops, teacher trainings, and retreats both nationally and internationally. She is passionate about inspiring and empowering herself and others to listen, wake up, and be guided by the infinite intelligence and wisdom of the body.

She currently lives in Boulder, Colorado with her husband and two sons. She loves to hike, ski, and play in the mountains! Learn more at **www.alisonlitchfield.com.**

One Good Thing!

BY KIRSTEN LIVINGSTON

"Be careful when a naked person offers you a shirt."
—AFRICAN PROVERB

I spent years of my life on profligate good deeds. I was so *moved* by the troubles of my family and friends, I believed it was my "calling" to assist in any way I could. And so, with little consideration for my own dwindling inner resources, I forged ahead. My story is not unique—illnesses, deaths, injuries, divorce—one incident followed another year after year as I "came to the rescue" time after time. Yet finally, when the crises were winding down and my own divorce was final, I became ill. And then, in the summer of 2017...I collapsed into utter darkness.

I was rescued from oblivion by a handful of people—friends, family... and professionals. Although some of my earlier "good work" had been misdirected I *had* actually provided relief for a few and developed some wonderful friendships. They cared enough to shine their love upon me—so much so that I could not help but feel it. If these people loved me so much, surely I owed them a look—could I see what they saw in me?

I had to start somewhere basic—the voice that assaulted me from morning until night—I noticed that was *my* voice. Would I accept that kind of treatment from anyone else? Would I treat someone I disliked to such a stream of wretchedness? The answer was a firm *no*. Painstakingly, diligently, I began to "catch myself in the act" of my own vindictive voice and alter both the words and the tone. Instead of "You idiot!" it became "That was a mistake, slow down next time." Simple, yet extremely difficult and this exercise required commitment minute by minute, day after day. Yet, as each day passed, my inner voice became kinder.

> *scraping sludge away*
> *allows me to see through the*
> *heavy dark of my heart*

During my time of recovery, I found myself drawn back to Yoga. I had studied Yoga for over twenty-five years, yet still found it difficult to integrate meditation and asana into my *daily* life and I yearned for more knowledge—more motivation—more understanding! Once I began to see value in life—in me, the idea of doing something for myself—**one good thing** came to me: Yoga Teacher Training. It was like a flashing neon sign that would *not* be ignored.

I found a ten-month 200-hour training at Karuna Center for Yoga & Healing Arts in Northampton, Massachusetts with the help of my teacher. The training began in January 2018, but because I had been ill I had to prepare; my collapse had taken a significant cognitive and physical toll. I began to read a *ton* and I added in academic work to engage my mind; take in and integrate concepts once again. I went to Yoga class regularly and practiced with my teacher.

I found the first training weekend *overwhelming*—and incredible and opening. It took *three* more months before I found my cognitive rhythm. It was amazing to have ten months over which I *had* to make Yoga a priority, where it became part of the fabric of my life. And the training deepened my understanding of self-kindness. Indeed, all of the practices of Yoga are toward stilling the *cittavrttis* or "thought waves"—our restless consciousness, which are considered to be at the root of all suffering.

I loved and was challenged by my studies *and* had some embarrassingly difficult moments where I did poorly or didn't feel I could perform adequately. In fact, one of the deterrents to teaching was my "idea" of what a Yoga teacher *is*—someone who teaches hour-and-a-half-long classes to groups of people in a large room. When I student-taught in such a situation, I didn't like it. However, as I continued student-teaching, I worked with individuals and small groups in their homes and my vision transformed. This more personalized teaching resonated for me and each time I met with students in smaller environments, I left ready to return.

That inspired me to design my teaching practice as *klivingyoga*—specifically for private and semi-private clients at their homes or places of business. It has been a way for me to meet the needs of people who might not otherwise feel able to attempt *any* of the Yoga practices—people like me, who need to be treated gently in some way—physically, mentally, spiritually, or all three. And, I absolutely love to design each practice or sequence specifically for each client.

I still study and practice and, yes, still struggle with my own practice at times. My life feels abundant and I hope some of that abundance spills forth and flows to those around me. I wish for everyone to have a place of peace. For me, that place is with my mat (and my props) doing Yoga.

I'm no longer in the business of leaping to the rescue of friends and family—bringing (perhaps unwanted) "shirts" to people as I deplete my own limited reserves. Instead I am able to offer Yoga where it is needed—to myself and to others. After all, Yoga has become my *renewable* resource!

> "If you can breathe, then you can do yoga."
> —SRI TIRUMALAI KRISHNAMACHARYA

Kirsten Livingston (RYT 200) has studied yoga for more than twenty-five years in California and New England. She completed her 200-Hour Yoga Teacher Training Certification with Paul Menard and Eileen Muir at Karuna Center for Yoga & Healing Arts in Northampton, Massachusetts.

Kirsten specializes in *bringing yoga to her clients* (at home or in the office) to create a relaxed environment. She uses experience, props, education, intuition, and common sense to develop customized breathing, meditation, or physical practices designed to support her clients' challenges and enhance their strengths. Kirsten works with individuals and small groups.

Kirsten lives in Guilford, Connecticut with her 16-year-old son, her dog (who was once mistaken for a large squirrel), and her best friends. Learn more at **klivingyoga.com**.

A Living Practice of Connection and Belonging

BY STEPHANIE LOPEZ

Many people practice yoga and meditation to discover a sense of ease, balance, and purpose. I believe there is a deeper motivation as well; a longing for connection with one's self and rest of the world. I've found this yearning is satisfied through the simplicity of Being.

Being refers to your inherent existence or presence. Hidden in plain sight behind all our thoughts, emotions, and actions is an undeniable ground of stillness. The practice of yoga—or any practice that fosters one-pointed, focused attention—may reveal an underlying ease of Being, well-being, and interconnectedness with all of life. Fostering an ease of Being brings forth a direct sense of wholeness that is unchanging regardless of life's circumstances.

What do you notice when you simply rest rather than being continually drawn by the movements of the mind or happenings around you? Take a moment, find a comfortable chair or position, knowing that for the next few moments there is nothing you need to do and nowhere you need to go. Let yourself rest and simply be. Thoughts can pass by without the need to attend to them. Notice how images and sounds come and go. All the while you are resting...being. Sense the space of the room around you. Sense your whole body. Notice the body breathing. Savor this moment of quietude, without striving or expectation of an outcome. Let attention shift from the changing sensations and perceptions to an ever-present ease of Being. Within your inherent presence is a sense of wholeness and underlying well-being with this moment, just as it is.

As you transition from this mini practice, what do you notice?

Living from the ground of Being is its own heartfelt offering.

As we begin to explore Being, we learn to welcome everything just as it is. To practice welcoming is to abide in nonjudgmental presence and simply allow whatever arises to arise. We learn that *welcoming* is not an extra something we do. Rather, it is an essential aspect of being human.

In contrast, struggle is accompanied by tension, contraction, anger, and fear. At its heart is the desire to have things other than what they are. You push away what you don't want and cling to what you desire. There is no denying the pain and struggle that is a part of life yet reconnecting to the ground of Being teaches us to meet these experiences without trying to fix or change them. Imagine the fierce grace of meeting pain as pure physical sensation and gently welcoming the emotions and beliefs it engenders. The act of feeling into and allowing pain to emerge can bring a shift in its intensity.

What happens when we let go of the struggle with life? What happens when we simply allow its challenges, heartbreak, and beauty? In my experience, there is a release of tension, an opening to freedom, and joy in full presence of all movements of life. At the heart of this welcoming is an underlying wholeness that cannot be broken—the ground of Being.

Through this compassionate welcoming you develop connection with all parts of yourself and begin to live authentically. There is trust in who you are and what you do—and this belonging with yourself flows into a connection with others. As you live life fully and with an undefended heart, you develop a sense of belonging in the world. This intimacy with yourself and others empowers you to live life to its fullest potential.

The spaciousness of Being widens your lens to take in more and more nuance in the immediacy of now. You open your attention more fully to others, expressing kindness and compassion more freely. Even difficult situations are a catalyst for your most authentic, heartfelt response. Rather than judging or trying to fix and change others, you learn to become curious and responsive to life's ups and downs.

Take time to nourish the ease of Being. Living and responding from your ground of wholeness will transform how you see and engage with the world. Deeply connected with all of life, you may discover wonder, joy, and delight.

Stephanie Lopez, LISW-S, C-IAYT, is a skillful and authentic teacher who brings the ancient yogic teachings to life. With a deeply embodied understanding of meditation, Stephanie holds space for students to awaken to their essential nature. Stephanie's offerings are informed by twenty-five years of immersion in the non-dual teachings of yoga. As a meditation teacher, yoga therapist, and psychotherapist, she bridges Eastern wisdom with Western psychology to support healing and transformation. Stephanie's compassionate presence, depth of knowledge, and ease of being create a welcoming space for insightful learning. As the Director of Operations, Senior iRest® Trainer, and Retreat Leader for the iRest Institute, she leads retreats and trainings internationally with a focus on living an authentic and awakened life. Learn more at **www.stephanielopez.org** and **irest.org.**

Phoenix Goddess Rising:
My Path to Love

BY CAROLINA GRACE LORENZO

I don't believe that people are defined by their worst mistakes, by their biggest traumas, or the stories that they believe about themselves. I believe that we can live and die many times while we are still living. I believe in instantaneous healing that can happen through the power of love. I know this as truth because I have been the giver and receiver of love's grace countless times along my humbled journey. It is through the mud of what we go through that the lotus nourishes itself; the mud becomes transmuted into the medicine with which we serve the world. Even as I write this story about "myself," I feel I am writing about a girl who died, and I am writing now as the phoenix goddess that arose from her ashes.

Her story makes me a little sad to share here. My story is not unique—it seems women of every shape and size have been taught to believe in a collective myth that as women, we are not enough, and because of this, we compete with each other, hustle for a sense of worth, and seek validation outside of ourselves.

I am thrilled to be alive in these times when we are rising to tell our story, coming out of the shadows and waking up to love. This is my story of waking up from a trance of unworthiness. This is my story of how I am learning to be the best friend, mother, lover, sister, partner, encourager to myself that I can be. My great prayer is that my story may touch your heart, beloved reader, and remind you of your own humanity and divinity, and the goddess within you, and leave you feeling compassion for the journey we are all walking back home to our hearts.

Before I found yoga I didn't love myself; I felt I didn't belong, I was too much and, conversely, not enough. The times I loved myself were when someone else loved me or told me I was good. Like many women who experience trauma and sexual violence, I felt broken. I didn't want anyone to know how much I struggled, and I had difficulty with trusting others. The first time I met my spiritual teacher, Simone, she looked at me like I was a beloved queen. I will never forget the way she took me in, as if she was beholding a great gem, and being taken in like this changed my life. In her eyes everything I had done or had been done to me was forgiven and transmuted back into love. She shared that her body filled with light and she told me yoga was an important part of my path. This was where the journey to yoga began for me. I saw a whole new way of living in love in our time together, and the path of healing began for me.

Some people may have a gentle slow-forming love affair with yoga, but for me the relationship was fast and furious. My first yoga class was a total game changer, and I started my first teacher training a month later, and six months after that I was headed to India to do my second teacher certification. My first yoga class was a strong, sweaty flow class, and these are my favorite. I remember the moment I rested into my puddle of sweat in pigeon pose toward the end of class. Here I heard a voice, a voice of a kindness I had never heard at that point, it was the voice of my spirit, Spirit, who knows. She said, "Rest there, my love."

In that moment I heard, I was safe, I was enough. I had the right to rest and be quiet and be still, and not hustle for my worth. Love is unconditional. This voice, this kindness, changed my life. The door of love opened and nothing would stop me from walking toward the light of this love. But I sank down into that puddle and I cried. I cried tears of fear, tears of knowing that I had problems with managing my emotions, that I couldn't stop using something outside of myself to deal with my emotions. I was lonely, and I knew something so beautiful wanted to emerge from within me, and I didn't know what to do or how to let it. I didn't know where to go. But Yoga was the guiding light.

Before I started yoga I felt the world inside of me, I could feel other people's pain and joy, other people's expectations and needs and I didn't have any space for myself inside. On my yoga mat I found my edges, I found the release button inside and I found the way to keep out feeling the world around me, and ever so slowly I began to feel myself. I am a huge advocate and tear enthusiast; crying is the greatest healer out there. Each tear seemed to release the pressure to perform, the armoring over my heart, and the fear from my eyes. It is on my mat that I thawed out and cried ancient tears that I had been holding onto. I cried for the women of my lineage who didn't feel their feelings. Their armor, too, would fall off of me and my vibration would shift. There I would find pleasure and enjoy the flow and freedom and power of my body.

From this deep place of inner connection and healthy space for myself, I would feel the breath of my neighbors, and the breath of their neighbors, and then together the whole room merged into the field of breath and oneness. On my mat I would come home to this temple. It would be years before I learned how to be and stay in my body off of my mat, but slowly I learned how to come home moment after moment, and I am still in the embodied school of the open heart today. In yoga I learned to take up space, to shine without others' approval or threat or rejection. And if I shined, there was infinite space for others to join me. It was on my mat that I became a leader of the heart.

A large part of my story in this life is about sharing my voice, my love as well as my pain, and not stuffing my feelings down. Finding my voice was about trusting that it is safe to sing my whole song and to take up space and trust that whatever other people say or do, I am always standing on sacred ground. When I sing, I am touched, caressed, bathed in light, and love pours out of me. For me to allow the singer to be born, another part of me had to die and stop hurting my throat with throwing up my food. I can still remember the day that I simply woke up to what I was doing, throwing up my food day after day, I was so sad for the cells in the back of my throat; I was hurting myself and my heart opened wide with love for this whole pattern and I cried. I reminded myself I was a singer and I was hurting my sacred temple. This day I became the caretaker of an instrument given to me on loan from Spirit, and a singer was born. This practice of coming home to my body as a sacred, holy place opened my heart to my own innocence and the inner child who lives inside of me. This wild-hearted unbroken spirit is my great teacher of life and forgiveness and of play, and my relationship with her has healed and brought me through the hardest times.

One day while living at a retreat center in upstate New York, after a hard break-up and surrendering to my path of recovery, I heard the critic in my mind making fun of my inner child for the way I *over*-shared with people and longed for love and attention. In a moment of motherly love, I pulled out a piece of paper and wrote down a poem to this sweet little girl in my heart, coming to her loving assistance against the bully of my mind.

I wrote:

Hey Care, queen of the TMI, yes you, way to go, you are an open-hearted love warrior and I am never letting you go. Your love is the river that I come to everyday. Your love is the river that I come to, to pray and to play.

I seek to live very closely with the little girl inside of my heart. For years I would imagine putting her at the foot of my yoga mat and do my practice for her. I would wake and see her in my eyes in the mirror and adore her. I would fall in love with her through play and making mundane moments more joyful with song and sass. She is my greatest teacher and teaches me how to love myself more, and she screams when I don't listen or when I abandon myself for someone else or for some outer authority.

I am still learning to be the integrated masculine and feminine to ground and protect that little girl in my heart, to listen and to surrender to the warrior goddess path I am here to carve. I am on a journey, and sharing it brings to my eyes—tears of joy.

Carolina Grace Lorenzo

I am a therapist, coach, and a devotional singer. I specialize in issues around EMPOWERMENT, voice and Body. I create transformational coaching programs to uplevel people's lives in every way. I am so excited to share my Sassy Lotus-3 Moons Program with the world, as this is an ongoing group-based online program devoted to creating an amazing relationship with yourself, with your life, with your body, and with a community committed to kindness and love. The program consists of a Daily Lotus Guidebook, meditation and embodiment videos, group zoom calls, and curriculum for 3 Moons, working with the Body (all things self-care), Bond (our relationships), and going Beyond where we have been out of any scarcity or limitation. I am so honored to be guiding people in really CLAIMING the gift of who we really are, and owning the painful parts of our story and our experiences, so that we can create a NEW Earth together. Thank you for being a part of this great LOVE! Together We RISE! For more information reach out to carelorenzo@gmail.com and check out my websites at **www.yogawithcarolina.com** and **www.sassylotus.life**.

Special Gift

Dear one, this song is about honoring the innocent place inside of each one of our hearts. It is about honoring the child and coming back into wholeness and into grace. I wrote it for my own heart and there I found all hearts. Sat nam.

Listen here: **https://youtu.be/al-nw9qY2zo**

Enlivening the Antennae of Consciousness

BY KANDY LOVE

Years on the mat, alone and among others in classes, have given me a depth of connection to my body and thoughts and sensations I had never imagined possible or even desirable. In the quiet, ideas and insights emerge spontaneously. I relish these times. No conversation, just exploration of being present for, with, and by myself.

I recently translated this familiar framework from my mat practice to achieve a higher quality of life off the mat. Showing up for myself from a deeper/higher level has evolved.

Before yoga, self-focus looked differently for me. As a single woman for thirty-four years, being alone was not foreign to me. Speed and intensity for production and success was my formula. During three previous careers—management with AT&T, high school English/Journalism teacher, and newspaper editor—I had readily put in long hours, always followed by periods of depleted energy and fatigue.

The outside world had been my focus. I thought that the way to become even more productive or successful was to find ways to go outside of myself—even escape myself—especially my thoughts. Being home alone was a time to unwind and regroup. However, it didn't provide much solace, as watching TV, studying, computer surfing, working, and questionable eating habits were my regular distractions.

The roller coaster ride was so familiar, it even felt friendly!

> "You do not need to seek freedom in a different land, for it exists *within* your own body, heart, mind, and soul."
>
> —BKS IYENGAR

Once yoga became part of my life, the mat and meditation offered moments of peace not often found in daily life. It was as if little antennae began perking up inside of me as the intelligence of my body was being awakened. I explored alignment, breath, balance, strength, flexibility, mobility, focus, quietness, relaxation, and self-love and the increased awareness within each. These values spilled into my life. A good yoga life evolved, including creating a successful community-oriented yoga and massage center.

However, even then, the choices I made were imperfect. Lapses of carelessness and even self-sabotage still happened. Poor choices affected my life in dating, business expansion, and taking little vacation time. My alone time off the mat often felt removed and lonely, which definitely was not the same thing as being alone.

Then in January 2018 at the age of sixty-nine, I was startled to receive a diagnosis of Hashimoto's Thyroiditis: My own immune system was attacking itself, and the target was the thyroid. I had gone for a blood test not for a particular problem but to simply have a baseline with an integrative medicine doctor—a preventative personal choice. But my surprise gave way to concerned curiosity. I spent hours with "Dr. Google," quizzing friends and associates, and researching symptoms of this ailment and recommendations from Yoga Asana/Pranayana, Ayurveda, nutrition, acupuncture, Chinese medicine, and the American Medical Association (AMA).

I had been experiencing all the symptoms of Hashimoto's as small body changes, nothing big really. I just hadn't grouped them together to discern a pattern. I had attributed afternoon fatigue, hair loss, and memory gaps to the aging process and to the grieving of several losses, including my dear mom, a great-nephew at eighteen months old, a love partner. I had sold my business, and my home had suffered smoke damage. I had handled these with my yoga tools of nurturing myself, "licking my wounds," thanking the Universe for my lessons, and continuing on.

However, there had been an overall toll. I couldn't see the forest through the trees. So once again I followed my Mom's advice, "If you always do what you always did, you will always get what you always got."

Change was called for on a whole new level. I evaluated and adjusted all aspects of my life: my mat and spiritual practices, food and supplement choices, social activities, and workload. Even my deodorant containing aluminum got tossed!

I noticed the effects. By April my journal entry reflected improvements: "Feeling...more focused. More creativity. More energy, longer. More directed internally. Lighter." Extra weight melted away, my hair grew thicker, my eyebrows filled in, and I had more vitality, more energy throughout the day, easier memory recall, and fewer thought gaps, and I made better personal choices. I was impressed!

A definable shift was in my ability to take notes. For many years I had easily written the entire sequence after a yoga workshop. Others often borrowed my notes. Gradually that had become less possible, which was weird and disconcerting. But, after just five months of my new routine, I could once again recall the content at the end of a workshop.

After seven months, I returned for follow-up blood work. The results were definitely affirming! The level in January identifying the Hashimoto Thyroiditis was a 10 (the normal range is 1 to 9). By August it had dropped to a 7. This was the first time that I had actual data to document the effects of my yogic lifestyle choices.

> "Yoga allows you to find an inner peace that is not ruffled and riled by the endless stresses and struggles of life."
>
> —BKS IYENGAR

Then the reflections began: "What had actually happened during those seven months?"

My life off the mat had mirrored my mat practice.

Off the mat I paid attention to my body, thoughts, and sensations in the same ways I had practiced for years. Hours of exploration in mat time and seated meditation had become the undercurrent to daily activities in my world. My awareness skyrocketed: Every single choice I made mattered, on the mat and off the mat. "One scoop or two? Or none!" sums it up.

> "Yoga does not just change the way we see things, it transforms the person who sees."
>
> —BKS IYENGAR

Each action was chosen to support and balance me, from the inside out. I had enlivened more of those little intelligence antennae so now every part of me was able to communicate and also respond to every other part. And now it was medically measured!

I felt more balanced and alert in all aspects of my life, and feedback from others reinforced this.

I realized these antennae are innate gifts for which I am responsible. They are the connectors and the unifiers of all that is greater and higher with all that is earthly. Ah yes, the definition of yoga! In just seven months I had walked my yoga talk in ways I had only experienced alone on the mat. Now my "alone-awareness" comes with me throughout the day, everywhere I go.

Kandy Taylor Love, Ph.D., CIYT, CYT, E-RYT-500, LMT#9704 has committed her life to teaching and touching people of all ages and abilities to guide them in improving the quality of their lives through healthy lifestyle choices. She founded the first healing sanctuary in Lee County, Florida in 1990, and it is still a well-respected yoga and massage business.

In 2011, Kandy created Love-Works, a modality that includes the eclectic skill set that made up her "kit" of healing tools: movement and touch with the ultimate foundation, love. This "kit" includes yoga in the Iyengar style, massage therapy including Swedish, deep tissue, and Craniosacral Therapy, whole-body healing based on Healing from the Core® and Integrated Awareness®, meditation, affirmations, journaling, nutrition, workshops, lectures, and writing. Kandy has offered LoveWorks in clinical, classroom, corporate, and private settings.

The richness of Kandy's abilities and skills has deepened and expanded through studying with world-renowned teachers such as B.K.S. Iyengar, Angela Farmer and Victor Van Kooten, Ramanand Patel, Bobbi Golden, John Schumacher, Dr. John Upledger, Lansing Barrett Gresham, and Dale Alexander. Her commitment to her daily personal practices creates a magic that fills her heart, heals her body, and quiets her mind. This regularity and longevity of practice manifests her life purpose, enabling her to guide students and clients in rediscovering playful, powerful, and peaceful aspects of themselves. Contact Kandy at **www.becauseloveworks.com** or email **yoginikandy62@gmail.com**.

Cradle of Comfort

BY ELIZABETH MCLAUGHLIN

I never intended to be a single parent.

Intellectually it's an understandable phenomenon; people become single parents for many reasons. Sometimes it's a choice, sometimes it's an unfortunate divorce, sometimes thrust upon one due to the death of a beloved spouse. But me? That was not the "plan."

There is a specific moment near the beginning of my new path that profoundly changed my entire perspective on life, the experience of joy, and sharing joy with others.

The first time I felt a quickening—that astonishing, alien, wonderful feeling of the life inside me moving—was a significant turning point. Interestingly, after the initial shock and realization of what it was, I quickly moved to a place of intense sadness. There I was experiencing something so amazing, and my natural instinct was to share it. But I was alone with no one there to put their hand on my stomach and feel what I was feeling. That moment must be so emotional for a couple, especially experiencing it for the first time. I imagined a loving couple, so excited about their coming child, and sharing this unique event. Once those tears were exhausted, something else followed. Suddenly it occurred to me, is it any less amazing and joyous because there is no one here to share it with me? Well, actually, no! Something just fluttered inside me, and that is probably one of the most amazing things I've ever felt. The tears turned to a smile, then something that can only be described as pure joy.

The joy stemmed from the experience itself and also from the freedom and permission to fully enjoy it all on its own. The shift that happened during that moment seemed to be a critical piece of life's puzzle for me—joy and happiness start from within and can exist on their own. No one can manufacture it for us; we are responsible for our own happiness. That doesn't mean that joy should always be held close and not shared; much of the richness and fabric of life comes from sharing and connecting with each other. To be able to sit in a place of unconditional love and truly feel another's happiness and celebrate with and for them is one of life's gifts. And to have others who care about you express happiness for your joys is just as important. It is how we can wrap each other in a cradle of comfort, safety, and love.

I know how and why that realization was accessible to me. It sprang from a practice that I had started several years earlier. I'm not even sure how I happened upon the Iyengar studio in Davis Square in Cambridge, Massachusetts, tucked away through an unmarked door, down an institutional-looking hallway. The studio space was nondescript but I quickly learned it was filled with some of the most amazing teachers and students and knowledge seekers to whom I have ever been exposed. I was a skier, runner and cyclist at the time, and the experience of yoga asana practice started slowly. I remember in an early class our teacher asking us to picture our practice like a thick phone book, the kind with really thin paper pages. Each time you practice, the progress you make was like flipping one thin page. It may seem subtle, but soon enough you have flipped through the book and are in a beautiful virabhadrasana 3.

My practice started with the physical. I took quickly to inversions because they were fun and started to crave that feeling of clarity when I came down from a handstand into child's pose. It was like all the cobwebs in my head were swept away—it was better than coffee. The practice quickly progressed from just the physical beyond to an exploration of the mind-body-spirit connection. I started to empty the junk drawer of stress, tension, and old emotions held in my body. And I discovered that my heart chakra was closed off from years of building up the fortress of protection I had apparently deemed necessary. I recall a backbend class where our teacher had us contorted backwards through a folding chair. It was extremely uncomfortable for me, not necessarily physically but because I felt so exposed and open and vulnerable. I stayed with it, but when we came out of the pose, I left the class, retreated to the changing area, and curled up in a ball unable to move. After class we talked about what happened, why it happened, what may have been releasing for me. Over the course of time and practice, there were many other such experiences of releasing and learning.

Once that door opened, once that exploration and growth started, it created such a thirst for more. I craved deeper, richer, realness in my life. The quest led me down new and interesting paths, including a retreat to an ashram in the Bahamas. If time and life had allowed at that time, I would have stayed for a month or more. I fell so easily into the rhythm of ashram life. Not being a natural morning person, I even came to enjoy the sound of the gong waking the community for morning meditation and yoga. That phase of life awoke something in me that I did not understand or cultivate in my earlier years. Looking back, I now see it was there but I hadn't known what to do with it.

As a teen and young woman, I remember having this powerful yearning, a gnawing sensation that sometimes manifested as wanting something so badly but not knowing what it was, or sometimes as a perception of lack. I knew something was missing and I recall, at various points, a restless search for love, for achievement, for change, for happiness—which invariably resulted in fleeting but not lasting satisfaction. When I started traveling down the royal road of yoga, I began to unravel my unruly waves of mental, emotional, and physical energy and channel it into spiritual energy, which allowed me to achieve a more real and accessible peace.

The clarity I get when I tune into my practice can be so visceral. I leave any asana practice and the world looks different than it did before the class. Colors are more vivid. Even a gray, slushy day in winter has a beauty—maybe the texture of the sky, or the crispness of the wintery sun-lit horizon seen through refreshed eyes.

Most importantly, the ability to move from a lofty place of reflection and clarity resulting from practice, to the here-and-now, everyday connection to people is made smoother with yoga. Real life can throw us many tests, including people who try to hurt us with their words, actions, or non-actions as well as difficult family members, others with differing political views, challenging co-workers, bad drivers ahead of us on the highway, and on and on. After a meditative session of yoga in any form, asana, or simply a remembering of my practice and the instant centering that follows, people suddenly all become my brothers and sisters. On a soul level we are all the same, all one. That scowling man at the grocery store? He may have just lost his wife and is figuring out his new reality. That car that cut you off? Perhaps it's a parent rushing their child to the clinic. Yoga is the portal that brings me back, time and time again, to clarity and loving kindness. And just like our monkey minds may wander off a hundred times when we try and sit in meditation, our lives also wander off into busy-ness and we may move away from our practice. The thing with practice is, the more you do it the easier it gets. The spans of time between remembering and living in that place of peace become shorter and shorter the more we practice. It's not called yoga perfection, it's called practice. Maybe an equally good term is yoga lifestyle, as what I practice on the mat weaves itself into all aspects of life.

Back to the cradle. It started as a literal cradle holding my new daughter. This small bundle graced the scene in all her glory and changed my life forever in ways small and large, obvious and subtle. Even though I had narrowed down a short list of names, she arrived and named herself—Grace. It just made sense; of course, she was Grace! We quickly became a team and got busy living life. Had I not experienced the study, meditation, and openness that evolved from the early years of my yoga practice, I'm not sure I would have shifted so readily to that place of awareness, joy, and acceptance of my life experience exactly as it was unfolding.

The rocking cradle holding that beautiful baby girl has now become college applications, and I know that all the years in between have been made better and the joys richer because of the virtual cradle created from a strong connection to my practice that kept me grounded. One of my greatest joys is that I have been able to pass on, and will continue to pass on to my daughter, some of the life lessons I have learned through the study of yoga, as she forges her own path and finds her way toward her destiny. One thing is for certain, I will always be here holding a cradle for her.

I believe that through the practice of yoga we can continually, gently bring ourselves back to our center. When we live within our own cradle of comfort, it becomes easier and more natural to hold those around us in that same cradle of unconditional love, acceptance, and support. Thank you, my practice, for opening my eyes and life to the "secret" portal that is open and available for anyone who is willing to enter and pass through.

Elizabeth McLaughlin is a lifelong learner and seeker of harmony and beauty. As the sole breadwinner for her family, she was fortunate to have a wise mentor early in her career that passed on sage advice—some of life's earthly systems, like work and money, can be thought of as a game. You get to decide if and how you want to play that game. For the past twenty years, Elizabeth has tapped into a  game with a purpose, college planning, with a goal of helping families avoid the crushing student loan debt that burdens our young people today. She works tirelessly to remind families that we don't have to do everything alone, we are in this together including the goal of college if our kids so desire. We can all tap into family and friends, community and villages to help, between birthdays and Bar/Bat Mitzvahs, Christenings and Quinceañeras, with the right mindset and tools, we can all work together toward this important goal.

Elizabeth and her daughter hit the road as often as possible, seeking adventures and cherishing time spent with dear friends, family and especially cousins. They both crave that feeling of driving out of town in a packed car or settling into their seats on a plane and heading off somewhere interesting.

Elizabeth lives in Connecticut with her daughter Grace and their rescue dog Maui, who is teaching both humans about unconditional love and patience.

Elizabeth gets on her mat as often as possible, and otherwise endeavors to live a yogic lifestyle off the mat.

Contact Elizabeth at **eliz.mcl21@gmail.com**.

Breath, the Divine Remedy

BY S. PAULINE MICHALOVIC

Energy to consciousness, the union of positive (+) and negative (-) is the basic core of yogic theory and taken further, all of life. Breath, alone, is the first rung on the ladder of life. It is our connection to the Divine.

As humans we are a balanced union of mother and father energies, heaven and earth, spirit and knowledge. Each cell, toroidal in nature, is electrically balanced by breath, affecting our pH, the oxygen carrying capacity of our blood and our brain wave patterning. These are human life's "true vitals".

I was born a gifted seer and from a young age was aware of extra sensory perception. Athletics was important, too, which eventually led me to world class recognition in telemark skiing. At 11,400 feet above sea level, year round, I found myself the nation's highest resident, a skiers' dream!

While here, my vision beyond this realm unfolded and I delved deeply into Eastern and Western teachings and other extreme disciplines of body and mind, as a traditional student. Eventually this passionate wisdom focus organically shifted into the healing arts, where flourished my greatest gift to share with others.

Through many soft tissue injuries and recovery, I became my own research subject, paying attentive detail to my health and breath focus (pranayama). Keeping mostly sane in a driven Renaissance lifestyle, I connected with cutting edge experts in the natural medicine field. Life continually returned to the inquiry, "How can I help humanity's health in the current model of disease? How can I help myself?".

My relationship with the body, a wonderful instrument of encapsulate light, has allowed me to see patterns in the biologique world. Over the course of my career, touching thousands of bodies (precious temples), I noticed patterns that offer age old wisdom and a "medicine for the people". Through the process of my research, I developed the Guardian of Life Model, a new paradigm of health.

The Guardian of Life, a unified, comprehensive and highly integrated approach to the divine spark and biomechanics of healing, began to take form and substance.

Pranayama or yogic breath technology, an effective balancing remedy, is life's highest technology available to us for free.

Through my own traumas, breath has allowed me to touch my infinite self with divine healing. Chi, life force, divinity, vitality and connection... these are some of creation's whispers, glimpses of breath's gift.

The Guardian of Life model lends an ability to see, sense and comprehend mental, physical and spiritual imbalances in place. This gifts a tremendous empowering wisdom and the ability to heal. When we balance the sparks of positive (+) and negative (-) charges, the results can be wholeness and magic, overcoming great obstacles.

We can observe and experience a dominant acidic, yang or patriarchal system in place, within ourselves and in the world around us. This distortion of wholeness feeds itself through repetitive neurology, in which we literally become addicted to our own "is-ness". As we repeatedly experience painful lessons, it can easily feel non consensual. Yet breath, the helm of connection to life, is an alkaline and stabilizing return spot.

Conscious breath rewires these connections, establishing new pathways and creating ease in developing new ways of being. Integrated brain hemispheres with "true vitals" addressed can result in more benefits than most all pharmaceuticals.

To work effectively, focused therapeutic breath requires dedication, discipline and devotion. Breath technology greatly improves all health conditions.

In Aramaic, Jesus' language, "prayer" translates to "breath". Through prayers of our own breath (ancient contemporary gnostic wisdom) we begin. When we look at brain wave patterning, pH and the oxygen carrying capacity of our blood as " true vitals", nourishing and sustaining health, balanced sparks are from ion to asana, pranayama primary.

The capacity of our blood to carry oxygen increases with pranayama practice and our beautiful grooves of dancing brain waves are synchronized optimally.

Breath is life. Water is life, with oxygen being the first rung on life's ladder. Including all oxygen therapies here, we have the divine remedy, which is yogic, abundant, available, sustainable, life force enhancing and highly therapeutic. Volumes of knowledge and wisdom exist here, integrating inspiration and our life force spark.

One can trace the imbalance of sparks yogically through soft tissue. This demonstrates the pattern of one-side dominance or imbalance throughout the body generated from "unsynced sparks".

Differences in your feet, hands or shoulders contain visible results of this one sidedness. Note the tone, shape and size of your dominant foot, hand or shoulder compared to your non dominant. Look for subtle clues, most often profound! Invite awareness of the dominant repetitive self by witnessing your own biomechanics of thought, movement, spirit and breath

Breath the easiest and most basic point from which to begin from, doesn't lie and can be used to objectively describe the moment, any moment.

Oxygen is primary in keeping our physical structure clear enough to contain the electrical system, bio dynamic and energy generating. Our context of life is embedded in our cells wall, psycho and somatic or mind and body connection, electric, and benefits most from a clear, stabilized frequency pure.

Breath provides the ultimate in self care with the living, breathing body as temple. Daily pranayama practice brings abundant blossoms of awareness, uniting with devotion, offering us whole being.

Breath is the primary and divine remedy, life's quintessential technology.

PRACTICE WISDOM FROM THE DOWNWARD DOG

collaborative
field of wisdom practicing
receive nurturance

catalyzing love
voices together transmit
creativity

higher consciousness
curriculum of teaching
a woven fabric

positive self talk
reach each opportunity
joyfully present

past the surface live
serving higher, together
trauma sensitive

for gaia we rise
medicine of supporting
she thirsts for sharing

loving collective
healing collaboration
all life is sacred

powerful, gentle
resilient channel of love
practices in life

we are all here now
students, teachers in beauty
effort with grace, ease

come to life, she breathes
wisdom, intrinsic, here now
joy and sorrow, one

calming monkeys mind
deep sense of intimacy
starting with ones self

crystalline body
sacredness geometric
essence messaging

rising joyfully
meeting opportunities
seeds planted fertile

vibration is love
vulnerable, heart open
chanting, for the one

with pure alchemy
equanimity touches
all hearts as one love

ETERNAL DANCE OF BREATH

you are the first rung
quintessential to all life
inhaling the now

expand, reflective
long deep full and slow breathing
system comes neutral

primal action first
pranayama technology
mother remedy

attentive to breath
creation, permeating
the living temple

all ways leading us
connecting, key to the art
reflective life dance

I rise and I fall
breath of life, wisdom holder
bowing, eternal

torsional movement
exhalation, we inhale
untwisting, practice

as the beginning
is always now, life happens

actions accumulate

technique specific
deeper breath, conscious, aware
quality practice

dynamic, static
every action, effect
focusing through breath

become possible
continuous attention
improving our life

few moments without,
life ceases, technology
kundalini rise

breathing lifts life force
pranayama, gold light
eternal breath dance

HEALING JOURNEY HAIKU

the healing journey
born sensitive, life long thread
divine alignment

study, continues
unify, guardian of life
devotional

return to essence
through my own recovery
a yogis journey

vital spark creates
vision of soul in balance
never ending path

moral observance
complete surrender to god
life long devotion

action, discipline
energy infinity
awakening now

BIOMECHANICS OF A YOGIS WELLNESS JOURNEY

yoga, self healing
wellness biomechanics
yogic as way of life

breath, the life divine
spirit self and collective
alignment quickens

self-realization
fulfillment of divine spark
surrendering now

spirit, mystical
divine align, awaken
posture and breathing

unified or lay
medicine of the people
guardian of life

time feels standing still
where the juice is in the now
breath, the highest tool

life force healing comes
chi, creation, smoothing the groove
brain wave patterning

infiltrate system
activate cell electric
living connection

pain pushing, vision
pulling, towards the ultimate
transformed freedom

RADICAL BREATH

with truth bearing light
vision of soul revealed
bringing in new life

faith, love, persistence
inhaling deep, full and slow
breath of life, we bow

remedy, living
human energy system
radical approach

YOGA ALCHEMY

moving, hatha
yogic alchemy, primal
kundalini rise

extend attention
expansion in awareness
opening the space

in observation
the art of yoga offers
slow motion, reflect

permeate the temple
awareness, intelligent
intend, creation

attune, natural
organic processes gift
self discovery

yoga alchemy
pure, simple and magical
begins where I am

ZEROPOINT

the turning away
when practice is needed most
always, returning

reference, empty
no charge, balance point zero
the mother of all

mirror seeing self
meeting, to unite spirit
a point unreached

physical practice
creation, life force, soul full
spirit and I, one

INTENSIFYING THANKFULNESS

abundance tonal
amplify reality
thanking creator

spirit of blessing
intensifying thankful
open vessel field

extending vastness
through the beloved petals
high hertz frequency

PRACTICE

observe objective
deepening in consciousness
introspective awareness

practice benefits
liberating freedom, from
source of suffering

sutras elevate
the spirit, nurturing inner
practice lends wisdom

absoluteness in
yoga theory, practical
super natural

STILL POINT

still point
sensitivity exquisite
funnel of light
entrance to surrender
learning, remembering, teaching
chalice of the heart
all channels awake
I am the veil
the scent of roses
bring you to me
dancing your alter
feeling gnosis
as a spark comes
lofting on the breeze
ancient tones bringing truth wisdom
the vessel
the veil
lightning strikes
shining star pulsing
flower of life frequency
electric

S. Pauline Michalovic is a holistic health practitioner, researcher and visionary, gracefully integrating thirty years of practice. Pauline is nationally certified and state licensed in massage therapy, contemporary cupping methods, visceral manipulation, and cranial sacral therapy. She is a yoga teacher, priestess initiate, sixth generation Reiki master, personal trainer, raw and whole foods chef.

A remarkable western Renaissance woman, traditional and contemporary medicine woman, master massage therapist, nutrition and detox consultant, Pauline offers unique perspective to transformational wellness in Cortez, Colorado under the gaze of Mesa Verde National Park. As a healing emissary, Pauline joyously celebrates the divine spark at Mesa Verde Morning Sun, ecco bella organique: spa, retreat and private practice, resting in the beautiful and sacred four corners region of Southwest Colorado.

Yogic in creation, Pauline's vision Miraclewrx nourishes, educates and shares in the facilitation of universal healing, from the ion onward. Offering cutting edge innovative health care perspective, Miraclewrx, "Guardian of Life", gifts all health conditions and modalities positive therapeutic adjunct, including: Western, Eastern, traditional, contemporary, allopathic and holistic practices, gifting a layperson's "medicine for the people". Mesa Verde Morning Sun, home to Miraclewrx, specializes in oils, analgesics, essential oils, medicinal baths, oxygen therapies, detoxification and organic lifestyle.

Pauline's professional and personal experience have led her to create The Guardian of Life model, a unified, comprehensive and highly integrated approach to the divine spark and biomechanics of health and wholeness. The Guardian of Life empowers health through simple and observable laws of nature.

Pauline has studied at the University of Colorado, Colorado School of Healing Arts, Yoga Institute of Houston, International Cupping Therapy Association, The Barrell Institute, Upledger Institute, West Winds Academy of Massage Therapy, 13 Moon Mystery School , with affiliations including U.S. Olympic Diving, U.S. World Mountain Bike, and U.S. Freestyle Skiing. Pauline holds World and National titles in telemark skiing.

To learn more... **infinitehealth@miraclewrx.com**

The Answer Is Within

BY AVITAL MILLER

Mid-practice breathing deep, weight on hands and feet, resting in downward dog to see through the fog.

The position of downward dog is like being the roof of a house where you can look inside. The Sanskrit name is adho mukha shvanasa. Shvanasana is another root for savasana, the rest position where we integrate our practice and take a step away to gain perspective. Yoga teaches not only to fully live life but also to simultaneously be the silent observer of yourself. It is similar to being in a human-size maze but also hovering above it at the same time looking at the whole picture. It allows us to have a broader perspective and be less emotionally reactive to what is happening in our lives. And when we look at the whole picture, we more closely achieve the purpose of yoga, to unite with all that is.

Everything seemed to be going perfectly. I had overcome growing up in a family of Holocaust survivors, my divorced parents living in two different countries. I had overcome a verbally abusive marriage and an autoimmune disorder. And I had given up being a program manager at Microsoft to travel the world and become a yoga instructor.

For almost four years I was living in a state of bliss in a spiritual community based on the teachings of the yoga guru Paramhansa Yogananda, author of Autobiography of a Yogi. I was surrounded by high-energy, joyful people. I had great jobs as a yoga teacher trainer and as a sales and marketing director for their book publishing company. I lived in a pristine new home that I helped design.

But one morning, after a peaceful sleep in my quiet white bedroom in the woods, I woke up in shock, eyes wide open, clutching the bed with the realization that something was wrong, yet I had no clue what it was.

I was scheduled to take vows promising my life to the community, but my mother passed away right before the ceremony. They rescheduled me to take the vows three months later, but something in me could not do it. Instead I asked for permission to stay in the community while spending a lot of time alone to figure out what was going on inside myself.

This discussion happened with my spiritual advisor while on vacation in Hawaii, listening to waves crashing behind our words. Tears were flowing. I felt like a failure to the community for not fulfilling their big vision for me. My advisor replied, "I don't know what to tell you. You have been doing everything perfectly."

Soon after, the spiritual teacher who founded the community also died. With his death died the physical form of inspiration I was seeking. I realized I couldn't feel it through the people and programs but only inside myself.

For the next three years, I walked around feeling like I had fifty swords sticking in my body. For a few of those months I experienced what some people would call the dark night of the soul. Nothing really bad was happening in my life, yet it felt like hell.

Why did this experience last for three years? If downward dog were the roof of a house, you would be able to see everything inside—but not if there was a veil blocking your vision. I realized I valued my interpretation of the beliefs of the community over the ideas and beliefs that were coming from inside of me. It was a constant battle between the messages inside me and the messages I heard, and I chose to take their word over my own.

The thought of leaving the community did not cross my mind because some of the members implied those who left fell off the spiritual path. My biggest fear was losing God. If staying close to God meant staying in a place that felt like hell, I would do so. But I was soon to learn that I was even further from God by forcing myself to be something I was not and to be in a situation that did not make me happy.

If I was really going to do yoga and create union with all that exists, I couldn't discriminate and call some things God and some things not. I woke up one morning with the intuition to dance salsa again and another morning to teach yoga. That led me to make friends in town. My lifestyle felt balanced until a membership advisor at the community told me I had to choose between the two and that I was "too big." After all those years of trying to be quiet, nice, and small I was still "too big"? On the contrary, that felt like a message to embrace my "bigness."

For a while I stayed there, secretly living both lives in and out of the community. If I was going to move it was only going to be because of intuition. Thus I waited until my conflicts with the people around me and inside myself subsided, and I was calm again. I saw a vision of writing, speaking, and running my own meditation group with a more universal understanding of spirituality that was integrated with daily life.

After so much time wondering if I should stay or go, the minute I drove away with all of my belongings I did not feel any longing for the community. If there were energetic cords tying me to the community, they were cut when I moved off the property.

There I was stepping out into the world to discover what a more integrated approach to spirituality would look like for me. It was overwhelming, and I did not have clear direction on how to make friends or start my work. I needed breaks from all the energies swarming around me in the city. And I needed time to understand the new me, what my new spiritual beliefs would be, and how I would live in the world. I spent a lot of time at home and didn't make much of a life for myself in Portland.

When I sat to meditate I heard a voice saying, "I hate you." Something in me told me to stop meditating unless I shifted my relationship with meditation. I realized that I mainly meditated to get rid of past karma, because I felt I would not be considered valid unless I did, and because there was knowledge I needed to seek that I didn't have. I sensed that by not accepting myself as I was, I was stuck in an energy of self-hatred.

When I started meditating again, it became something to do for fun, to relax, to connect with myself, and to quiet the outside world without having a need or expectation of what meditation would give me. I learned to float between Yogananda's techniques and practice them only when the inspiration naturally arose. I discovered I had a gift to guide meditations for others with creative visualizations.

My new relationship with meditation became a model for my overall relationship with spirituality and how to live daily life. The less definition, the less I would live in the mind and the more I live in the moment. The less judgment, the more I respond positively to the environment around me and be in the energy of love. The more I focus on working off my "bad" karma, the more I get stuck in it. But the more I believe it is just a story, the less it holds me back and the freer I feel. Spirituality evolved from rituals practiced separately from the rest of my day to an experience of living life authentically.

After so much time staying home alone in Portland, I moved into a quiet house on the coast of Oregon to write my book *Healing Happens: Stories of Healing Against All Odds*. As soon as my book launched in April 2018 my community became the people I chose to visit on my worldwide book tour. Many invited me to stay in their homes, fed me, and told me fascinating stories from their lives. Now my community is both inside me and spread throughout the world.

These realizations and changes have led to a great sense of calmness and peace within myself. I have been able to follow my inner guidance without as many questions. I appreciate the growth and experiences the spiritual community offered me and I also love the life I have manifested. I feel more connected with all that is with a greater sense of love. Now in downward dog I don't just see "my house" but the entire world.

Special Gift

Healing Happens: Stories of Healing Against All Odds brings you insight and inspiration from health and healing experts who cured themselves and others despite dire medical prognoses from over twenty illnesses including cancer, diabetes, and autoimmune disorders. Enhance the power to heal yourself through natural healing techniques and awareness in order to comfortably, energetically, and joyfully live your passions. Fatal pronouncements do not have to be your fate. Get your free chapter of Avital's Book, *Healing Happens* at **www.healinghappensforyou.com.**

Avital Miller, best-selling author of the book *Healing Happens: Stories of Healing Against All Odds*, inspires others to experience boundless energy, absolute happiness, and true success in order to live the best life possible. For more than 15 years, Avital has been serving thousands of people worldwide as an award-winning international keynote speaker, healing breakthrough facilitator, and global dancer.

Avital's leadership background includes being a program manager at Microsoft, lead coach for Success Resources America, sales and marketing director for Crystal Clarity Publishers, yoga and fitness teacher trainer, and fitness director. Her articles have been published in *Toastmasters International Magazine*, *Fitness Professional Online*, *30 Seconds*, and *Sacred Dance Guild Journal*. In 2018 she received the Exceptional Woman of Excellence award from Women Economic Forum and *Healing Happens* was recognized by TopShelf, Dan Poynter Global eBook, Living Now Book Awards, and NABE Pinnacle Book Achievement.

Spirituality has entered Avital's life through becoming Yoga Alliance E-RYT 500 certified and an ordained minister, as well as living and teaching in a yoga community for almost seven years. She is also an energy healer in Pranic healing and Ananda healing.

In April 2018, besides launching her book *Healing Happens*, Avital founded HealingHappensForYou.com and released the Healing Happens Podcast. These programs share research from health and healing experts about the connections between physical health and emotions, mind, and spirit. Discover how to embody vibrant health through natural techniques you can do yourself.

A graduate of Washington University in St. Louis, Missouri, with a bachelor of science degree in mechanical engineering and a major in dance, Avital has performed and taught dance since 1993. She is known for offering beyond-cutting-edge wisdom with authenticity, delightful energy, and infectious joy. Connect with Avital at **www.avitalmiller.com**.

So I Breathe...A Journey To Inner Peace and Self-Empowerment!

BY DENA OTRIN

I sit on my mat, this place is my oasis
How I long for the calm from the storm.

The storm of life's upsets, daily tasks, household chores and setting boundaries from others' expectations galore.

So I Breathe!
I breathe in through my nose so my belly will rise, and breathe out through my mouth, pulling my belly button back towards my spine
I breathe in cool calming air with each inhale and blow out what I no longer need with every exhale.

I am ready to be one with myself, on my own little island for grounding and inner peace
Peace that can only come from within, radiating outwards, connecting me—mind, body and spirit.

My spirit is longing for attention, "remember me," it calls
Calling out to me as an old familiar friend with a wave and a smile to light up the room.

In this room my mat brings me back to my center, to my
intentions, to mindfulness.
Being mindful of the love and self-care I need to give myself today.

So I Breathe!
I breathe in worthiness, I breathe in love
I breathe in strength from spirit guides, guardian angels and loved ones
from above.
I breathe in guidance and direction for my path in life
I breathe in the words "I Am Enough" and things will be alright.
I breathe in to be strong, be fearless and shine my light.

I take comfort in knowing I am here and I am safe
Safe from the storm that life seems to bring.

Bringing me to a place to see my inner strength,
my conviction is strong
Strong enough to break down barriers and destroy any walls.

Walls hold little purpose except to hide,
Hide from negative thoughts and feelings that are deeply
held inside the mind.
Mindful this is not, it actually gets in the way of living heart centered and
impedes in every way.

So I Breathe!
As I exhale I release the worries and thoughts that move me
away from inner peace;
Inner peace and self-love cannot co-exist with worry and negativity.

So I breathe in unconditional love and light and breathe out
what I want to release.
I release expectations of my own and from others;
I release what I cannot control and release fear by pulling
back its covers.

I release unspoken words and actions I wish I would have done or said,
I release past decisions and regrets and the tears I have shed,
I release the condemning thoughts that swim in my head.

I release what no longer serves me in my life;
I have let go of stress and fear with delight,
Delight of what is to come into my life and how it can
be amazing for me.

For me I can see the strength in myself and accept what life can offer.
Life can offer me a vision of endless possibilities since I have made space
for goodness, strength and positivity.

Positive and strong is how I feel, and I can handle lives moments with
conviction and grace,
Gracefully I can embrace each moment with optimism, a smile and
knowing it will be a great day.

Day after day I will mindfully respond to daily situations, stresses and
things that go wrong,
Wrongful thoughts and habits can cover truth like a glove, so I have to
adjust and be mindful to no longer react, but come from a place of love.

Love is the intention when I am on my mat because I am taking time to
cultivate inner peace and self-empowerment,
Self-empowerment is like energy radiating within me filling every cell with
love, light and authenticity for who I am meant to be.

I am meant to be here, now on my mat, so I can mindfully be present and
connected to my truth,
My truth is my values; my truth is my soul; my truth is my vision; my truth
is my goals.

My goal is to present in the here and now and mindfully honor me and my
future self.

My future self is able to make dreams come true as long as I stay focused on my mat and breathe it all through.

My future is brilliant, my future is bright, but I have to continue mindfulness daily in my life.

My life is a gift ready for me so when moments get tough I can let go,
Let go of what I don't want and fill myself back up with what I need;
for this reason I will inhale and exhale...
So I Breathe!

Dena Otrin has been in the health and wellness field for 20 years as a Licensed Professional Counselor and in private practice for 18 years, currently at Bayside Counseling in Westbrook, Connecticut. Dena is a certified Reiki III practitioner, a Life Transformation practitioner, health and wellness consultant, facilitator of women's retreats, workshops and empowerment Groups, and a self-empowerment blogger through her business An Empowered Life. Adding to her repertoire of holistic services for health, wellness, self-care, and self-love, Dena recently became a Certified Yoga Teacher and a Certified Yoga Teacher for Kids. Dena embodies empowerment as she assists others on their journey of personal or business transformation and success. Learn more at **www.AnEmpoweredLife.net.**

Goodbye Hustle: How I Discovered Life is a Forward Bend

DANNY POOLE
WRITTEN BY WINDY COOK

Playing basketball was my "golden ticket." My one-way golden ticket out of the hood and into a full-ride college scholarship. I was the third of eleven children, born in Jackson, Michigan to the hardest working people I ever knew.

My dad was up before the sun and never missed a day of work, and my mother ran a tight ship. An old school work ethic was my driving force, and I was ready to succeed. Be prepared, be on time, and hustle. There were eleven mouths to feed and money was tight, but the world of athletics offered a chance to achieve the American dream.

Other members of my family found their golden ticket, too. Tony Dungy of the Indianapolis Colts is a former professional American football player and coach. He's a cousin of mine—and gratitude runs deep.

In 1967, I received the first basketball scholarship Grand Valley State University ever awarded to an African American athlete—and I played to win. We won far more than we lost, and I walked down that golden Hall of Fame.

Being an athlete was strenuous, and the wear and tear on my physical body was the nature of the beast and I played on.

I eventually became a basketball coach to Aspen, Colorado's high school girls basketball team. We took fourth in the state. My old school work ethic was at the heart and soul of my coaching. To this day, my students still tell me that they "hustle" if they want to win.

Hustle.

That was my world, and I walked, breathed, and lived it.

It wasn't until a girlfriend took me to my first yoga class that I knew what it meant to just relax.

I was introduced to the "corpse" pose as my first Shavasana. The experience blanketed my being. I was floating on a cloud, and right then and there my life transformed and took a different direction.

Yoga was my guide and my coach. It took me on a journey of doing the opposite of what I knew how to do really well: hustle.

As athletes, it's quite simple. We run and jump...And jump and run...and do it all over again.

Same motions, same muscles. In sports, it's all about *moving forward* and *moving forward fast*. Time and speed are all that matter.

But life is a forward bend.

Yoga was the window into the "yin" of the yang in my life. I wanted more than being a Physical Education major. I wanted the opportunity to practice yoga every day, and in the back of my mind, I knew that becoming a yoga teacher would allow me to do that.

I wouldn't have a choice. The hardest part is showing up and doing it. Right?

My wish was granted, and the Integrated Yoga Therapy course offered a certification to teach yoga in my area for the first time.

It was a two-week seminar, and I relished this new world to explore the "yin" of life and the opposite of what I had always known: moving backwards, bending backwards, twisting, and putting my feet up. I learned how to stretch in a whole new way and at my own pace. For an athlete, being able to stretch your hamstrings and twist your back is worth its weight in gold.

I've been teaching yoga for more than twenty years now, and my gift is bringing this home to the world of college and professional athletes. I naturally gravitate toward where the jocks are.

In the world of professional sports, the motto seems to be, "If things aren't broken don't fix it." I have to remind these athletes that yoga is preventative. One reaps the benefits of yoga *over time*. If you practice yoga, and it's a daily or weekly practice, injuries can be avoided. I also have to remind these tough guys that yoga isn't just some "woo-woo," mystical, for or something only for women in cute yoga pants. Yoga is for everyone, and its benefits are long-lasting. Yoga can be practiced anywhere and at any time. I'll often get down on the floor in the airport and do the sphinx while waiting to board a flight.

You won't need repairs if you grease the machine.

I can't help but think of Steve Atwater, one of the best defensive Bronco football players of all time, telling me that if he would have continued to practice yoga, he could have extended his career for several more years. Several more years to an athlete is a lot of time and, of course, a lot of money. There is fruit to this hard-earned labor.

Regrets...how not to have them, right?

Unfortunately, it's the same story for other professional athletes I've known. Brandon Marshall, a well-known wide receiver for the Broncos, practiced yoga with me—only to stop practicing for good, which in my opinion, led to a pulled hamstring and a shorter athletic career. Marshall was quite an athlete and playing longer would have brought joy to many of his fans, not to mention the inner sense of satisfaction he would have felt in his own heart.

Interestingly, I was able to practice yoga with the current Broncos linebacker, who is also named Brandon Marshall, but he also stopped doing yoga, which possibly led to an injury and several missed games.

My own satisfaction is knowing that I was able to bring the "gift" of yoga to four NFL Hall of Famers: John Elway, Terrell Davis, Shannon Sharpe, and Willie Roaf. Practicing yoga with these athletes gave them an opportunity to experience what had transformed my life, the preventative benefits of flexibility, deep stretching, and relaxation.

People call me "GOAT" (greatest of all-time yoga teachers for athletes) or "YogaDanny.". You might see me on Facebook or other social media with a humble smile and a sense of humor wearing a long brown goatee.

When I'm not working with professional athletes, I teach regular people and seniors. They might not get to a hip yoga studio. So, I bring my yoga to them. My Jeep is my office. My bumper sticker should read, "I have yoga and will travel!"

Fast and forward motion...Fast and forward motion...

My goal is to help people do the opposite of the typical "forward motion" energy of our lives. Instead, I help them to bend backwards in a sphinx position. I also guide them to twist and detox their organs. Then, I guide them into the "Waterfall" position with their feet up in the air against a wall.

Ahhhhhhhhhhhh.

When was the last time you just stopped moving and put your feet up a wall and breathed out into a loud verbal "Ahhhhhhhhhhhh?" Try one right now. And, while you're there, don't forget the easy backbend, the Sphinx.

If we could all practice more backbends and Waterfall yoga poses, we could say goodbye to life's hustle and bring some balance into our "forward bend" lives. Balancing the yin to the all too familiar yang.

Ahhhhhhhhhhhh.

Danny Poole, 69 years young, was given the name "Yoga Danny," by the football players at the University of Colorado during his four years as their yoga instructor. Danny grew up in Jackson, Michigan and attended Grand Valley State University (GVSU). He went to GVSU on its first basketball scholarship in 1967 and was hired after graduation to be the Assistant Coach in charge of recruiting high school basketball players in the state of Michigan. Later, he was named to the GVSU basketball Hall of Fame.

While coaching Aspen High School's first girls' basketball team, a national Pepsi cola commercial was filmed in Aspen for the 1976 Olympics in which Danny was cast a part to play the quarterback. It ran on TV for three years and launched his move to New York City to pursue a modeling career with the Gilla Roos modeling agency. Danny practiced yoga in NYC and scored an acting role in a Schick razor blade commercial in Sydney, Australia. He fell in love with that country and Australians' passion for sports. Homesick for soul food in Sydney, Danny started a restaurant called Hog Heaven Sydney and, later when he returned to the United States, he started Hog Heaven Denver.

Danny has taught Hatha Yoga in a variety of settings, including corporate stress management, mental health, health care, health clubs, senior care, team sports, and privately one-on-one.

Over the past eighteen years, Danny has stretched and practiced yoga with members of the National Football League (NFL), Colorado Crush, Broncos, Nuggets, and Rockies. He's worked with the Women's National Basketball Association (WNBA), the Colorado Men's Open Golf Tournament, the University of Colorado Athletic Department, Leprino Foods, and Lakewood Country Club. He has worked with many professional athletes, including linebacker Brandon Marshall and wide receiver Brandon Marshalls, San Francisco Giants great Barry Bonds, Olympic skier Jeremy Bloom, and four NFL Hall of Famers: John Elway, Shannon Sharpe, Terrell Davis, and Willie Roaf. Contact Danny at **yogadanny@gmail.com.**

Healthy Relationships: Yoga as a Portal into Your Sovereign Nature

BY RACHEL ROMANO

I awoke one morning with one word buzzing through my body: "Sovereignty." For the first time in my life, I truly knew what that word meant. I could literally feel freedom, ownership, and benevolent rulership pulsating from the most remote corners of my being. Sovereignty signifies loving from a place of integrity and true knowing, without sacrificing the soul. It took many years of practice for this homecoming to manifest at a cellular level.

In a world with constant distractions from our truth, it's easy to believe that we will be loved more if we modify our actions, allow others to bend our will, say "yes" to things that are really a "no", or deny our heart's deepest desires. Look at any advertisement and you will feel *not good enough*. Our hair, dress, makeup, and bodies are all under constant bombardment from media, peers, and often even friends and family. We attempt to modify our nature to fit into some perfect ideal that doesn't actually exist. I cringe to think of how I used to hate my body, my hair, and my features. Sadly, this body shaming is the norm. How can we fully express love if we are shaming ourselves or others?

Compassion is the antidote. It is the key to sovereignty and embodies the full expression of love and acceptance. Every time we show up to the mat, we have the opportunity to practice full compassion. Feeling our bodies. Accepting them as they ease into the poses. Backing off when it becomes too intense.

We manifest life through the body. To hate the body is to hate the self. At any given moment, each cell is performing miraculous functions—without even being told to do so! No external factors can change this wonder. Yoga connects us to the exquisite nature of who we ARE without modification, without persona: that which is pure love, pure truth, pure existence. Cells just doing their best. Yoga is the art of BEING: not doing, thinking, judging, or shaming. If we listen to our bodies while we practice, we can feel a joyful celebration of life in every cell. When we value every cell, no one can defile it. We no longer accept abuse or bad behavior.

We are taught that negative feelings are "bad," so we brush them aside, doing more and feeling less. In our formative years, we are told to do things that we don't want to do, and often we must do them without protest. Over time, we faithfully ignore our body's wisdom. We look for external validation based on external factors: the way we look, dress, talk, perform, and what we accomplish. For me, compliments from others used to be the goal. I needed to be the best, the most effective at whatever I did. I became a human "doing"—always on the go, doing more, working several jobs, achieving more. But in Yoga, LESS is more! It doesn't matter what others say or think. Others who boldly compliment us today can just as boldly drag us through the mud tomorrow with criticisms. We must rely on our INNER TRUTH to uphold us through this noise. In doing less, we hear this truth.

In yoga, we become the observer, witnessing our own experiences, practicing how to do this without judgment. At first, we judge ourselves on the mat: "Look at that person—she's so much better than me!" or "I'm the best in here!" or "I really hate this pose" or "I wonder if I look fat in these leggings." With practice, these judgments quiet down as we focus on making fine-tuned modifications, feel the body, and tune in. This focus is called *Swadyaya,* or Self Study.

We are all born with inner Wisdom, but integrating into a buzzing society makes it easy to forget, then ignore and abandon. This separation from True Self that leads to deep unhappiness. With record-breaking numbers of people are diagnosed with depression, it is time for us all to find our way back to ourselves, our joy, and our knowing.

Plenty of people are willing to provide guidance when it means that we will serve their desires or their ego. The test of a true guide and teacher is someone who will lead us to our own Inner Voice. The practice of yoga is one that leads to inherent wisdom. But only if there is enough pause between the motions to allow us to feel and hear.

True love is listening without judgment. Applying compassion toward all beings starts with the self. When we become the nurturers of our emotions, our bodies, our souls, and our wisdom, we experience true freedom. We choose our actions and reactions by becoming the observers of our thoughts. This is our power. When we step into this power, we step into our sovereign selves.

Some relationships must end when we step into our power. When we claim our right as a free being in relationships, we must surrender control and allow others to choose to stay or go...grieve those who are not capable of true love...feel...cry. Then walk toward bliss.

This allows room for more authentic relationships with people who respect and treat us as the sovereign, worthy beings we truly are. So have faith that your heart will heal and continue to love yourself. This way, you'll attract other souls who have chosen wisdom, freedom, and true love, as well.

Find your Sovereign body, mind, and soul on the mat. Tune in. Observe. Detach from thoughts. Detach from what you "should" be doing. BREATHE. Do this every day, even if just for a few moments, and you may just hear the whisper that has been waiting to be heard, guiding you back home to yourself. Where healthy relationships start.

Namaste.

Rachel Romano combines global experience as a consultant and researcher with her expertise as a yoga teacher and performance coach to help her clients create healthier, happier lives. She is a 500-hour yoga teacher and certified coach with two master's degrees and a heart of service. Her favorite yoga styles focus on healing through the breath and are influenced by teachings from  Sivananda and Iyengar. Rachel is a mom of two girls and a rescue dog, and she is thankful for every day she gets to put her mindfulness skills to practice!

Rachel customizes each engagement to meet the needs of her clients, always with the outcome in mind. She is adept at leading groups and guiding practices that lead to cohesiveness, connection, authenticity, and the resulting higher performance that comes with those experiences. She has been working in healthcare research and wellness programs since 2005, working as a Manager and Director for large corporations until 2012, when she stepped into her sovereignty as a consultant so that she could focus on clients who are looking for deep, actionable insights and tools.

To learn more about Rachel or to contact her about retreats, group coaching, or corporate wellness programs, visit **breathofwellbeing.com**.

The Garden of Love: Planting the Seeds of Intimacy

BY VALERY SHERRIN

CREATING SPACE FOR GROWTH

There is power to be in community. For me, that power comes in the form of confidence, contentment, and safety in my being. It is there that I find deep intimacy with others through a reconnection that gives a soulful sense of truth, love, and authenticity. It is a place that I long to be.

However, for that connection to be real, I've learned that it must come from within yourself first. Yoga can be a vehicle into this powerful relationship with self. It can be a journey of love, trust, and honor, if you allow it to be. It is only when you are ready to make the leap into discovering how to create more intimacy with yourself that this beautiful relationship can form. Self-intimacy is necessary so that we can offer a deep sense of grounded intimacy with others.

Discovery happens when I take the time to tune in and connect. A yoga teacher by trade, I am a student first. I stay open to learning lessons in life that come my way. I know that every lesson has a purpose, good or bad, toward deepening my self-awareness. It starts by getting still, closing my eyes, and giving myself permission to let go and just be.

Our body innately knows exactly what it needs, but listening is a requirement. We can hear our heart speaking to us from a place of deep love and care. For most of my life, I've made decisions by telling my body what it needed and listening only to cues from the world around me. Today, I tune inward for my answers.

> "At the center of your being you have the answers."
>
> —RUMI

It's all a practice. I take one day at a time. Lesson by lesson. Practicing.

PLANTING THE SEEDS

I remember when I was five years old. We were in between living arrangements during some intense custody battles between our mom and dad. One birthday weekend, my sister and I were invited to have a celebration with our mom. She made a beautiful birthday cake topped with candied, violet flowers—a French tradition. After dessert, we were told to go out to the neighborhood playground where she would meet us. A brown Chevy van pulled up to the playground. The door flung open. Our mom was inside and called out for us to get in. I remember her frantic yelling as she called our names and waved her arm at us to hurry. There were several people inside the van with her. One, I recognized was the private investigator that had been working with her during the divorce. We got in the van trusting our mother's signal. The doors shut and the van sped off.

There was a large cardboard box behind the seats filled with children's clothing. Boys clothes. My mom used scissors and chopped my hair short. We were told to put on the clothes which covered us from head to toe. We arrived at a train station, boarded the train, and embarked on a journey which eventually ended in the New York LaGuardia Airport. Once in New York, the plan was for us to board the airline to take us out of the country to our mother's home in Annecy, France.

Things didn't go as planned. In the airport, the police who had been notified several hours prior about our kidnapping, and were on high alert. An officer noticed us at the ticket counter and approached us to ask a few questions. Their suspicions were correct and she was handcuffed and taken into custody. I was directed to go to an office was given some crayons, paper, and was left with no explanation. That was the last I saw of her.

My identity was lost from that moment on. As well as my voice. Through yoga, I was able to discover who I truly was from the answers I found deep within my soul.

As a child, I was confused without many explanations. All I knew was that my mother was taken away and never came to find me. I took the blame for her being gone. I didn't feel good enough for her to keep and not worthy enough to be found again. I was ashamed and felt like I had been thrown away. I became numb and began to reject myself. I lived in a void, with no sense of self-love.

Our father was around and did the best he could. But it was rare to receive a hug. Birthdays were just another day. My sister and I fought a lot... and I never won. Her words were stronger than mine, and I was influenced to be silent. From the incident in the van, I never had a voice. It was the safest place to be. Rejection was a recurring theme, and in our own ways we both wandered into places of shame.

I had to learn things on my own. I had to figure out how to become a woman. Being led by the world around me was a scary place to be, because when one feels empty on the inside, the outside world can feel extremely unstable and not safe.

I became completely vulnerable to the world and sought love from external sources. I was lost and felt like a ship without a navigator, floating away from land. Because of the circumstances of my childhood, I wasn't exposed to my own truth about who I was or my value to the world. I wasn't told what my talents and abilities were or cheered on and supported, or that I was loved, valued, even adored.

My home life prepared me to become a warrior, a fighter—and to figure out how to get my needs met with determination. I had grit, and I had to prove myself to my mother, if she ever decided to come back, to my father, and to the world. Proving became my default.

With endless determination, I made several fast leaps up in my career. Within two years, my company relocated me from Philadelphia to Atlanta to San Francisco and finally Salt Lake City. I trained in various markets. My determination grew a voice of its own within the company. I grew to have a booming six-figure income with accompanying feelings of validation and self-worth. I was hearing my own voice in the world for the first time.

Money became no object. Neither was sleep. My morning white chocolate lattes were followed by skipping lunch and self-medicating so I could keep going. I worked long hours and went on frivolous shopping sprees. It felt good. But I felt stuck, and I could feel it in my body.

I felt unhealthy on the inside. I enrolled in a class at a swanky, local yoga studio. The first several practices, I only remember the space and the Savasana, often falling asleep on my mat. My body knew it needed rest.

I was learning about self-awareness. I liked going to the studio and felt connected to the people there. They were gentle, kind, and often offered me a warm embrace. The hugs were softening my hardened heart.

Tiny seeds were being planted in my soul.

I had an offer to go further out west to work with the vice president of the company to train for another position. This would be another huge leap up the corporate ladder. I reacted, true to form, and jumped on a plane. Once settled in a new apartment, the seeds that were planted began to open.

I found myself craving time alone and taking meditative walks on the California seashore. I noticed my breathing. I noticed the tension and the unsettled feelings inside my body. I began asking *myself* questions about what I was really doing and why was I doing it. A level of self-curiosity developed—I was seeking answers about what was missing in my life from deep within my heart.

NURTURING THE SEEDS

With my new-found awareness, I decided to leave my fast-paced career. I longed for balance, a different lifestyle, and connection. This decision was sporadic but honest. I was determined to trust my heart! My ship set sail back home to Florida.

I found my way back to college to finish my degree. My heart needed that closure. I began noticing how closure was nurturing to me. It was something that brought a sense of peace.

During this new season, I met and married my husband, Randy. It was hardly one of those love-at-first-sight things. His assurance in himself was different. I wasn't sure he would understand a girl like me. But I felt honest love and deep connection with Randy. His heart and love for me was authentic. He seemed to understand me even though I was still figuring myself out. We moved in with his family and started a small business together. My heart began to swell as I saw for the first time what deep family connection looked like. I was so grateful.

We had children and moved close to the beach. Both of our souls were ignited when we were near the ocean. I felt connected to myself and to God there. I knew that was the place where we wanted to raise our family.

Practicing yoga several times a week now, I started seeing exactly how broken I had been and how alive and whole I started to feel again. I felt love, acceptance, and understanding for myself. I felt the unconditional love that was constantly being given to my from my family. I was feeling worthy and loved. Grace and forgiveness began to replace my shame and rejection.

My connection to people started to change along with my perspective. I was able to extend the same love that I was feeling inside now to others around me. I decided that it was okay to be imperfect, and I found peace in that.

DIGGING DEEP

I came to a season where I had to really dig deep. I received a phone call about my mother. It had been over three decades since I last saw her and she was losing her third battle with breast cancer. This time the cancer, too, had grit. She had a year to live.

There were so many unanswered questions surrounding her disappearance in my life. Things like: *Where had she been? Why didn't she try to find me or try to reconnect with her daughters? Did she even think about us?*

At least now, I knew she was alive, a question I'd never been sure of before. I felt a drive to connect with her, to look into her eyes again, to reignite what had been lost so long ago. I wanted the uncontrollable groan in my soul to be gone.

WATERING AND NURTURING

Without yoga, I would have reached externally for my answers to respond to the pain I was feeling inside. Instead, I chose my mat and turned inward. I chose differently. Knowing what was ahead of me, I chose empathy, forgiveness, and love.

I also knew I wanted to walk through this painful period as an observer in my story instead of a victim. *What could I learn from this? How could I use this for my good?* I knew I had a chance of deepening my level of forgiveness, love, and intimacy.

I prioritized each day with yoga. It helped me slow down and connect with my heart. I received the support my family and community offered me instead of resisting it. I continued to serve the people around me by choosing to not to abandon motherhood, by being a wife, staying present in sisterhood and in friendships.

Reaching out to my mom took a huge amount of courage and strength. Expressions of love poured out of me in various forms: love letters, photographs, art, words of forgiveness, and offerings of gratitude. I approached it all with no expectations.

My phone calls weren't accepted—neither was the visit from my family. Her husband said, "She grew too ill and too weak." And that my visit would, "stir up too many painful memories for her." I assured him that "I was here only to make peace" and I promised not to talk about the past. He relayed the message to her and walked back to where I was standing with my family, his chin bowed low in disappointment. She refused to see us.

I was confused. The sting of shame resurfaced. I acknowledged it and chose to let it go because I also felt her shame, her regret, fear, and sorrow. Somehow, empathy made the sting of her rejecting us go away.

FERTILIZING AND WEEDING

After her death, I deepened into my yoga practice. I started tapping back into my creative brain and spent long periods in deep meditation. I observed and honored the feelings that came up. If I needed rest, I would honor my body with rest. If I needed to weep, I wept.

I started piecing together the answers I had been searching for with her absence. All the answers I found within myself during meditation after sifting through her old belongings.

I found sitting still for long periods of time were necessary but difficult. I read about Japa meditation and how to use mala necklaces as a tool to help sit still and recite mantras. My creative mind went right to work creating my first mala necklace with an intention set behind it of "I am whole, I am healing." The creative process usually took several hours and became a meditation of its own.

Many days this is how I got through my grief. The necklace became a gentle reminder of my journey to healing.

RECEIVING THE BOUNTY OF THE HARVEST

Each season that followed needed new intentions as my life began to move forward. With each intention came a new mala necklace. I began to fall in love with the process of setting intentions and used them throughout my day to find mental clarity. I set mantras at the beginning of my yoga practice which added more meaning to it making it more of a moving meditation. I started living life more intentionally and that intimacy grew deeper still.

I began offering my new craft of mala making with others as a way for others to process their own grief. I found joy in doing and teaching yoga and workshops as a way to guide others on their own quest of self-discovery, healing and wholeness.

Being a yoga teacher allows me to connect by sharing how I found my own personal power. It's incredible how we, as a collective unit of yogis, can create change just by practicing loving kindness to ourselves, each other, and our communities.

Today, I guide people in classes, in workshops, and on retreats. I love to teach about the importance of living a life with intent through devotional practices both on and off the yoga mat. I feel a richness in my heart, and joy in the depth of intimacy with my community.

The garden of my inner self has flowered and continues to bring abundance to my life. I am forever grateful for the lessons I've learned and the intimacy that fuels my heart every day.

Valery Sherrin, RYT 200, is a yoga student and teacher at The Mix Yoga Studio in Neptune Beach, Florida (www.yoga-mix.com). She has been a yoga practitioner for over a decade, beginning her practice while living in Salt Lake City, and has made yoga part of her daily devotional practice since 2013. She obtained her yoga teacher certification from the inspirational Alyson Foreacre at Jacksonville's Yoga  Den, where she also studies Bhakti Vinyasa. She resides in the Jacksonville Beaches with her husband, Randy, and their two boys.

Her teaching style is a balance of playfulness and authenticity as she guides practitioners through individual sessions, group classes, workshops, and yoga retreats. Having several years of experience as a long-distance runner and studying biology and human anatomy has made her a multi-dimensional teacher with a focus on injury prevention through body awareness, proper alignment, and self-acceptance.

Valery shares her yoga journey to others through the lens of mindfulness, self-kindness, and common humanity. She offers Mala necklace making workshops as a way of service to others looking for a way to process their grief or other blocked emotions to find healing and wholeness through the practice of daily meditation. She views yoga as much more than a practice of postures and more of a process of self-curiosity. She honors the importance of making self-love part of a daily and intentional practice that we all must find so that we can return that same sense of loving kindness to others in our lives. Connect with Valery at **valery-sherrin.com** or on **instagram @valery.sherrin**.

The Power of a Headstand: How I Found My Self-Care Groove Again

BY DEBBIE SODERGREN

As an entrepreneur, I empower others to practice self-care. It's so important, because, as women, we give, give, and give to everyone but ourselves. It's no wonder we are cranky, short with people, and, well, dare I say, pissed off!

Recently, I realized that I was not practicing what I preach with my own clients. I had dropped the ball on one piece of my own self-care—movement and exercise. This felt like a lack of integrity within myself that I did not want to model for my clients, and it was seriously bugging me. I mean, just writing this piece gives me angst!

One of my challenges is taking on other people's judgment regarding my exercise regimen...or lack thereof. (I mean, I know I have slacked off. No one needs to give me shit about it; I am hard enough on myself!)

It can be so easy to get stuck in needing external validation and taking on other people's issues that get projected onto us. I mean, don't we all sometimes take on other people's opinions about our health as our own?

You sit in your chair all day...
You need to get out and walk...
Why don't you start running?...
Maybe you should join the gym again...

I'm so fed up with the judgment. Enough already!

I have learned, however, to use these reflections as an opportunity to look inside myself and see what needs my attention. I've thought really long and hard about this, and have made it a point to not sit at my desk for longer than an hour without getting up to either dance to loud music, go for a walk, or do jumping jacks while I make tea. I've gotten really creative in making sure I move for 10 minutes out of every 60 minutes at my desk.

The gym? Okay, fine. Maybe I will rejoin the gym. After all, I do live in a cold weather climate for six months out of the year, and I don't like it—but I am not ready to make any major moves. Thinking back to what gave me pleasure when I was younger, I was a dancer from the age of 4 all the way into my 20s. This brought me real pleasure and kept me in tip-top shape and feeling great. A decade ago, I regularly took yoga flow classes at the gym. I got the same feeling from these classes as I did from dancing when I was younger, and I loved the yoga postures. But then I got busy with the kids and running around doing mom stuff. Their commitments on teams and in clubs clashed with my yoga flow class times, so I stopped going.

My spouse is a runner. He has run at least thirteen marathons throughout the years. As I reflect on that, I realize I am envious of him and his practice. He *never* lets anything come between his running practice. He runs in the cold, in the rain, even went traveling out of town. The man is amazing with his level of commitment to his self-care routine of running. I wanted to be *that* committed to my yoga practice, but I doubted myself and felt I didn't have his level of tenacity.

One day I typed in "yoga" in the search bar of YouTube. *Voila!* Endless free yoga videos! I was so excited and began to do yoga again in my home. I set aside a time in my day when I was alone and rolled out my yoga mat, grabbed my water, and hit play. Because I hadn't practiced yoga in so long, I searched for "Beginner 30-day yoga." I found that I really liked doing these 30-day yoga practices at home on YouTube.

As time marched on, I noticed a pattern. I had allowed my yoga practice to slip during the summer months so that by September, I was starting at ground zero again. I was allowing my business, traveling, and family commitments to take priority; *everything* was coming before my yoga practice. I could feel myself beginning to get angsty and pissed off again. Why was I so inconsistent? And so hard on myself about it? Looking back, I see how I was repeating a pattern of self-sabotage. And I was so done with this behavior.

It was time to make a change and actually give *myself* an opportunity for transformation.

I recently got active on Instagram and started to follow a few friends, and through one friend I discovered this thing called a Yoga Challenge. No matter where she was, she would do a pose, take a picture and post it. She even did poses while we were having fun at the beach or at Universal Studios. She was committed.

And then, my ah-ha moment showed up.

I decided that I wanted to set a goal to do a headstand—the kind of headstand without a wall or anyone holding my legs—since I'd never done one. When I shared this goal with my friend, she suggested I should participate in a Yoga Challenge.

Since then, I have done quite a few yoga challenges on Instagram, and they don't get old. These yoga challenges keep me committed to my practice, and for that, I am thankful. My stress level is lower, my body is stronger, and my mind is more focused.

Yoga, for me, has become a friend.

I enjoy spending time with it and get *so* much out of it. My commitment to my "friendship" with yoga has supported me in discovering a deeper sense of self-love. I know no one else can do this for me—no one but me. So I don't say no to myself anymore. Now, I feel my own tenacity, strength of spirit, and dedication to my body as a temple.

Yoga fills me and keeps me happy and full of gratitude, so that I can walk my talk for myself, my family, and my clients.

Debbie Sodergren, founder and owner of Up Vibrations, LLC, has been helping her clients live their fullest lives for nearly 20 years. Debbie is nationally certified as a Reiki Master Teacher, certified to teach Metaphysics and Meditation, and is an Infinite Possibilities Trainer. She has studied the human energy field in areas of chakra balancing, vibrational medicine, channeling, death  and dying, meditation, astrology, and mindset work of infinite possibilities and has a deep understanding of the body-mind-spirit connection. We are all connected, and everything is made up of energy, and Debbie loves how infinite possibilities ties this all together. Learn more at **www.upvibrations.com**.

Special Gift

Enjoy these free 4 Vibrational Tools to up your vibration at **www.upvibrations.com.**

Before Yoga, There Was Fear: Finding My Ground on the Mat

BY ANDREA TRANK

I don't know how it all began.

Fear of thunderstorms. Fear of getting some dramatic illness. Fear of losing my children in department stores or museums. Fear of my husband getting into a car accident on his way home from work. Fear of flying. Fear of environmental catastrophes. Fear of starvation. Fear of alienation. Fear of not having enough money or love or friends.

Maybe if I look deep enough, I will see that the fear started when my mother remarried when I was seven. I went from being one of three children in a single parent household to one of ten in a household with several angry older brothers and a grumpy step-father.

My mother wanted security and she got it, but her own children may have been sacrificed in this exchange. My brothers and I were not loved by our stepdad until *much* later. In fact, there were many occasions when I heard my mother arguing to give her children the same luxuries that were afforded his children. I did what any typical kid would do—I escaped. I spent most of my time away with friends in their homes. Then I went off to college and only returned home for vacations.

My stepdad changed once my children were born and he realized that I was a loving daughter to both he and my mother. In fact, it was my husband and I who took care of them in their last decade of life, debilitated from Alzheimer's.

The first time that I was debilitated by fear was during a sickness in my mid-thirties. At that point, I had two young boys. I lay in bed days at a time, unable to eat. I had been diagnosed with gastroparesis, a disease that can be debilitating. I, of course, was imagining the feeding tubes that were going to be in me. "What can I eat?" was my mantra. Six months into this disease, I threw out the pills that were causing depression as a side effect and came up with a new mantra: "I am going to heal!"

That is when I walked into my first yoga class. A slender blonde teacher greeted me with a whimsical smile. Sensing my trepidation, she said, "Just do what you can. And then assume child's pose to rest." Fifteen minutes was all I could muster during the first several weeks, but the lyrical sound of her voice and her use of metaphors held me captivated. I was beginning to land and find a sense of safety in this cocoon of healing.

During this time, I had just started my career as a public school teacher in an inner-city high school in Charlottesville, and had gone on medical leave halfway through the year when I became ill. I had hoped my students would have responded to me the way I was responding to this yoga teacher. I didn't understand how to reach them. Earth Science was not their priority, finding food on the table and secure home was. But it was not until later that I could see the disconnect. My failures with them contributed to my insecurity and illness during that time of my life.

I had studied so hard to be a teacher, learning both the art and science of it, but my passion for the subject could not break through to these young people and I was really frustrated. I finally did get well and returned to teaching armed with many new tools such as positive behavior management and a different mindset that led me to a breakthrough in my teaching career. I was so determined to show up for these students that I doubled my efforts to learn to be the best teacher I could be—and ended up winning a Golden Apple in my teaching job in another public high school.

I continued to practice yoga, and my teacher offered the perfect message of healing and inspiration. Every class seemed made just for me. It was if she was addressing whatever was in my mind and heart that day. During this time, I also discovered a new community of like-minded people that I loved so much, so I stuck with her yoga classes for ten more years.

Many small crises were solved weekly on that yoga mat. Job changes, financial hardships, and the boys' struggles in school kept us busy, while I tiptoed through my life hoping to avoid the next scary life event that was lurking around the corner. I took painstaking measures to keep myself and my family safe from what I perceived to be life's great dangers. When big thunderstorms arrived, I quickly piled the kids into an indoor room or a closet. When trips were planned, I avoided flying and chose car or train travel. Europe was *definitely* out of the question! I tried to allay my fears of the world by avoiding violent movies, violent people, and by supporting environmental programs.

Still the fears persisted. I wanted to make sure my children grew up in a safe clean world and I felt all my efforts could not guarantee this. And then the shoe dropped.

I had moved my family to Fort Myers, Florida to take care of my parents. But the stress of hidden agendas by some of my siblings and unhealthy family dynamics really was building on me. Everything collapsed quickly, including the housing market, and the stress of it all was straining my relationships and my body.

And then, on Mother's Day 2013, I received even worse news regarding a family member as I was exiting a yoga class. I sat outside on the stairs of the yoga studio and broke down weeping. Two years later, after dealing with what felt like endless struggles, I walked back into that studio and signed up for Yoga Teacher Training. Educating myself about the healing effects of yoga was going to rescue me one more time. I started eight months of training. I was fifty-three. Facing my fears one more time, I opened myself up to the wisdom of the Sutras, the beauty of the language and movement of asana, and the support of a class of students as we sat in Satya passing the tissue box around, revealing our deepest secrets and giving each other space to grow.

This is how I teach my yoga classes. I open up my home and heart to anyone who needs a safe place to heal, to laugh, to explore their bodies and breath through movement. We try new things together and we never judge. Sometimes we listen to soft music, other times loud birds or the sounds of the neighborhood around us. There are few rules in my classes, and my students usually hang around afterward playing with the dogs or listening to each other with kindness.

My life has settled again—even in the midst of more loss. We evacuated during Hurricane Irma. I was diagnosed with Hashimoto's, an autoimmune thyroid disease. I lost my mother to Alzheimer's. But we survived that evacuation, I studied nutrition, and I got on a plane for the first time in thirty years so that I could see my son get married in Brazil.

Now, when my body shows up with another sign of the aging process, I explore it with curiosity, rather than fear. I keep upping my game in the healing arena. I am up for the challenge and walking my path as I help others find the courage to living life fully, no matter what is thrown at them—thanks to the healing powers of yoga.

Special Gift

Receive a free 30-minute consultation on yoga for healing, nutrition, or essential oils with Andrea—simply mention this book at **www.heavenlanecreations.com/contact/.**

Andrea Trank, a yoga teacher and lifestyle and wellness coach, uses the wisdom of yoga, Ayurveda and Functional Nutrition to support her clients to live more vibrantly, no matter what their current diagnosis. Andrea has an Ed.S. in Curriculum and Instruction, an M.Ed. in Science Education and a B.A. in Speech Communication. She has long been a student and teacher of yoga, environmental issues, essential oils, functional nutrition, digestive health, Ayurveda and herbs, giving her keen insight into her clients' needs and how best to support their transformation to greater health.

For most of her life, Andrea has suffered from what is now known as autoimmune diseases. It started with panic attacks in her twenties, IBS and gastroparesis in her thirties, weight gain and hormonal issues in her forties, and thyroid, prediabetes, and bouts of chronic inflammation and other autoimmune diseases in her fifties. Today, thanks to the yogic lifestyle, she doesn't take any medications.

When Andrea is not studying or teaching, she designs jewelry (available at **etsy.com/shop/Heavenlanecreations**) and enjoys time with her family. She has been married to her lifelong sweetheart since 1984 and has three amazing boys, now men who have always kept her on her toes literally and figuratively. For more information on her services or to read her blog, visit **www.heavenlanecreations.com.**

Purifying Thoughts: The Power of Positive Self-Talk and Affirmations

BY MICHELE TSIHLAS

Growing up, I was challenged with a parent who was diagnosed mentally unstable, and I received quite a bit of psychotherapy as support between the ages of nine and fifteen years old. I also developed obsessive-compulsive behaviors as coping mechanisms. For example, when I was nine, I used clapping and specific movements as an energetic and ritual practice to get my big brother out of my safe space and protect myself from his bullying antics. Later I learned that this physical action of clearing the energy around the body is similar to that of a yogic practice to help one cope with negative influences while chanting *Aum Tat Sat*. This movement in conjunction with this most powerful ancient mantra is a healing brain remapping tool that is now a huge part of the foundation of my yoga practice. Interestingly, the obsessive compulsive behavior was actually serving me in an instinctive way. It's so strange to see how the threads of healing come through in different ways at each phase of life. We all have these lessons that manifest in our life.

Through all the diagnostic labels, I found myself being put in a box. But yoga has allowed me to create safety and repattern my beliefs and find a sense of belonging in the world. I fully embrace a practice of purifying thoughts (those that do not serve us being at our highest potential) and using positive self-talk and affirmations as they offer the simplest ways of obtaining and/or sustaining happiness in our lives, regardless of circumstances. Lots of Yamas and Niyamas (the do's and don'ts of yoga from the Sanskrit Sutras of Sage author Patanjali—not unlike the Ten Commandments) are practiced with this one.

Self-esteem is instrumental for happiness, and many of us do not realize that what we say—whether verbally or mentally—has a vibration or energy, and if the energy isn't positive it most certainly doesn't feel good. Yoga guru Paramhansa Yogananda said, "Simplicity of living plus high thinking lead to the greatest happiness." Whether silent, spoken out loud, or even uttered in jest, words impact us profoundly, even to the point of experiencing serious health conditions. Our inner and outer monologue becomes a reality in the vibration of our lives.

What are you magnetizing energetically? If your intentions are positive and nourishing, then hopefully you're telling yourself, "I *can* choose to communicate in a more positive manner," rather than telling yourself something critical or negative. We are what we feed ourselves—in our thoughts, in our diet, and in our enjoyment—or lack thereof—of life. Our beliefs are what give us power and fortify our will. Our will is what fuels our actions.

We make choices along the way mentally, physically, and spiritually, and those choices are our path. I choose to say the most positive things to myself, because it is empowering, and it feels great. There was a time when I was unaware I was making a choice each time I made a self-deprecating comment. This little story using *Ananda Yoga*® *asana affirmations** shares my narrative.

With a strong will, and no direction except for a gut feeling to move toward the light, I began my journey, with conviction, in search of my happiness and being at my highest potential. *"Left and right and all around, life's harmonies are mine,"* I said to my friends and family as I headed off on my mission. It wasn't very long until I met my shadow while walking along a wildflower-speckled path in the forest, and it was so mysteriously startling I nearly fell. My shadow offered no support or assistance; she only mimicked my coming out of balance. I asked her for directions, but she remained silent. Even though she behaved this way, I found myself attracted to her darkness; something familiar was there.

"I am calm, I am poised," I said to myself as I found my footing and my breath. I stretched upward and could feel *"Strength and courage fill my body cells."* Even though it was hard, I chose to listen to a whisper inside to look away from her intriguing darkness and continue to walk toward the light

on the path, saying to myself, *"I radiate love and goodwill to soul-friends everywhere."*

My shadow persisted and followed me even though I had turned my back on her. After a while, it became a distraction. Swiftly I spun around to confront her and I stumbled, this time losing my balance completely and falling into a rocky ravine. Sprawled, face-down at the very bottom of the gorge, and riddled with pain, I lost consciousness. When I came to, anger reverberated within me as I wondered why the one responsible for my fall did not help me. Although it was terrifying at rock bottom, I was still breathing, and *"Within my every breath is infinite power."*

"Don't just lay there," I said to myself, *"Awake, my sleeping powers, awake!" "I am master of my energy, I am master of myself." "My body is no burden; it is light as air."*

I finally gathered just enough strength to sit up, and when I did, my vision was blurred with outrage. I could no longer see the light or the path. Time passed and I managed to survive a while in the darkness, furiously telling my story to anyone who would listen, following their opinions and desperately stumbling from one numbing vice to another in search of the light. My happiness and my highest potential felt so far away. Filled with defeat and consumed with angst, there was a day I closed my eyes and asked for help, even though there was no one there to hear my request. I remembered my gut feeling to move toward the light, and somehow even just thinking about the light was soothing.

"I relax from outer involvement into my inner haven of peace."

In this state of being I realized that I had choices. I could choose to come to this place of peace instead of stewing in sorrow. *"Energetic movement or unmoving peace: The choice is mine alone! The choice is mine!"* I said to myself. *"With shafts of will I pierce the heart of worries."* Once again I felt a spark of inspiration to continue with my journey to find my happiness and highest potential. *"I relax and cast aside all mental burdens."* And, *"I offer every thought as a bridge to divine grace."* Now I had hope, for I found *"in stillness, I touch my inner strength."* My enthusiasm grew each time I affirmed something positive. In my mind's eye I saw the brilliant setting of the burning Sun and the rising of a brilliant full moon in the darkness.

"Salutations to the sun, to the awakening light within, to the dawning of higher consciousness in all beings," I exclaimed. I discovered that as *"I rise*

above all thoughts of past and future, into the Eternal Now and expand fully into this moment." And in this moment, if *"I attune my will to the source of all power, I joyfully manifest the power of God!"*

If you have a vision for a higher quality of life, ask yourself, "What am I telling myself on a cellular level?" "What kind of master (*to my body and brain cells*) am I?" No matter the circumstances, if you're willing, the practice of one single Ananda Yoga® asana with its affirmation, or even a single affirmation on its own, will transport you to better place.

And so, friend, remember the opportunity to choose thoughts that empower by using this phrase, *"I choose to [insert empowering words here] in this moment."*

More power to you!

* As published in *Spiritual Yoga: Awakening to Higher Awareness* by Gyandev McCord, Crystal Clarity Publishers, Nevada City, California.

Michele Tsihlas is a native New Yorker who now lives just outside of Nevada City in the tranquil Sierra forest. She was diagnosed with Multiple Sclerosis in 1995 and injected herself for ten years with intramuscular interferons. Her MS was crippling and her muscle atrophy was severe, but she refused to let her happiness be overridden by her illness. In 2001 Michele took a holistic approach to her health and engaged in a total lifestyle change, and in 2005 her physicians recommended she stop taking the interferons since she had been symptom-free since 2003.

Michele is passionate about and dedicated to sharing the joyful pursuit of wellness, health, and fitness from the inside out. Knowing that no single approach is right for every individual, she has been trained in a range of modalities. As a wellness professional, Michele's mission is to help people live healthy, fulfilled, authentic lives that reflect their passions and values and feel good doing it, regardless of circumstances. Her educational background includes being a certified Ananda Yoga Therapist C-IAYT, E-RYT Yoga Teacher, Personal Trainer and Group Fitness Instructor. Her career journey took her through many diverse occupations: retail manager, spa and salon manager/cosmetologist, aromatherapist, life enrichment director, actress, teacher, and wellness professional. All along the way her passion for writing found its way to manifest.

She facilitates creating new, positive beliefs that empower people to craft fun and effective habits, inspiring them to find their unique gifts and talents to bring the greatest level of fulfillment and wellness into their lives.

For the latest on what Michele is manifesting, visit her website at **www.zanyinteractive.com**.

Released by My Ujjayi, No Longer Prisoner of My Disease

BY NEREYDA VARIAS

It all was found within my breath, the breath of life, the breath of battle, the breath of self-forgiveness, the breath of rebirth. The breath is where I found my light once again. I was training for a marathon when I experienced a surreal injury that included four disc herniations and severe nerve damage. As a thirty-one-year-old mother of two, suddenly I was faced with not being able to walk. Pain was not prejudiced. I was in full-blown pain regardless of my age, color, race, gender, disability, sexual orientation, or religion.

The ten-minute ride to the hospital felt like an eternity. Sitting felt like the sensation of a vice compressings, clamping my hips and causing crushing, drumming responses within my body. An MRI showed severely progressive degenerative lumbar spinal stenosis, severe nerve damage, and four herniated discs from my L5 and S1. No one, least of all me, could believe that running had caused this. Further testing showed that I had been silently living with a debilitating degenerative disc disease for some time. It had slowly crept in and grown. Injuries that I sustained as part of marathon training led to a much faster deterioration of my structure. Being a yogini, I understood how running was my meditation; it was my state of being wild and free! But little did I know, my running life was forever gone.

The arsenal of Western medicine methods began as I desperately tried to rid myself of this disease. To manage pain and allow for healing in my body, I tried physical therapy for two years without success, chiropractic adjustments that caused me great pain, epidural injections that left me unable to walk for three days, and my doctor's first line of defense: narcotics, muscle relaxers, and anxiety medication.

An orthopedic specialist shared a little secret with me, urging me to try yoga, acupuncture, and any holistic healing before even thinking about surgery. With that doctor's advice, I began movements once again and have since learned this simple truth:

Movement is never fully lost.

The physical and physiological destruction I experienced compelled me to seek alternative ways of movement that would aid my body to heal naturally. My self-healing journey had begun.

The first real sacred space where my rehabilitation took place was in a yoga studio after so many other failed attempts of other therapies years ago. I was embraced by something unspeakable. It had created space I did not know I was missing. Yoga was calling me. My renewed health and Yoga Teacher Training followed, although I lived my path as a teacher with lingering pain. Today, the science of yoga is my pain management tool. Restorative Yoga became my niche, and I quickly learned that teaching and practicing gentle yoga was my purpose, inside and out.

A grand moment in my life was my first acupuncture session. I walked in seeking healing. My first encounter was the most visually and emotionally stimulating session I have had experienced. My intuition was heightened by stimulated points and aromas of herbs and oils. I was nervous and excited as the session progressed and began to chant mantras to ease my conscious mind as the meditation began to take hold. I fell into a deep trance and the images and vision began to flood my psyche.

The mantra I repeated was *Teyata Gate Gate Paragate Parasamgate Bodhi Soha*. In Sanskrit, it means, "Going, going, going on beyond, always going on beyond, always becoming Buddha." It is from *The Heart of the Prajna Paramita Sutra* and, as always, it is up to the interpretation of the individual. Deva Premal's version has changed my life, and the profound vibrational frequencies of the Gyuto Monks is intoxicating. The sounds take you to another plane of existence; the octaves that the Gyuto Monks reach is my pure definition of mysticism.

As my first acupuncture session concluded, I arose off the table and felt as if I had traveled to a distant place and returned filled with bliss, ready to share with the world my illuminated spiritual energy.

Body work and glass cupping therapy have been for years a bi-weekly necessity for my body maintenance, and the physical and emotional transformation has been miraculous! The whole experience is inspirational, loving, and offers an incredible physical understanding of how the mind, body, and energetic spirit are all intertwined. The healer and client connection becomes more than hands-on contact; it becomes a dance between two bodies of water. Teaching yoga and my self-practice require this healing art for optimal daily function and pain management.

Meditation and guided imagery, including Yoga Nidra, was my post-healing reintroduction to breath and restorative yoga, along with self-guided hypnotherapy resulting in deep trance. My meditations reached higher levels of frequencies.

I used all my power to relieve the pain I was in. Then, last year, my body fully shut down. My orthopedic surgeon shared that I was moving down the severity scale of severe nerve damage and had now almost ninety percent loss of disc. My health dropped drastically in a matter of weeks. I went from being a fully active yoga instructor to a semi-active gentle yoga teacher to being a full-on disabled individual. I felt lost, alone, afraid, and filled with so much pain.

When patients do not positively respond to some of the Western medicine modalities shared above, surgical procedures are now options. My particular medical procedure was called Anterior Lumbar Interbody Fusion (ALIF). The surgeon entered my body from the front, placed a metal cage into the diseased area and overlaid pieces of my own bone (shavings of my hip bone) into the cage for bone growth so that the fusion would take place over time. Studies show that this procedure reduces pain in the back and allows for more sustainable movement.

My family and I prepared not only physically but environmentally, emotionally, spiritually, and profoundly. The morning of April 24, I went into surgery and all I could hold onto was my mantra:

Teyata Gate Gate Paragate Parasamgate Bodhi Soha.

As I awoke for the first time, a rebirth per say, my first breath was that of the "Ujjayi" breath. Like I child, I learned to roll over and to walk. The pain was immediate and intense. As I was supported by my nurse onto a walker, my "Ujjayi" breath was automatic. I didn't even notice until my daughter said, "Mom, breathe calmly." I responded, "This is the only way I can walk." My Ujjayi breath was my warrior's breath. The depths of my breath were as if the ocean was literally rising from the center of the darkness, ascending, spiraling up toward light. The nurse was upset and kept telling me to stop, to stop breathing so hard so I told her, "This is my breath and I will breathe as I need to…to walk again!"

I took only five steps, but these were the steps out of my metamorphosis, expanding my wings for the first time in what felt like years. However, little did I know as I stood up for the first time, the inner incision to my abdominal wall had unraveled and my lower intestines spilled out. All that was stopping them from descending to the ground was my outer layer, the skin of my belly. This was a severe complication, and I wasn't even aware of it for about a year. The symptoms that followed were unimaginable, but that is a whole other story to tell…

My path consists of change. Change is inevitable, and whether shared vocally or kept inside, it will happen nonetheless. My path is in perpetual motion, even as I am restricted to more seated or reclining positions. Today, my path has taken a more spiritual approach, and in the spiritual realm my ability to move is boundless. My Ethers are moving within micro movements, but rest assured micro movements bring progress. My journey is grander than I could have ever imagined, and my feet are what will take me there—one step at a time.

When reflecting on the ways that the rules of the road will return me to the path of living the life I want, the formula is simple to me now. To stop and see myself in a whole healthy light, time is of the essence to raise my vibrations. Time to myself will be key to returning to the life I desire and deserve. I deserve love, compassion, honor, gratitude and, above all, self-care. This self-care begins with me, because when I put myself first above all else, I will be able to be there for everyone and travel everywhere. To live my life to the fullest, I must first honor each sacred breath.

Nereyda Varias was born into a Nicaraguan family in Los Angeles and was taught at early in life to express her passion and energy through movement. Unknown to her, a routine marathon training session caused considerable injuries and her body could no longer move at that level. Nereyda sought another form of movement that would aid the body to heal in a holistic way, and her

inquiries led her to the science of yoga. Her yogic path evolved into a passion for reaching fellow beings though cultivation, teaching yoga and sharing movement, showing love to all walks of life, speaking with purpose, and inspiring self-expression. To create a sacred space, a moment in time which to nurture the higher vibrations of all who cross her path and with encouragement allow their colors of energy to paint the cosmos. This was her transmutation.

Nereyda was blessed to immerse herself in the magnificent Santa Barbara mountains of The White Lotus Foundation, where she graduated from a 200+ Hour Yoga Teacher Training Program. Nereyda also graduated from Southwest Institute of Healing Arts, majoring as an Integrative Healing Arts Practitioner, specializing in Spiritual/Life Coaching and Guided Imagery/Hypnotherapy and was ordained as an Interfaith Priestess through the Universal Brotherhood Movement. Nereyda's passion expanded into energy healing, and she earned certification as Crystal Reiki Master.

Nereyda's intention is, through Integrative Healing, to share the art and balance of energy and compassion to the body, mind, and spirit. To connect with Nereyda, send her a direct message via **Facebook @nereydas_illuminations** or **Instagram @nereydasilluminations.**

> "Our deepest fear is not that we are inadequate. Our deepest fear is that we are powerful beyond measure."
>
> –MARIANNE WILLIAMSON

Yoga: The Art of Release, the Art of Being

BY DEBRA MICHELLE VEGH

I stand on my yoga mat, my rectangular sanctuary, 24 inches by 68 inches, it is all I need at this moment. Heel to heel, toe to toe, tummy tucked, spine straight, shoulders back, head up. Hands together, fingers interlocked, knuckles under my chin.

I am so grateful. The thought rolls dreamingly through my mind. I am grateful to have found this yoga practice, these rooms, especially with all that has been unfolding over the past couple of years. Through this process of grieving, I have turned to my yoga practice to re-balance my emotions and soothe my soul.

The sweat beading on my forehead makes its way down my cheek. *Is that a tear?* I wonder. Sometimes, sweat and tears blend in these rooms. The tears and sweat flow together. It's a safe place to let them go.

Brian, my Bikram instructor, tells me to inhale, "Inhale through your nose, raise your elbows to the ceiling, keep your eyes open and breathe." My drista, or gaze, locks on the space between my eyes, reflecting back at me from the foggy mirror. The fog reminds me of the emotional state I was in after a doctor prescribed an antidepressant for my grief, which he referred to as depression. Grief manifests itself in many forms: anger, sadness, resentment, depression...the list goes on and on.

I took the prescription for a few months before I recognized that my emotions had flat-lined and I felt nothing. Good or bad, there was nothing but indifference and a numbness to everything and everyone. I soon realized I missed my emotions so I went off the anti-depressant. Safely weaning off the medication, I replaced a regular yoga practice for antidepressants, and found release. The healing I so desired was here for me now.

In a few minutes I will no longer be able to see my reflection in the mirror, I think as the heat and humidity rise around me and fill the room. This room has become my sanctuary, my oasis. A place of escape and solitude, if only for an hour and a half at a time.

I don't need to see my reflection to stay focused. I learn to view myself from my third eye, my internal sight. I look straight ahead while traveling within, inhaling deep into my body, sending my breath past my lungs into my belly. I take a long-drawn inhale, willing the oxygen to infiltrate my entire being, to fill every pore, and to travel the core of my cells.

"Open your mouth and exhale," Brian instructs. I open my mouth gently exhaling. I push my chin back, pulling my elbows together, parallel to the floor.

Awwwww...
I Release...

I release the day's stresses, the ringing phone. The tension in my neck, the unpaid bills. The pain between my shoulders, the anxiety about the future. The ache in my lower back, the financial worries. I exhale the stale air that has been trapped within, waiting for an exit valve to open.

Awwwww...
I Release...

I am so happy, I think. My mind begins to slow down, and I enter a state of bliss. I allow the process to permeate me. I am so happy in this moment. The heat. The humidity. The sweat glistening from my pores. Detoxing my body, detoxing my mind, detoxing my soul.

Awwwww...
I Release...

I remember the intention I set for this class,

> *Be here*
> *Be present*
> *Breathe...*

It's all that is required as I take my next inhale,

> *Be here*
> *Be present*
> *Breathe...*

The knowledge that the next hour and a half is mine—all mine—settles in. I relax. I separate from the chaos of the outside world, the stress of owning a hair salon and managing a staff while continuing to work behind the chair six days a week. I separate from the demands of clients, staff, family, and pets. I separate from the responsibilities of life, if only for now.

Only me, my breath, and my soul.

> *I Exhale*
> *I Release...*

In the yoga studio, I find the peace, the oasis, and the space I need to let go, to release, to recharge, to be free. For me, yoga has never been about learning to stand on my head, hanging out in crow, or how far I can twist my body and push beyond my limits. For me, the true purpose of yoga is to reconnect me to my breath, to slow my manic, overactive mind, and to remember that although I have a body, I am not the body, and to reunite with my soul.

> *To remember I am a soul.*

Yoga uses the asanas, or poses, to teach me how to connect to my body and breath through movement. To release the resistance, the control, and the struggle. Releasing it all, yoga teaches me to focus on my breath and the pause in between. It's a practice that I can take with me in to every moment of every day. Focusing on my breath, releasing, and finding the bliss in every moment.

Just as it takes practice on the mat, it takes practice in my daily life. It's a constant reminder in moments when stress appears, when fear comes to pay a visit, or when anxiety threatens to take over and shut me down. The practice of yoga gives me the tools to stop, to focus on my breath, and to calm my racing heart. To return to the present moment. To find things to be grateful for as I name them off one by one in mind: The sun is shining, the window is open, and the sudsy warm water feels pleasant as I shampoo my client's hair. My client is happy. I am present.

Yoga teaches me to return to the present moment, to be grateful, and to simply Be.

Yoga is the art of release,
the art of being.

It's a tool that has the ability to teach us how to take our practice into our everyday lives.

The practice, the peace, the oasis, the sanctuary—we find it all in a yoga studio. We find bliss on the mat that lives inside of us. It's so simple, really. All we have to do is,

Be here
Be present
and simply be.

Namaste.
I love you all so.

Debra MicheLLe Vegh is an author, organic hair stylist, Reiki Master, yoga instructor, licensed relaxation masseuse, and certified health coach. She is currently studying to be a Master of herbology, advanced nutrition, Iridology, and vibrational healing.

Debra MicheLLe calls upon her ancestral right as a Native American to assist her in healing, with the use of stones, feathers, bark, plants, oils, and Mother Earth''s vibrational magnetic energy. She has been on a conscious mission for all of her life, studying, learning, and accepting the Universe's gifts of love though several healing modalities. Having journeyed through a period of the shadow and a battle with addiction, Debra MicheLLe awakened to a life of higher vibration, manifestation, and joy, and she is called to share what she has learned. Through her experience, strength, and hope, she connects with those who cross her path, planting what she calls "seeds of possibilities" within their hearts—seeds, she prays that will sprout and take root as we all come together, collectively to raise the vibration of the world.

Her motto, "Keep your face to the sun" has served her well in times of unrest and dis-ease, reminding her that what we focus on manifests to create our own world.

Debra MicheLLe is being called by the One True Source to share the message of joy, to bring Love and Light into the world, to Illuminate this existence beyond our wildest imagination, and to demonstrate how to have fun along the way. Connect at **DebraMichelleHealing.com**.

Special Gift

To receive your **7-minute meditation** as my gift to you, email debra@DebraMicheLLehealing.com requesting it—and be sure to mention this book *Practice: Wisdom from the Downward Dog.*

Getting Lost: A Homecoming

BY ELIZA WHITEMAN

What does it feel like to lose yourself?

To me, I feel cold, empty, and isolated. It seems like an imposter has taken over my body, or someone else is driving while I am just a passenger. It's like shouting into a cave where the only reassurance that anyone is home is the sound of your own voice.

I have never been diagnosed with depression, but I do know when I have drifted just far enough into the shadowed periphery that jolts me awake and back into living. If my life was a graph, you could see the peaks and valleys of my mental highs and lows. I notice my lows come around when I am influx with doing for everyone else. This was first noted when I moved to be with my then-boyfriend who became my husband. He was active duty military, and I made the decision to move to be with him. I physically gave up everything and moved to another state. I didn't have a job or friends, and my self-identity felt like it got lost in the move, too. We married and moved again less than a year later, and I started all over again in another place. But this time was different. This time I stumbled into a yoga class—and not a moment too soon.

My husband was deployed for a year-long tour right during the height of the Iraq War. Not only that, he was Special Operations, which was not part of a traditional post, and this made communication irregular. During this period, my time on the yoga mat was pivotal in getting to know myself. I had to learn and relearn—both figuratively and literally—how to hold myself up all on my own.

Fear and anxiety consumed me, so I cocooned for the first couple of months and focused on setting up our house and finding a job. I wasn't sure exactly what I wanted to do, but I had the realization that I could, in fact, create a new pathway. My love for yoga deepened as it allowed me the space to listen, discover, and be present with the direction my life wanted to take. By the next year, I had my husband back, a new job as a school teacher—which I absolutely loved—and had made new friends. I had emerged from my cocoon and found my way back to *me*. The next few years were a renaissance, of sorts. I was in a groove and felt really connected to what was going on in my life.

And of course, nothing ever stays the same.

Four years later we moved across the country so my husband could go to business school...and I just had a baby. The graph on my time-line would show another dip. I loved motherhood, but as time wore on, I knew deep down that I wanted to also be something more. What was that? Once again, I had no community, no yoga studio, and no friends. I did have a local gym where I would try to practice yoga as best as I could on my own. That is where I slowly listened to an inner call to be a new kind of teacher—a yoga teacher. Months later, I found a teacher training program. The gift that yoga and teacher training gave me was the opportunity to build my own community and allow me to have a home practice.

As the years wore on, I had lots of ups and downs in coming to terms with my new way of life. But I held fast to my vision of wanting more. I held tightly to this lifeline of being a yoga student and yoga teacher. Even after having subsequent children, I realized that yoga was what I wanted more of. There was a passion inside of me—an excitement that kept my inner fire stoked. I started to wake up from my hibernation.

By listening to what I actually desired, I knew my next step was to open my own studio—to deepen my practice and teaching but also to reach out and provide a refuge for others to make space for themselves and provide a sanctuary that would foster their souls. Getting on my mat was integral for me through some of my toughest days, and giving this gift to others will always be hugely important to me. My husband and I opened our studio in July 2015.

We both put our heads down and worked long days while also juggling our young family and pursuing various yoga trainings. During these first few years, I was always on the go and had very little downtime. Year after year, our classes, workshops, trainings, revenue, responsibilities, and stress doubled. With every season I could feel a little bit more of myself getting caught up in over doing for others.

I was losing myself again. While growing my business, I was again doing everything for everyone else.

This past fall, we won best studio *and* I won best yoga teacher. This should be been one of my happier moments. It was supposed to be the ultimate of what I had worked so hard so for all these years, but all I could feel was emptiness. It felt like someone else was driving and I was just being taken for a ride. Over the summer I ran myself ragged doing the summer camp shuffle for the kids, running my studio, teaching classes, and leading trainings. I was barely practicing my own yoga.

All I wanted to do was curl up and take a nap and avoid it all.

Again, I was in a cycle of overdoing and underperforming (notice a pattern, anyone?). As a closet introvert, the outside world sees me as larger than life—loud, outgoing, personable, welcoming, smiling, laughing—but it's tough to keep that all up. I felt depleted, tapped out, worn out, and running on minimum operating levels just so I wouldn't have a full breakdown. Finally, I had what us Southerners call a "Come to Jesus meeting." I could not continue to live this way; it was unsustainable.

Once again, I had lost my way. And this time the thing that had always been my shovel to dig my way out of my funk—yoga—was the thing that was shoveling the dirt on top of me. It reminded me of when I had moved to each new post in my military spouse days. In the age before Google Maps or even TomTom, you had two options: Drive around to find your way, or get a physical map. I always chose to drive around, get lost, and find my way back home. This is what I chose to do this time. Find myself, through myself.

First, I had to locate myself, physically. As hard as it was, I had to get to a yoga class. As hard as it was to be in my own studio, I knew I had to be an example of how to begin again. So I went back to the homing device that brings me back to me—my mat. But this wasn't all rainbows and unicorns, I assure you. It was an all-out dogfight. Having to show up for myself after pushing "me" away for so long was almost unbearable. I felt shame for being an imposter in this beautifully perfect yoga world. I felt blame for letting things get to this point, and I felt terrible for beating myself up—because berating myself only hinders the process of coming home.

I consistently made my date with my mat. I also cut my caffeine, ate lots more green veggies, took vitamin supplements, hiked outdoors, and took our dog on long walks. And then, something started to happen: The fog began to lift and I began connecting back to my physical body. As I regained my strength and stability, I was proud of what my body could do and how good it could feel by doing the work.

I realized that the farther I get from my practice, the farther I get from who I am.

Mindful breathing and meditation gave me pause to reflect on who I was and who I wanted to become. My energy levels went up, and I had more awareness over how what I eat contributes to how I feel for the rest of the day. My drive to create and make was piqued again. But this time, I took more time to create for myself by writing, brainstorming, journaling, and setting goals.

But hang on, this is not the end. I'm not walking off into the infinite sunset just yet! This journey is *never* complete. Who you are, what you do, and where you go is never over, just a work in progress. Isn't that great? We are never 100 percent cured, 100 percent fixed. There will be ups and downs and all arounds. We have to be ready for it all. But that is what this practice does for me. It keeps me aware of when I am off track, and this awareness allows me to have the choice to take action or not.

Our drishti, breathing, body awareness, discipline, and passion all builds until we are in the glorious hum of humanity with ourselves. Some days on our mat, the connection is instant. Some days the magic is just being able to hear the slightest truth inside. And sometimes, I need to get totally lost to find myself. Because I cannot be a mom, a wife, a boss, an entrepreneur, a leader, a yogi, or a yoga teacher if I am not a stand for myself.

Today, I choose to take care of myself first and allow yoga to cultivate a deeper listening to my highest self. When I keep tuning in and listening at this level, I can reconnect on a cellular level and find my way back home.

Eliza Whiteman is the co-founder and director of FlyDog Yoga in Charlottesville, Virginia. She is a Master Baptiste Teacher and former collegiate athlete at Auburn University. It was through sports that she learned the value of teamwork and the power of community to lift one another up, which has led FlyDog Yoga to be recognized as one of the top yoga studios in Virginia, serving thousands of people monthly.  As a result of the success of FlyDog Yoga, Eliza was chosen as a 2017 Tory Burch Foundation Fellow for women entrepreneurs.

Eliza found her yoga practice at a time when she felt lost and alone when her husband left for a year-long active duty military deployment. Yoga literally and figuratively showed her that she could hold herself up all on her own. She strives to give her students this same feeling of belonging, possibility, and empowerment.

In addition to business ownership, Eliza is involved in public speaking, the MilSpo Project, Yoga Teacher and Leadership Trainings as well as various workshops and trainings. Eliza's commitment to service reaches beyond her immediate yoga community and includes international, national, and local nonprofits such as Africa Yoga Project, Veterans Yoga Project, VETOGA, and various local military and first responder organizations. Eliza lives in the Charlottesville, Virginia area with her husband/business partner Brad and their four children. Learn more at **flydogyoga.com**.

Grace of Pain

BY SASANNA YEE

Spiritual teachers say that all the answers we need are already within us. But what if going inside is scary because you live in a painful body? For decades I waged a bloody battle against myself, until I surrendered in 2018.

It was 1987 in San Francisco. Three-year-old me jumped up and down in our kitchen, ecstatic that Dad was taking me to buy a toy. I sat in the front seat without a seatbelt. We were driving along a winding mountain road when Dad swerved to avoid an oncoming car and totaled his 1967 Ford Mustang against the barricade. He frantically looked over at me and saw my head smashed an inch into the glove compartment. This happy day turned into a horrific one.

The years went by and I grew up like any other kid. I excelled in both academics and sports. Yet physically, my jaw was misaligned and the rest of my body had organized around the asymmetry. When I looked in the mirror, I saw ugliness staring back at me—my sad asymmetrical face, my droopy breasts, the scoliosis causing the right and left curvatures of my torso to be uneven. As my inner critic became louder and more unforgiving, I became more depressed and insecure. I was very susceptible to stress. My fight-flight pounding heart mirrored the noise in my mind. My body screamed as if she carried the crippling pains of the world.

Every day, I'd wake up fatigued and aching. Hot burning pain would radiate down my low back into my thighs and into my toes. I couldn't sit for long, stand for long, have sex for long, do anything for long. From the moment I opened my eyes in the morning until the moment I closed them at night, my pelvic floor would be clenched bracing against life.

I've seen an eclectic spectrum of doctors and mystical healers. I've had Botox shot into my back. I've had a Chinese healer "gua-sha" (scrape) me until I was raw. I have three different kinds of heat packs. Sometimes alone in my car, I'd wail uncontrollably just to release the emotional pain. Other days, I'd be so debilitated that walking to the bathroom was difficult because moving my legs hurt my hips and back. I'd feel possessed, writhing on the floor or convulsing on the bed as the muscle spasms and physical pain overtook me. Some nights, I'd silently cry myself to sleep. Many times, I've envisioned ending my life.

When I was at the end of my sanity, yoga came into my life. Like a chiropractor, yoga connected and realigned my mind-body-spirit. I came to this ancient practice for the physical relief; what I didn't anticipate were the emotional and spiritual gifts I'd receive. I began to experience relief from the grief and fear I had been carrying as a result of the car accident.

One of the most important lessons I've learned from yoga is that there is an inextricable connection between our physical sensations and emotions. A physical manifestation of pain can signify a much deeper pain beneath the surface. Because emotional pain is something we are not often taught to address, our souls bring it out in our physical bodies in order to get our attention.

"The body keeps the score," says Dr. Bessel van der Kolk, a psychiatrist noted for his research in the area of post-traumatic stress. "As long as you keep secrets and suppress information, you are fundamentally at war with yourself...The critical issue is allowing yourself to know what you know. That takes an enormous amount of courage."

Yoga gave me that courage. This practice taught me how to tap into my own body's wisdom. *"Our issues are in our tissues,"* said one of my yoga teachers. My tissues have locked in that trauma from long ago. Understanding this was key to untying the knots and unraveling the mystery of chronic pain. The more consistently I practiced yoga, the more my nervous system calmed and the fiery pain cooled. Yoga helped me to face my fears, to trust myself and my body, and to be more audacious. Wholeness was taking hold.

Camel was the first posture to give me this visceral sensation of courage. A luxurious revitalizing breath came when I dared to fully commit to the posture. It was as though a paramedic had jolted my heart. My heart pounded anxiously as I lifted my head, leaned back, rested my hands on my heels, and gently settled into the posture. Kneeling and anchored on the ground, my rounded shoulders rolled down and back, my caved chest stretched opened, my constricted windpipe exposed, I allowed invigorating oxygen to rush into my throat, heart, and ribs. A long sigh of "Ahhhh" escaped my mouth as tingling energy coursed throughout my whole body. Camel was like a trust fall with myself, and I saw that I had my own back.

Armed with this newfound courage, I began to venture deeper into my chronic pain experience with compassionate curiosity. Instead of resisting pain, I embraced her. As a result, I developed a more intimate relationship with my body and mind, and my practice began to reveal more questions than insights. This puzzled me until I realized: THE INSIGHT IS ASKING THE RIGHT QUESTIONS. Instead of asking, "Why is this happening to me?" I asked, "What can I learn from pain?", "How can I accept pain without judgment?"

I let pain be my light, my spiritual teacher, my guru—one who dispels the darkness of ignorance. I trusted this extreme discomfort in my body to guide me toward my liberation.

Carefully listening and discerning the messages from pain has been incredibly humbling and healing. I learned how big my ego was and how much self-doubt, self-hatred, and mistrust I carried. I noticed that my back and hips have been the dumping grounds for layers of toxic emotions that have kept me limited, in pain, and spineless. Pain forced me into a corner and she asked the real question: "What do you really want?" The answer is simple: I want ME. Not what I think I should be, and not what others want of me. I learned how to say NO and set boundaries. It turns out the safest place to be is within my own truth.

*I am no longer a victim.
I am empowered to co-create with this experience.*

Pain led me to take immediate action towards my dream of long-term travel. I gifted myself time and space—a year sabbatical to move at my own pace around the world. Without a plan, I quit my jobs and life as I knew it. I took a blind, courageous leap into the unknown. With only a backpack to my name, I ended up traversing six Asian countries in six months, discovering different aspects of humanity while exploring who I really am. For two months, I lived at a Sivananda Yoga Ashram in Northern India. Our school was right next to the roaring Ganges. I immersed myself in the yogic way of life, practicing daily meditation, *pranayama* (controlled breathwork) and *asanas* (postures), eating a vegetarian diet, studying *Vedantic* philosophy and the *Bhagavad Gita* (Hindu scripture), singing the *bhajans* (Indian devotional songs), and giving back with some *karma yoga* service to the ashram.

This transformative experience in the ashram gave me tremendous gifts. In the absence of the usual distractions, I began the real healing work of reconnecting authentically with myself. I discovered that when I change, the world changes. I cracked my emotional armor and embraced ALL my feelings with love and acceptance. Leonard Cohen said, "There's a crack in everything and that's how the light gets in." Yoga allows me to let in that light and shine it into the dark recesses of my being. As a result, I've tasted tremendous freedom and joy in my body, mind, and spirit.

Through this harrowing journey of self-discovery, a profound answer surfaced from my core. That traumatic car accident had linked *happiness* with *danger* in my subconscious mind. I had spent life never allowing myself to feel real happiness because I believed it was unsafe. The grace of pain led me to yoga, and to a healthier way of relating with my emotions. The grace of pain has given me the strength and courage to be comfortable with the uncomfortable. The grace of pain led me back to that deep sense of safety, love and peaceful silence that is always present. Through the grace of pain, I have let go of my fear of happiness, and I am finally truly happy in my own skin.

I do not know if I will ever be free of pain, but we have become friends, and she has transformed my life into one worth living and sharing.

Sasanna Yee is a social justice activist and bilingual yoga teacher who has made it her life's work to bridge the health and wellness gap for people of color. She teaches yoga through the lens of access and trauma providing compassionate support to underserved and underrepresented communities such as at-risk and immigrant populations. She received her training from Niroga Institute in Oakland,  CA and Sivananda Yoga Vedanta Center in India. Sasanna first sought out yoga, qi gong and meditation to help manage chronic pain. Her own healing journey led her to reunite with her true self, to live simply, and to find stillness through movement. She deeply believes that when we apply the right tools and the right mindset, we can heal our own bodies and transform our lives. Learn more at **sasannayee.com.**

Flower of Life Press Books

The New Feminine Evolutionary: Embody Presence—Become the Change

Pioneering the Path to Prosperity: Discover the Power of True Wealth and Abundance

Sacred Body Wisdom: Igniting the Flame of Our Divine Humanity

Emerge: 7 Steps to Transformation (No matter what life throws at you!)

Sisterhood of the Mindful Goddess: How to Remove Obstacles, Activate Your Gifts, and Become Your Own Superhero

Path of the Priestess: Discover Your Divine Purpose

Sacred Call of the Ancient Priestess: Birthing a New Feminine Archetype

Rise Above: Free Your Mind One Brushstroke at a Time

Menopause Mavens: Master the Mystery of Menopause

The Power of Essential Oils: Create Positive Transformation in Your Well-Being, Business, and Life

Self-Made Wellionaire: Get Off Your Ass(et), Reclaim Your Health, and Feel Like a Million Bucks

Oms From the Mat: Breathe, Move, and Awaken to the Power of Yoga

Oms From the Heart: Open Your Heart to the Power of Yoga

The Four Tenets of Love: Open, Activate, and Inspire Your Life's Path

The Fire-Driven Life: Ignite the Fire of Self-Worth, Health, and Happiness with a Plant-Based Diet

Becoming Enough: A Heroine's Journey to the Already Perfect Self

The Unfucked Code: Transform Your Relationships from Fighting to Uniting

The Caregiving Journey: Information. Guidance. Inspiration.

Visit us at **www.FlowerofLifepress.com**

www.ingramcontent.com/pod-product-compliance
Lightning Source LLC
Chambersburg PA
CBHW022102150426
43195CB00008B/239